JIM MANTHORPE wrote the first edition of this book. He has trekked in many of the world's mountainous regions from Patagonia to the Himalaya and Scandinavia to the Canadian Rockies. He is the author of three other Trailblazer guidebooks: *Pembrokeshire Coast Path*, *Tour du Mont Blanc* and *Scottish Highlands – The Hillwalking Guide*. He has also researched and updated numerous other Trailblazer titles. Jim lives on the west coast of the Scottish Highlands and now works as a wildlife cameraman and film-maker. See ⌨ www.jimmanthorpe.com.

This **fifth edition** of *South Downs Way* was updated by Bryn Thomas.

Authors

South Downs Way

First edition: 2004, this fifth edition 2015

Publisher Trailblazer Publications
The Old Manse, Tower Rd, Hindhead, Surrey, GU26 6SU, UK
info@trailblazer-guides.com, www.trailblazer-guides.com

British Library Cataloguing in Publication Data
A catalogue record for this book is available from the British Library

ISBN 978-1-905864-66-9

© **Trailblazer** 2004, 2007, 2009, 2012, 2015: Text and maps

Series Editor: Anna Jacomb-Hood
Cartography: Nick Hill **Layout**: Bryn Thomas
Proofreader: Anna Jacomb-Hood **Index**: Jane Thomas
Photographs (flora): C3 Bottom right, © Jane Thomas
All other photographs: © Bryn Thomas unless otherwise indicated

The maps in this guide were prepared from out-of-Crown-
copyright Ordnance Survey maps amended and updated by Trailblazer.

Acknowledgements

We're grateful to everyone who helped us with information and advice along the way, in
particular Andy Gattiker & Tim Squire; Tim Muddle, Juliet Bray & Alison Thomas for
company on the trail. Thanks also to all those readers who've written in with comments and
suggestions, in particular, Heather Babb, Steve Bramwell, Stuart Blackburne, Anne
Conchie, Rodney Duggua, Rachel & Karl-Peter Hammer, Richard Marshall, Nick Price,
Trudi & Andy Rintoul, and Sue Wood.

Thanks, as always, to everyone at Trailblazer: Anna Jacomb-Hood and Nicky Slade for
editing and research; Nick Hill for the maps and Jane Thomas for the index.

A request

The author and publisher have tried to ensure that this guide is as accurate and up to date
as possible. Nevertheless, things change. If you notice any changes or omissions that should
be included in the next edition of this book, please write to Trailblazer (address above) or
email us at ▣ info@trailblazer-guides.com. A free copy of the next edition will be sent to
persons making a significant contribution.

Warning: coastal walking and long-distance walking can be dangerous

Please read the notes on when to go (pp13-15) and outdoor safety (pp66-8). Every effort
has been made by the author and publisher to ensure that the information contained herein
is as accurate and up to date as possible. However, they are unable to accept responsibility
for any inconvenience, loss or injury sustained by anyone as a result of the advice and information given in this guide.

Updated information will be available on: ▣ **www.trailblazer-guides.com**

Photos – Front cover: The Seven Sisters. **This page**: Paragliders over Ditchling Beacon.
Previous page: The cliffs above Beachy Head Lighthouse.
Overleaf: On Fulking Hill. © Jim Manthorpe.

Printed in China; print production by D'Print (☎ +65-6581 3832), Singapore

South Downs
WAY

WINCHESTER TO EASTBOURNE

60 large-scale maps & guides to 49 towns and villages

PLANNING – PLACES TO STAY – PLACES TO EAT

JIM MANTHORPE

FIFTH EDITION RESEARCHED AND UPDATED BY
BRYN THOMAS

TRAILBLAZER PUBLICATIONS

Contents

INTRODUCTION

About the South Downs Way

PART 1: PLANNING YOUR WALK

Practical information for the walker

Budgeting 27

Itineraries

What to take

Getting to and from the South Downs Way

PART 2: THE ENVIRONMENT & NATURE

Flora and fauna

Conservation of the South Downs

PART 3: MINIMUM IMPACT WALKING & OUTDOOR SAFETY

Minimum impact walking

Outdoor safety and health

PART 4: ROUTE GUIDE AND MAPS

Contents

ABOUT THIS BOOK

This guidebook contains all the information you need. The hard work has been done for you so you can plan your trip from home without the usual pile of books, maps, guides and internet research.

When you're all packed and ready to go, there's comprehensive public transport information to get you to and from the trail and 60 detailed maps and town plans to help you find your way along it.

The guide includes:

● All standards of accommodation with reviews of campsites, camping barns, hostels, B&Bs, guesthouses and hotels
● Walking companies if you want an organised tour and baggage-carrying services if you just want your luggage carried
● Itineraries for all types of walkers
● Answers to all your questions: when to go, degree of difficulty, what to pack, and how much the whole walking holiday will cost
● Walking times in both directions and GPS waypoints
● Cafés, pubs, tearooms, takeaways, restaurants and food shops
● Rail, bus & taxi information for all villages and towns along the path
● Street plans of the main towns both on and off the path
● Historical, cultural and geographical background information

---

❏ MINIMUM IMPACT FOR MAXIMUM INSIGHT

Nature's peace will flow into you as the sunshine flows into trees. The winds will blow their freshness into you and storms their energy, while cares will drop off like autumn leaves. **John Muir** (one of the world's earliest and most influential environmentalists, born in 1838)

Why is walking in wild and solitary places so satisfying? Partly it is the sheer physical pleasure: sometimes pitting one's strength against the elements and the lie of the land. The beauty and wonder of the natural world and the fresh air restore our sense of proportion and the stresses and strains of everyday life slip away. Whatever the character of the countryside, walking in it benefits us mentally and physically, inducing a sense of well-being, an enrichment of life and an enhanced awareness of what lies around us.

All this the countryside gives us and the least we can do is to safeguard it by supporting rural economies, local businesses, and low-impact methods of farming and land-management, and by using environmentally sensitive forms of transport – walking being pre-eminent.

In this book there is a detailed and illustrated chapter on the wildlife and conservation of the region and a chapter on minimum-impact walking, with ideas on how to tread lightly in this fragile environment; by following its principles we can help to preserve our natural heritage for future generations.

Break clear away, once in awhile, and climb a mountain or spend a week in the woods. Wash your spirit clean. **John Muir**

INTRODUCTION

The South Downs are a 100-mile (160km) line of chalk hills stretching from the historic city of Winchester, in Hampshire, across Sussex to the Pevensey Levels by Eastbourne. For centuries travellers and traders have used the spine of the Downs as a route from one village to the next.

> **For centuries travellers and traders have used the spine of the Downs as a route from one village to the next.**

Today that route is still used by walkers, outdoor enthusiasts and others who simply need to escape from box-like offices in congested towns and cities. London, Brighton, Southampton and other urban areas are all within an hour or two of the South Downs, making these beautiful windswept hills an important recreational area for the millions who live in the region.

A traverse from one end to the other following the national South Downs Way trail is a great way of experiencing this beautiful landscape with its mixture of rolling hills, steep hanging woodland and windswept fields of corn. Add to this the incredible number of pretty Sussex and Hampshire villages with their friendly old pubs, thatched cottages and gardens bursting with blooms of roses, foxgloves and hollyhocks and one begins to understand the appeal of the Downs as a walking destination.

The Way takes you through, or close by, numerous pretty English villages, such as South Harting, with their thatched cottages, cosy pubs, village greens and ancient churches.

The start of the South Downs Way:
Winchester Cathedral ...

... and the end – Eastbourne.

Arundel and its castle, five minutes by train or
90 minutes on foot from Houghton Bridge.
© Jim Manthorpe

The South Downs Way begins in the cathedral city of Winchester from where it heads across rolling hills and the Meon Valley with its lazy, reed-fringed chalk-bed river and charming villages. At Butser Hill the Way reaches the highest point of the Downs with views as far as the Isle of Wight and, in the other direction, the North Downs. Continuing along the top of the ridge the Way passes through ancient stands of mixed woodland, past the Roman villa at Bignor and on towards the sandstone cottages of Amberley. Close by is the fascinating town of Arundel with its grand cathedral and even grander castle rising above the trees on the banks of the River Arun. Then it is on to Chanctonbury Ring with its fine views across the Weald of Sussex. The next stretch climbs past the deep valley of Devil's Dyke and over Ditchling Beacon to Lewes with its crooked old timber-framed buildings and the famous Harveys Brewery. Finally, the path reaches the narrow little lanes of Alfriston with more historic pubs than one has any right to expect in such a small village. The walk's grand finale includes the meandering Cuckmere River and the roller-coaster Seven Sisters chalk cliffs – before reaching the final great viewpoint of Beachy Head, overlooking the seaside town of Eastbourne.

Walking the Way can easily be fitted into a week's holiday but you should allow more time to be able to explore the many places of interest such as Arundel, Lewes and Winchester itself ... not to mention the lure of all those enchanting village pubs that are bound to make the trip rather longer than intended!

History

There has been a long-distance route running along the top of the South Downs for far longer than walking has been considered a leisure activity. The well-drained chalk hilltops high above the densely forested boggy clay below were perfect for human habitation and were certainly in use as far back as the Stone Age.

From this time onwards a complex series of trackways and paths developed across the land and it is believed that by the Bronze Age there was an established trade route along the South Downs. All along the crest of the Downs escarpment there is evidence of Iron Age hill-forts and tumuli (ancient burial grounds), many of them very well preserved, particularly the Old Winchester hill-fort site in Hampshire.

In more recent times the land was cleared and enclosed, and the flat hilltops were put under the plough. Although this process erased many of the lesser tracks the most significant of them remained; the one which ran east–west along the edge of the escarpment. It was not until 1972, amid rapidly growing public interest in walking, that the then Countryside Commission designated the 80 miles from Eastbourne to the Sussex–

The Way passes through the Queen Elizabeth Country Park with its ancient stands of mixed woodland.

Hampshire border the first long-distance bridleway in the UK. Later, the final section through Hampshire was added bringing the length of the South Downs Way to one hundred miles and giving it a spectacular start in the historic city of Winchester. Today the route is growing in popularity with walkers, cyclists and horse-riders alike, all of whom tend to mingle with ease.

How difficult is the path?

The South Downs Way is one of the most accessible and easiest of Britain's long-distance paths.

The South Downs Way is one of the most accessible and easiest of Britain's long-distance paths. Those on foot will find the route usually follows wide, well-drained tracks in keeping with its designation as a long-distance bridleway, catering for cyclists and horse-riders as well as walkers. If anything walkers may, on occasion, crave a few more lightly trodden paths since the route always sticks to the well-beaten track.

This 100-mile walk can be conveniently divided into sections starting and stopping at any of the numerous little villages that sit at the foot of the escarpment or in a fold in the hills.

One thing to note, though, is that because the Way generally follows the high ground along the top of the South Downs, to reach the villages offering accommodation, pubs and shops you usually have to descend steeply off the Downs and climb back onto them to continue, which can make pub lunches less attractive! When cal-

Famous local landmarks, the two windmills above Clayton are known as Jack and Jill (see p138); this is Jill.

INTRODUCTION

culating the day's timings you need to bear in mind this extra walking time involved.

(**Below**): The chalk cliffs between Cuckmere and Birling Gap are known as the Seven Sisters.

How long do you need?

The whole route can be tackled over the course of a week

Walkers will find that the whole route can be tackled over the course of a week but it is well worth taking a couple of extra days to enjoy the beautiful downland villages that are passed along the Way. It is also worth taking time to explore the former capital of Saxon England, Winchester, a historic town with a beautiful cathedral. At the other end of the walk Eastbourne, to be polite, is perhaps a little less interesting but will keep those who like to sit on a windy seafront happy for hours.

See pp28-32 for suggested itineraries covering different walking speeds

The practical information in this section will help you plan your walk and design an itinerary to meet your particular preferences.

When to go

The south-east of England has probably the best climate in a country maligned for its fickle weather. By best climate I mean not too much rain and more hours of sunshine than other parts of the UK. The route can be followed at any time of year but clearly the chances of enjoying good weather do depend on the season.

SEASONS

Spring

A typical spring is one of sunshine and showers. From March to May a day

Harveys Brewery in Lewes supplies many of the pubs in the region.

walking on the Downs may involve getting drenched in a short sudden shower only to be dried off by warm sunshine a few minutes later. However, the weather can vary enormously from year to year, sometimes with weeks of pleasantly warm sunny weather and in other years days of grey drizzle. In general this is a great time to be on the Downs. Walker numbers are low and the snowdrops, bluebells and primroses decorate the bare woodland floors.

Summer

It can get surprisingly hot and sunny from June to September but again the weather can vary from one year to the next. Always be prepared for wet weather but also be confident of enjoying some balmy summer days too. Occasionally it can be a touch too hot for walking. This can be a problem as there is not much water on the Downs so bring plenty of full bottles. Visitor numbers are high at this time of year, as you might expect, so it can be a little difficult to enjoy a solitary day on the Way. The hills are colourful in summer with wild flowers in bloom in the meadows, red poppies among the corn and fields of bright yellow oil-seed rape. Hay-fever sufferers may not agree that this is such a good thing. However, everyone seems to be in a good

Lewes Castle was built shortly after the Battle of Hastings in 1066.

mood and the pubs are brimming with all sorts of folk, from fellow walkers to country gents. The big advantage of summer walking is that it remains light until well after nine in the evening so there is never any rush to finish a day's walk.

Autumn

Autumn is probably the season when you can reliably expect to be rained on. The weather from September to November tends to be characterised by low-pressure systems rolling in from the Atlantic one after another, bringing with them prolonged spells of rain, mist and strong winds. On the positive side those who enjoy a bit of peace and quiet will find very few fellow walkers out and about at this time of year. Furthermore, it is not all rain and wind. Sometimes the weather can surprise you with a day of frost and cold sunshine that can make a day on the Way a real treat. It's important to remember that some businesses shorten their opening hours at this time of year or even close all together.

Winter

Southern England doesn't experience as many cold snowy winters as it used to some ten to twenty years ago. From December to February these days it's usually relatively mild with wet weather and occasional spells of colder, dry weather. Any snow that does fall is usually during January and February.

You'll find a good range of traditional pubs, such as the 14th-century George Inn in Alfriston, in the villages along the route.

It is more likely the further east you go since it is the south-east corner that gets caught by the snow showers that roll in from the North Sea, when the wind is from the north or east. Many walkers will appreciate winter walking for the wilder weather it offers and the days of solitary sauntering along the high windswept crest of the Downs. The best days are the cold, frosty ones when the air is clear and the views stretch for miles. Bear in mind that in winter many businesses, particularly in the more remote villages, are closed. It is always wise to call a guesthouse or pub before turning up expecting a bed or dinner.

TEMPERATURE

Generally, temperatures are comfortable year-round. In winter, warmer clothes will be needed as the temperature drops towards and, on occasion, just below freezing. Summer is usually pleasantly warm with temperatures around 16°C to 23°C but temperatures as high as the low 30s Celsius do occur on at least a few days during July or August which can make walking on exposed sections of the Way uncomfortable.

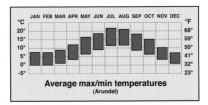

Average max/min temperatures
(Arundel)

RAINFALL

The weather in England is affected mostly by the weather systems that come from the south-west. These are usually low-pressure systems that contain a lot of rain. Rain can and does fall in any month of the year but dry weather is usually more likely in the early summer.

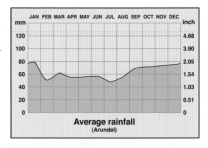

Average rainfall
(Arundel)

DAYLIGHT HOURS

If walking in autumn, winter and early spring, you must take account of how far you can walk in the available light. Also bear in mind that you will get a further 30-45 minutes of usable light before sunrise and after sunset depending on the weather.

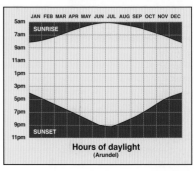

Hours of daylight
(Arundel)

(**Opposite**): A hot summer's day and classic South Downs rolling landscape: the view towards Truleigh Hill (see p135).
© Jim Manthorpe

❏ MAIN FESTIVALS & EVENTS

May/June

● **Charleston Festival** (🖥 www.charleston.org.uk) Held in Charleston Manor (see p156) in the last week or two of May. Arts and literature abound.

● **Goodwood Festival of Speed** (🖥 www.goodwood.com) Held over three days in late June on the Goodwood Estate a few miles south of Cocking; see box p102.

    Horse-racing takes place at Goodwood Race Course between May and October.

July/August

● **Winchester Hat Fair** (🖥 www.hatfair.co.uk) Originally a buskers' festival, now a celebration of street arts and community; all events are free but contributions are welcome – just put your money in the hat. First weekend of July.

● **Winchester Festival** (🖥 www.winchesterfestival.co.uk) A 10-day festival in early July which includes classical and choir music in the cathedral, folk music in the pubs, dancing in the street, art exhibitions, comedy events and plenty more.

    For details of other festivals throughout the year in Winchester visit: 🖥 www.festivalsinwinchester.co.uk.

● **Arundel Festival** (🖥 www.arundelfestival.co.uk) takes place over the last 10 days of August in the castle's grounds featuring folk, rock and classical music as well as plays (Shakespeare) and comedy.

September

● **Goodwood Revival** (🖥 www.goodwood.com) A festival of racing involving rare and unusual racing cars held at Goodwood over three days in mid September.

November

● **Lewes Bonfire Night Celebrations** (🖥 www.lewesbonfirecelebrations.com) Largest bonfire-night celebrations in the country, held on 5 November unless it's a Sunday.

(**Below**): The South Downs Way is very well signposted which is helpful since it crosses several other waymarked trails.

Practical information for the walker

ROUTE FINDING

There is very little opportunity to get lost along the Way. It would be an easy route to follow even without the waymark posts, which are usually marked with the National Trail 'acorn' symbol. An acorn on a

yellow chevron indicates that this route is a footpath, ie exclusively for pedestrians. A **blue** background indicates that the trail is a bridleway and can therefore also be used by horses and cyclists. A **purple** background quaintly adds a pony and trap. A **red** or **white** background warns that the route can also be used by motorbikes. Bear in mind that other footpaths may be indicated on the waymark posts so **follow the acorn**.

Nevertheless, it is hard to go astray. Should you find yourself erring from the path the chances are a fence on one side or the steep Downs escarpment on the other will deflect you back in the right direction. In addition there are usually other walkers around who you can ask for directions.

Using GPS with this book

Given the above, modern Wainwrights may scoff while more open-minded walkers will accept that GPS technology can be an inexpensive, well-established if non-essential, navigational aid. In no time at all a GPS receiver with a clear view of the sky will establish your position and altitude in a variety of formats, including the British OS grid system, to within a few metres.

The maps in the route guide include numbered waypoints; these correlate to the list on pp182-5, which gives the latitude/longitude position in a decimal minute format as well as a description. Where the path is vague, or there are several options, you will find more waypoints. You can download the complete list of these waypoints for free as a GPS-readable file (that doesn't include the text descriptions) from the Trailblazer website: 🖳 www.trailblazer-guides.com (click on **GPS waypoints**).

It's also possible to buy state-of-the-art digital mapping to import into your GPS unit, assuming that you have sufficient memory capacity, but it's not the most reliable way of navigating and the small screen on your pocket-sized unit will invariably fail to put places into context or give you the 'big picture'.

Bear in mind that the vast majority of people who walk the Way do so perfectly well without a GPS unit. Instead of rushing out to invest in one, consider putting the money towards good-quality waterproofs or footwear instead.

South Downs Way app
A Trailblazer South Downs Way app is under development. For more information see the Trailblazer website 🖥 www.trailblazer-guides.com.

ACCOMMODATION

The South Downs lie in a populous area so there are plenty of villages and towns within easy reach of the Way, most of which offer accommodation for the walker. However, the Way generally follows the high ground along the top of the South Downs escarpment while the villages lie at the foot of the hills. This tends to leave the walker with a small detour to reach a bed at the end of each day. Bear this in mind when calculating times and distances from the maps in Part 4. As a general rule it is a good idea to allow an extra hour each day for the walk to and from your accommodation.

Camping
Unfortunately, there is little to no opportunity for wild camping on the South Downs so campers will have to rely on organised campsites of which there are few. Refer to the itinerary chart for campers on p32 to organise a schedule. Most of these campsites charge from around £5 per camper. Some of the more organised sites have showers and washing facilities while others are merely a place to pitch a tent in the grass. You can also camp at some YHA hostels.

It is difficult to arrange a camping trip along the length of the Downs without being forced into more solid accommodation for one or two nights. Those who have the urge to camp in greater isolation where there is no recognised site may find it worthwhile asking a landowner for permission to set up camp.

Those who do camp will certainly appreciate the experience: the pampered comforts of a bed and breakfast are outweighed by the chance to sleep under the stars and be woken by the sun, should it happen to be showing.

Hostels and camping barns
There are five **YHA hostels** within easy reach of the Way but all are between Truleigh Hill and Eastbourne.

Despite the name, anyone of any age can join the YHA. This can be done at any hostel or by contacting the **Youth Hostels Association of England and Wales** (YHA; ☎ 0800-0191 700 or ☎ 01629-592700, 🖥 www.yha.org.uk). A year's membership costs £15/20 if paid by direct debit/credit card (£5/10 for under 26s), or £25/30 for family membership.

YHA hostels are easy to book, either online or by phone and you can stay even if you aren't a member though expect to pay £3 per night more. It is now possible to pay by credit card at all the hostels.

❏ **Booking accommodation**
You should always book your accommodation in advance because of the competition for beds in summer and during events such as those held at Goodwood; also because some places close in winter. It is often possible to book online but if not phone the establishment. When booking check the rate and facilities and if walking with your dog, check this won't be a problem. You may be asked to pay a deposit, usually 25-50%. Always let the owner know if you need to cancel so that they can free the bed for someone else.

If you are having problems finding accommodation some tourist information centres (see p40) provide a booking service. The majority take a 10% deposit towards the cost of the first night's accommodation, though the deposit is then deducted from the bill. Some also may make an additional charge for the service.

Each hostel has a drying room, showers and a fully equipped kitchen. Telscombe (see p154) is self-catering only but has a small shop; the others offer meals. Bedding is provided but not towels though they can be rented for £2 (deposit £5).

There's an **independent hostel** near East Meon called Wetherdown Lodge (p92) and a **camping barn** run by the National Trust near Bignor Hill, which goes by the charming name of Gumber Bothy (p114).

Bed and breakfast

Some B&Bs can be quite luxurious and come at a price but in my experience all the Downs walker really wants is a warm bed and a hot bath. For this reason most of the B&Bs listed in this guide are recommended because of their usefulness to the walker and convenience to the Way, not for how many stars the tourist board has awarded them.

Bed and breakfast owners are often proud to boast that all rooms are **en suite**. This enthusiasm for private facilities has led proprietors to squeeze a cramped shower and loo cubicle into the last spare corner of the bedroom. Not having an en suite room is sometimes preferable as you may get sole use of a bathroom across the corridor and a hot bath is just what you need after a day's walking – and you will also probably save a few pounds each night.

You may find it hard to find establishments with **single** rooms. **Twin** rooms and **double** rooms are often confused but a twin room usually comprises two single beds which can either be pushed together for a couple or kept separate. A double room has one double bed. **Triple/quad** rooms are for three/four people and usually consist of a double bed and one or two single beds or bunk beds.

B&Bs do of course provide **breakfast** (see p20). Some also provide a packed lunch or an evening meal but you will need to give them advance warning and there will be an extra charge. Most B&Bs, however, are close enough to a pub or restaurant but if not the owner may give you a lift.

Rates Note that all per person (pp) rates are based on two people sharing a room. **B&Bs** in this guide vary from £25pp in the most basic accommodation to £50pp (or more) for the most luxurious, en suite places; most charge £30-40pp.

PLANNING YOUR WALK

Remember that many places do not have single rooms so they add a supplement (£20-30) for single occupancy of a room. Prices can drop during the winter months and if you are on a budget you could always ask to have a room-only rate (ie no breakfast) which will usually be less.

Guesthouses, hotels, pubs and inns

Guesthouses are usually more sophisticated than B&Bs, offering evening meals and a lounge for guests; rates are around £40-50pp for two sharing.

Pubs and inns offer bed and breakfast of a medium to high standard and have the added advantage, of course, of having a bar downstairs and also generally offer food, so it's not far to stagger back to bed. However, the noise from tipsy punters below your room might prove a nuisance if you want an early night. Prices usually range from £30 to £50pp per night for two sharing. Generally, **hotels** tend to be more expensive, ranging from £35 to £100pp for two sharing. There are now also a few **restaurants with rooms** which are great for a treat. Expect to pay £35 to £70pp for two sharing.

FOOD AND DRINK

Breakfast and lunch

If staying in a B&B, guesthouse or hotel you'll usually be served a full cooked breakfast which may be more than you are used to. However, some places offer a lighter continental breakfast which you may prefer first thing in the morning; alternatively, ask to have a packed lunch instead of breakfast, particularly if you are planning an early start. If requested in advance, and for an additional cost, many places can also provide you with a packed lunch.

Alternatively, breakfast and packed lunches can be bought and made yourself. There are some great cafés and bakeries along the Way which can supply both and if you are lucky you will be in town on the day of a farmers' market (see box p22); they are great places to pick up fresh food and try something from the local area. Remember that certain stretches of the walk are devoid of places to eat so check the information in Part 4 to ensure you don't go hungry.

Evening meals

The **pubs** that grace the pretty flint villages of the Downs rank as some of the most authentic country inns in England. Many of them date from the 14th or 15th centuries and have fascinating histories. Food can vary from cheap traditional bar food to high-quality cuisine served in a pub restaurant. For the serious 'connoisseur' drinker the best thing about the downland pub is the range of real ales on offer (see box opposite).

While evening meals in the villages are often limited to whatever the local pub is serving, some of the larger towns such as Winchester, Eastbourne, Petersfield and Midhurst are home to some quality **restaurants** with specialities ranging from fish to Italian fare. Those on a budget, or walkers who stumble into town late in the evening, will find a number of late-night **takeaway** joints offering everything from kebabs and pizzas to Indian and Chinese and, of course, traditional fish and chips.

Self-catering supplies

If you are camping, fuel for the stove and other equipment is an important consideration. Supplies can be found at any of the outdoor shops in Winchester and Eastbourne, whilst en route there are outdoor shops in Petersfield and Lewes. Check Part 4 for more detailed information about these shops.

Drinking water

Depending on the weather you may need to drink as much as 3-4 litres of water a day. If you're feeling lethargic it may well be that you haven't drunk enough, even if you're not feeling particularly thirsty.

Although drinking directly from streams and rivers can be tempting, it is not a good idea. Streams that cross the path tend to have flowed across farmland

---

❑ LOCAL FOOD AND DRINK

Food

Food in Hampshire and Sussex is varied and tasty. Local farm produce concentrates on beef and pork but there is also a variety of local cheeses and other dairy products. Look out for traditional English dishes such as steak and ale pie, shepherd's pie and ploughman's lunch which can all be found on pub menus.

Fruit farms are a common sight in the south. Most of them invite people to '**pick your own**'. That is not an invitation to get off their land and pick your own elsewhere but to help yourself to their strawberries, raspberries, blueberries and other fruit growing in the fields. Once you have picked enough, you take the fruit to be weighed and paid for.

Hampshire has also long been well-known for its **watercress** beds, particularly around Warnford, Overton and Hurstbourne Priors. The large-scale propagation of watercress in these areas dates back to the 19th century and is much aided by alkaline water provided by the chalky streams of Hampshire. Some of the original watercress beds are still used today.

Cream teas can be ordered in many of the cafés along the South Downs Way. Partaking in this quintessentially English activity is usually done in the mid-afternoon and involves a pot of tea accompanied by scones, clotted cream and jam.

Drink

There's a plethora of local breweries for the real-ale connoisseur to get excited about. Probably the most famous Sussex brewery, and certainly the oldest, is **Harveys** of Lewes which dates from 1790. Beers to look out for include their Sussex Best and Armada Ales while in September they release their seasonal Southdown Harvest Ale which they proudly describe as the 'taste of the South Downs'.

There are also several newer local breweries. You can try **Flowerpots Bitter** at the Flower Pots Inn in Cheriton. **Rectory Ales** of Plumpton Green, a tiny brewery set up in 1996 by the rector of Plumpton to raise funds for the local parish, a once-common tradition. Their most popular brews are Rector's Pleasure (4%) and Rector's Revenge (5%). On tap at the The Five Bells at Buriton is real ale from **Ballard's Brewery**, which was founded on a farm near Petersfield in 1980. Finally, there is the **Gribble Brewery** from Chichester whose ales deserve awards not just for flavour but for decorating beer pumps with some of the quirkiest names. Look out for Pig's Ear and the dangerously named Plucking Pheasant but go steady on the Winter Wobbler which, at 7.2%, is probably one of the most dangerous concoctions ever to drip from a beer tap.

PLANNING YOUR WALK

❏ **Farmers' markets**

Farmers' markets are held in a number of towns and villages throughout Hampshire and Sussex. These give local farmers a chance to showcase their produce and give consumers the opportunity to purchase locally grown stuff in the knowledge that they are helping not just the local economy but the environment too. Buying local produce helps cut down on the wasteful long-distance carriage of food both nationally and internationally – plus, of course, the food is much fresher.

To find out more about farmers' markets near the South Downs Way check out the websites 🖳 www.localfoods.org.uk, 🖳 www.hampshirefarmersmarkets.co.uk and 🖳 www.westsussex.info/farmers-markets.shtml (covers all of Sussex)

The following farmers' markets are all close to the South Downs Way:

● **Winchester** The biggest of its kind in the UK. Held on Middle Brook St on the second and last Sunday of the month; also in the Cathedral grounds on the third Saturday of the month
● **Petersfield** On the first Sunday of every month in The Square
● **Midhurst** In Capron House car park, North St, on the fourth Saturday of every other month starting in January
● **Arundel** On High St on the third Saturday of every month
● **Pulborough** In the village hall on the fourth Saturday of every month from February to November (Pulborough is just one stop on the train from Amberley)
● **Steyning** In the main car park off the High St on the first Saturday of every month
● **Lewes** On Lower High St by the river on the first Saturday of the month

where you can be pretty sure any number of farm animals have relieved themselves. Combined with the probable presence of farm pesticides and other delights, it is best to avoid drinking from these streams. Drinking-water taps are marked on the route maps. Where these are thin on the ground you can usually ask in a shop or pub for them to fill your bottle or pouch – from the tap, of course.

MONEY

While Eastbourne and Winchester at each end of the Way have plenty of banks and ATMs (cashpoints/cash dispensers), the villages in between do not. Bear in mind that some of these ATMs charge up to £1.75 per withdrawal. However, if you find yourself without a penny on the Way it is only a short detour to some of the larger towns; banks with cash dispensers can be found in Petersfield, Midhurst, Arundel, Storrington, Steyning, Lewes and Meads Village. Nevertheless, it is worth having more cash than you think you might need since small local shops will require you to pay in cash, as will most B&Bs, camping barns and campsites. Shops that do take cards, such as supermarkets, will sometimes advance cash against a debit card (a transaction known as 'cashback') as long as you buy something for at least £5 at the same time.

Getting cash from a post office

Several banks in Britain have an agreement with the post office allowing customers with a debit card and PIN to make cash withdrawals at post office counters throughout the country. For a full list of banks that are part of this scheme contact the Post Office (🖳 www.postoffice.co.uk/making-withdrawals-in-branch). This is a useful service particularly if no ATM is available.

OTHER SERVICES

Most villages and all the towns have at least one public **telephone**, a small **shop** and a **post office**. Post offices can be useful for sending unnecessary equipment home which may be weighing you down. In Part 4 mention is given to services that may be of use to the walker such as **banks**, **cash machines**, **outdoor equipment shops**, **laundrettes**, **internet access**, **pharmacies** and **tourist information centres** some of which can be used for finding and booking accommodation among other things.

WALKING COMPANIES AND BAGGAGE CARRIERS

There are several companies who will arrange all your accommodation and baggage transport for you. Some of the best are listed below.

Guided holidays
● **Footpath Holidays** (☎ 01985-840049, 🖳 www.footpath-holidays.com, Wiltshire) Offers 'highlights' itineraries.
● **Ramblers** (☎ 01707-386800, 🖳 www.ramblerscountrywide.co.uk, Welwyn Garden City) Offers an itinerary for five nights along sections of the Way.
● **HF Holidays** (☎ 020-8732 1250, 🖳 www.hfholidays.co.uk, Elstree, Herts) This long-established company runs at least one guided walk of eleven nights along the length of the trail (Winchester to Eastbourne) in summer.

Self-guided holidays
● **Absolute Escapes** (☎ 0131-240 1210, 🖳 www.absoluteescapes.com, Edinburgh) Offers itineraries of 6-9 days, and can tailor make as required.
● **British & Irish Walks** (☎ 01242-254353, 🖳 www.britishandirishwalks.com, Cheltenham) Offers itineraries along part of the Way.
● **Celtic Trails** (☎ 01291-689774, 🖳 www.celtic-trails.com, Chepstow) Offers set itineraries and walks tailored to individual requirements.
● **Contours Walking Holidays** (☎ 01629-821900, 🖳 www.contours.co.uk, Derbyshire) Has a variety of South Downs packages from short three-night sections to the whole walk.
● **Explore Britain** (☎ 01740-650900, 🖳 www.explorebritain.com, Durham) Offers a selection of self-guided trips with luggage transfer and accommodation in inns, from two-night excursions around Alfriston to the entire route.
● **Footpath Holidays** (☎ 01985-840049, 🖳 www.footpath-holidays.com, Wiltshire) Offers itineraries for the whole of the South Downs Way or part of it. Bespoke holidays available.
● **Footprints of Sussex** (☎ 01903-813381, 🖳 www.footprintsofsussex.co.uk, West Sussex) Does seven- to ten-night self-guided holidays with accommodation and baggage transfers. Also organises an annual, supported rather than guided, South Downs Way Walk each June (🖳 www.southdownsway.com).

● **Freedom Walking Holidays** (☎ 07733-885390, ▭ www.freedomwalking holidays.co.uk, Goring-on-Thames) Can accommodate variations of requirements within holiday packages.
● **Load Off Your Back** (▭ www.loadoffyourback.co.uk, Welwyn Garden City) Offers a variety of options for the whole Way.
● **Macs Adventure** (☎ 0141-530 8886, ▭ www.macsadventure.com, Glasgow) Operates a number of self-guided walks lasting seven to nine nights; can tailor-make to suit.

❏ **Information for foreign visitors**

● **Currency** The British pound (£) comes in notes of £50, £20, £10 and £5, and coins of £2 and £1. The pound is divided into 100 pence (usually referred to as 'p', pronounced 'pee') which comes in silver coins of 50p, 20p, 10p and 5p, and copper coins of 2p and 1p.

● **Money** Up-to-date **rates of exchange** can be found on ▭ www.xe.com/ucc, at some post offices, or at any bank or travel agent. **Travellers' cheques** can be cashed only at banks, foreign exchanges and some of the large hotels; it is probably better to use a debit card or bring cash.

● **Business hours** Most **shops and supermarkets** are open Monday to Saturday 8am-8pm (sometimes up to 15 hours a day) and on Sunday from about 9am to 5 or 6pm, though main branches of supermarkets generally open 10am-4pm or 11am-5pm; the Spar chain usually displays '8 till late' on the door. Occasionally, especially in rural areas, you'll come across a local shop that closes at lunchtime on one day during the week, usually a Wednesday or Thursday; this is a throwback to the days when all towns and villages had an 'early closing day'. Main **post offices** are open at least from Monday to Friday 9am-5pm and Saturday 9am-12.30pm. **Banks** typically open at 9.30am Monday to Friday and close at 3.30pm or 4pm though in some places they may open only two or three days a week and/or in the morning only; **ATMs (cash machines)** though are open all the time as long as they are outside; any inside a shop or pub will only be accessible when that place is open.

  Pub hours are less predictable; although many open daily 11am-11pm, often in rural areas opening hours are Monday to Saturday 11am-3pm & 5 or 6-11pm, Sunday 11am/noon-3pm & 7-10.30pm. Last entry to most **museums and galleries** is half an hour, or an hour, before the official closing time.

● **National (bank) holidays** Most businesses are shut on 1 January, Good Friday (March/April), Easter Monday (March/April), first and last Monday in May, last Monday in August, 25 December and 26 December.

● **School holidays** State-school holidays in England are generally as follows: a one-week break late October, two weeks over Christmas and the New Year, a week mid February, two weeks around Easter, one week at the end of May/early June (to coincide with the bank holiday at the end of May) and five to six weeks from late July to early September. Private-school holidays fall at the same time, but tend to be slightly longer.

● **Documents** If you are a member of a National Trust organisation in your country bring your membership card as you should be entitled to free entry to National Trust properties and sites in the UK.

● **EHICs and travel insurance** Although Britain's National Health Service (NHS) is free at the point of use, that is only the case for residents. All visitors to Britain should be properly insured, including comprehensive health coverage.

● **Mickledore** (☎ 01768-772335, 🖳 www.mickledore.co.uk, Keswick) Have itineraries offering the whole route in 6-10 days, or each half of the Way, and a short break two-day circular walk.

● **Sherpa Walking Holidays** (☎ 020-8875 5070, 🖳 www.sherpaexpeditions .com, London) Offers eight-day and ten-day self-guided inn to inn walks from Eastbourne to Winchester covering 9-11 miles per day.

● **Sherpa Van Project** (☎ 01609-883731, 🖳 www.sherpavan.com, North Yorkshire) Offers just an **accommodation-booking service**.

The European Health Insurance Card (EHIC) entitles EU nationals (on production of the EHIC card so ensure you bring it with you) to necessary medical treatment under the NHS while on a temporary visit here. For details, contact your national social security institution. However, this is not a substitute for proper medical cover on your travel insurance for unforeseen bills and for getting you home should that be necessary.

Also consider cover for loss and theft of personal belongings, especially if you are camping or staying in hostels, as there will be times when you'll have to leave your luggage unattended.

● **Weights and measures** The European Commission is no longer attempting to ban the pint or the mile: so, in Britain, milk can be sold in pints (1 pint = 568ml), as can beer in pubs, though most other liquid including petrol (gasoline) and diesel is sold in litres. Distances on road and path signs will continue to be given in miles (1 mile = 1.61km) rather than kilometres, and yards (1yd = 0.9m) rather than metres.

The population remains divided between those who still use inches (1 inch = 2.5cm), feet (1ft = 0.3m) and yards and those who are happy with millimetres, centimetres and metres; you'll often be told that 'it's only a hundred yards or so' to somewhere, rather than a hundred metres or so.

Most food is sold in metric weights (g and kg) but the imperial weights of pounds (lb: 1lb = 453g) and ounces (oz: 1oz = 28g) are frequently displayed too. The weather – a frequent topic of conversation – is also an issue: while most forecasts predict temperatures in Celsius (C), many people continue to think in terms of Fahrenheit (F; see the temperature chart on p14 for conversions).

● **Smoking** The ban on smoking in public places relates not only to pubs and restaurants, but also to B&Bs, hostels and hotels. These latter have the right to designate one or more bedrooms where the occupants can smoke, but the ban is in force in all enclosed areas open to the public – even if they are in a private home such as a B&B. Should you be foolhardy enough to light up in a no-smoking area, which includes pretty well any indoor public place, you could be fined £50, but it's the owners of the premises who carry the can if they fail to stop you, with a potential fine of £2500.

● **Time** During the winter, the whole of Britain is on Greenwich Meantime (GMT). The clocks move one hour forward on the last Sunday in March, remaining on British Summer Time (BST) until the last Sunday in October.

● **Telephone** The international country access code for Britain is ☎ 44 followed by the area code minus the first 0, and then the number you require. Within Britain, to call a landline number with the same code as the landline phone you are calling from, the code can be omitted: dial the number only. If you're using a mobile phone that is registered overseas, consider buying a local SIM card to keep costs down.

● **Emergency services** For police, ambulance, fire or coastguard dial ☎ 999 or ☎ 112.

PLANNING YOUR WALK

● **South Downs Discovery** (☎ 01925-564475, 💻 www.southdownsdiscovery .com, Cheshire) Offer set itineraries with 6- to 9-day options for the whole route as well as short breaks; can also tailor walks to suit individual preferences.
● **South Downs Way Tours** (💻 www.southdownswaytours.com, Hampshire) Based on the South Downs Way they organise personalised walking and cycling holidays for the full Way or part of it.
● **Walk & Cycle** (☎ 0844-870 8648, 💻 www.walkandcycle.co.uk/southdowns, Petersfield) Offers a wide selection of walking and cycling holidays and short breaks for the South Downs Way; accommodation is in top hotels and inns.

Baggage transfer
● **Footprints of Sussex** (☎ 01903-813381, 💻 www.footprintsofsussex.co.uk, West Sussex) offer a standalone baggage transfer service subject to availability.
● **South Downs Discovery** (see above). Offer baggage transfer along the Way.
    Note that for an agreed charge some **B&B owners** may be prepared to take your luggage on to your next accommodation; it's always worth enquiring. Some **taxi companies** – such as **14U cars** in Petersfield (☎ 07795-101895, ☎ 01730-300738) – are also prepared to transfer your luggage on an ad hoc basis.

MOUNTAIN BIKING

The South Downs Way is perfect for cyclists. It is Britain's first long-distance bridleway so it is specifically geared to horse-riders, cyclists and walkers. The entire route can be followed on two wheels on wide tracks which are, on the whole, well drained, with only a few very steep sections either side of the major river valleys. There are some sections where walkers and cyclists must follow different routes but these are well marked with blue chevrons indicating byways and yellow chevrons for footpaths.

TAKING DOGS ALONG THE WAY

Dogs are allowed on the South Downs but should be kept on a lead whenever there are sheep around. Considering the Downs is a prime sheep-farming area this is most of the time and it is worth remembering that farmers are perfectly within their rights to shoot any dog they believe to be worrying their sheep. See p186 for detailed information on long-distance walking with dogs.

DISABLED ACCESS

Many of the councils are taking steps to improve access to the Sussex and Hampshire countryside but, unfortunately, some parts of the South Downs Way are still quite inaccessible to disabled people.
    Nevertheless, there are stretches of the Way that can be followed quite easily, particularly where roads provide direct access to the top of the hills such as at **Ditchling Beacon** (see p143). Here there are gates designed for wheelchair users and there are also plenty of benches at intervals along the path to the west of Ditchling Beacon. **Devil's Dyke** (see p139) is another good spot where access is

relatively easy and the path not too rough. The **Seven Sisters Country Park** (see box p167) has good facilities for the disabled both in the park and at the visitor centre and access to the beach at Cuckmere Haven is quite straightforward.

Further west the easiest stretches of the Way can be found to the west of **Bignor Hill** (see p112), where there's a car park near the top, and on **Harting Down** (p101) which has a relatively long stretch of gentle, level pathways. **Queen Elizabeth Country Park** (p93) has wide, level tracks and easy access.

For more information see 🖥 www.accessiblecountryside.org.uk/southeast/.

Budgeting

CAMPING

Campsites generally charge £5-10 per person (pp) so if camping and cooking all your own food expect to need £10-15pp per day. However, it is always best to allow for more than you think necessary to cover those inevitable luxuries such as a warm bed after a day walking in the pouring rain. If you like a pint at the end of the day remember that one costing less than £3 is a rare thing in the south of England. Bearing this in mind it is worth counting on at least £15-20 per day.

CAMPING BARNS AND HOSTELS

The **camping barn** called Gumber Bothy (see p114) will set you back just £10 per night. **Hostels** along the route cost £13 to £20 (less £3 if you're a YHA member), making this kind of accommodation a bargain. The YHA charges for beds in its hostels following the modern online model with lowest prices during quieter periods and rates increasing with popularity of location and date. Rooms are surprisingly good for such a budget price.

Hostels usually have a self-catering kitchen allowing you to survive on cheap food from the supermarket or local shop. However, if you want to make use of their meals expect to pay £4.95 for breakfast, around £5 for a packed lunch and £6.50-9 for an evening meal. Now and then, however, you may prefer to eat out which would add to your daily expenditure. To cover the cost of a night in a hostel, the occasional bar meal and drink count on at least £25 per person per day. If you eat out most nights this figure is likely to be £30pp per day or more.

B&B-STYLE ACCOMMODATION

B&B rates can be as little as £25 per person (pp) per night but are usually nearer £30-50pp for two sharing a room (most places add a single occupancy supplement of £10 or more). Breakfast is, of course, almost always included in the total cost but you will need to allow about £5 for a packed lunch (more if eating in a pub or café) and about £10-15 for an evening meal. If you decide to treat yourself to quite a few meals in pubs or restaurants, drink beer and have other goodies you will probably need around £45-75pp per day.

EXTRAS

Don't forget all those little things that push up your daily bill – postcards, beer, ice-cream, buses here, buses there, more beer and getting to and from the Way. All these will probably add up to between £50 and £100.

Itineraries

This guidebook has not been divided up into rigid daily stages. Instead, it's structured to make it easy for you to plan your own itinerary. The South Downs Way can be tackled in any number of ways, the most challenging of which is to do it all in one go. This requires about one week. Others may prefer to walk it over a series of short breaks, coming back year after year to do a bit more. Some choose to walk only the best bits. To help plan your walk the **planning maps** (see end of the book) and the **table of town and village facilities** (pp30-1) give a rundown on the essential information you will need regarding accommodation possibilities and services. Alternatively, you could follow one of the **suggested itineraries** (see below for B&Bs, opposite for hostels and p32 for camping) which are based on preferred type of accommodation and walking speed. There is also a list of recommended **day and weekend walks** (see pp33-4) which cover the best of the path, all of which are well served by public transport. The **public transport map** is on p45.

Once you have an idea of your approach turn to **Part 4** for detailed information on accommodation, places to eat, and other services in each place on the

PLANNING YOUR WALK

STAYING IN B&BS

Night	Relaxed pace Place	Approx distance miles/km	Medium pace Place	Approx distance miles/km	Fast pace Place	Approx distance miles/km
0	Winchester		Winchester		Winchester	
1	Cheriton	8/13	Cheriton	8/13	Exton	12/19.5
2	Exton	7/11	East Meon	13/20	South Harting	16.5/26.5
3	East Meon	6/9.5	South Harting	12.5/20	Amberley	20/32
4	Buriton	8.5/13.5	Graffham	10.5/17	Pyecombe	20.5/33
5	Cocking	11/18	Amberley	9/14.5	Kingston	11/17.5
6	Amberley	13.5/21.5	Steyning	13/21	Alfriston	13/21
7	Steyning	13/21	Kingston	20/32	Eastbourne	12.5/20
8	Pyecombe	9.5/15	Alfriston	13/21		
9	Kingston	11.5/18.5	Eastbourne	12.5/20		
10	Rodmell	5/8				
11	Alfriston	8/13				
12	Eastbourne	12.5/20				

route. Also in Part 4 you will find route descriptions to accompany the trail maps.

WHICH DIRECTION?

There are many criteria that will determine in which direction to tackle the Way. It always seems a good idea to finish a walk with something that was worth walking towards. With this in mind Winchester is a far more attractive place to finish in than Eastbourne. Thus, east to west seems a good choice of direction. However, the scenery improves towards the eastern end and what finer place to conclude the walk than by the sea and on top of the white cliffs of the Seven Sisters and Beachy Head. Another factor is the prevailing wind which normally comes from the south-west. Having the wind at your back is a great help so this would also suggest starting at Winchester and finishing at Eastbourne.

Although the maps in Part 4 are arranged in a west to east direction, times for walking in both directions are always given so that the book can be used back to front.

SUGGESTED ITINERARIES

The itineraries below are based on different accommodation types – B&Bs, hostels/camping barns and campsites, with each one divided into three categories of walking speed. They really are only suggestions and all of them can be easily adapted by using the more detailed information on accommodation found in Part 4. Don't forget to add your travelling time from/to your accommodation both before and after the walk.

PLANNING YOUR WALK

STAYING IN HOSTELS/CAMPING BARNS

Night	Relaxed pace Place	Approx distance miles/km	Medium pace Place	Approx distance miles/km	Fast pace Place	Approx distance miles/km
0	Winchester*		Winchester*		Winchester*	
1	Cheriton*	8/13	Cheriton*	8/13	East Meon*	18/29
2	East Meon*	13/20	East Meon*	13/20	Buriton*	9/14.5
3	Buriton*	9/14.5	Sth Harting*	12.5/20	Bignor	19.5/31.5
4	Cocking*	11.5/18.5	Bignor	16/25.5	Truleigh Hill	20/32
5	Bignor	9/14.5	Truleigh Hill	20/32	Rodmell	21/33.5
6	Washington*	12.5/20	Ditchling*	10.5/17	Eastbourne	20.5/33
7	Truleigh Hill	8.5/13.5	Rodmell	13.5/21.5		
8	Ditchling*	10.5/17	Alfriston*	8/13		
9	Kingston*	10/16	Eastbourne	12.5/20		
10	Rodmell	5/8				
11	Alfriston*	8/13				
12	Eastbourne	12.5/20				

* No hostels/camping barns at places marked; alternative accommodation available

TOWN AND

Place name (Places in brackets are a short walk off the SDW)	Distance from previous place approx miles/km (+) = distance from SDW	ATM (cash machine) Bank	Post Office	Tourist Information Centre/Point (TIC)/(TIP)
Winchester	0	✔	✔	TIC
Chilcomb	2/3.5			
(Cheriton)	4.5/7 (+1.5)		✔	
Exton & Corhampton	5.5/9			
(East Meon)	5/8 (+1)		✔	
(Buriton)	7.5/12 (+0.5)			
(Petersfield)	(+2)	✔	✔	TIC
(South Harting)	3.5/5.5 (+0.5)		✔	
(Cocking)	7/11 (+0.5)		✔	
(Heyshott)	2/3 (+0.5)			
(Graffham)	1.5/2.5 (+1)		✔	
(Sutton & Bignor)	4/6.5 (+1)			
(Bury)	2.5/4 (+1)		✔	
Houghton Bridge	1/1.5			
Amberley	1.5/2.5		✔	
(Arundel)	(+4)	✔	✔	TIP
(Storrington)	3/4.5 (+1.5)	✔	✔	TIP
(Washington)	3/4.5 (+0.5)			
(Steyning, Bramber & Upper Beeding)	4/6 (+1)	✔	✔	TIP
(Fulking)	6.5/11 (+0.5)			
(Poynings)	2/3 (+0.5)			
Pyecombe	2/3			
(Clayton)	1/2 (+0.5)			
(Ditchling)	1.5/2 (+1.5)		✔	
(Plumpton)	2/3 (+0.5)			
(Lewes)	1/1.5 (+3)	✔	✔	TIC
(Kingston-nr-Lewes)	5/8 (+1)			
Rodmell & Southease	4/6			
(West Firle)	3.5/5.5 (+1)		✔	
(Alciston & Berwick)	2.5/4 (+1)			
Alfriston	2/3		✔	
Litlington	1/2			
Exceat/Westdean	1.5/2.5			TIC
Birling Gap	4/6			
Beachy Head	3/4.5			
Meads Village	1.5/2.5	✔	✔	
Alternative (inland) route from Alfriston				
(Milton Street)	1/2 (+0.5)			
(Wilmington)	(+1)			
Jevington	2.5/4			
Eastbourne	4/6	✔	✔	TIC

Total distance 100 miles/162km (via Seven Sisters), 97.5miles/158km (via Jevington)

VILLAGE FACILITIES

Eating Place ✔ = one; ✔✔ = two ✔✔✔ = three+	Food Store	Campsite	Hostel YHA or H (Ind Hostel) camping barn (CB)	B&B-style accommodation ✔ = one, ✔✔ = two ✔✔✔ = three+	Place name (Places in brackets are a short walk off the SDW)
✔✔✔	✔			✔✔✔	Winchester
			✔[1]	✔	Chilcomb
✔	✔			✔	(Cheriton)
✔	✔		✔[2]	✔✔	Exton & Corhampton
✔✔	✔		✔[3]	✔✔✔	(East Meon)
✔				✔✔	(Buriton)
✔✔✔	✔			✔✔	(Petersfield)
✔	✔			✔✔✔	(South Harting)
✔	✔		CB	✔✔✔	(Cocking)
✔					(Heyshott)
✔✔	✔	✔		✔✔✔	(Graffham)
✔	✔[4]		CB[4]	✔✔	(Sutton & Bignor)
✔				✔✔	(Bury)
✔✔		✔		✔✔	Houghton Bridge
✔✔	✔			✔✔	Amberley
✔✔✔	✔			✔✔✔	(Arundel)
✔✔✔	✔			✔✔	(Storrington)
✔		✔			(Washington)
✔✔✔	✔	✔	YHA[5]	✔✔	(Steyning, Bramber & Upper Beeding)
✔					(Fulking)
✔✔		✔		✔	(Poynings)
✔	✔	✔		✔✔✔	Pyecombe
✔				✔	(Clayton)
✔✔	✔			✔✔✔	(Ditchling)
✔		✔			(Plumpton)
✔✔✔	✔			✔✔✔	(Lewes)
✔		✔		✔	(Kingston-nr-Lewes)
✔		✔	YHA; YHA[6]	✔✔	Rodmell & Southease
✔	✔			✔	(West Firle)
✔✔				✔	(Alciston & Berwick)
✔✔✔	✔			✔✔✔	Alfriston
✔✔					Litlington
✔✔			(CB schools only)	✔	Exceat/Westdean
✔				✔✔	Birling Gap
✔					Beachy Head
✔✔	✔			✔	Meads Village
				Alternative (inland) route from Alfriston	
✔					(Milton Street)
				✔	(Wilmington)
✔✔				✔	Jevington
✔✔✔	✔		YHA	✔✔✔	Eastbourne

¹ 30- to 45-minute walk from village; ² in Corhampton; ³ two miles from village;
⁴ at Gumber Bothy 10-20 mins from SDW; ⁵ at Truleigh Hill on SDW; ⁶ at Telscombe, a 30- to 45-min walk from Rodmell or Southease but 20-30 mins from the Way itself.

CAMPING

Night	Relaxed pace Place	Approx distance miles/km	Medium pace Place	Approx distance miles/km	Fast pace Place	Approx distance miles/km
0	Winchester*		Winchester*		Winchester*	
1	Cheriton*	8/13	Exton	12/19.5	East Meon	18/29
2	Exton	7/11	Sth Harting*	16.5/26.5	Cocking	19.5/31.5
3	East Meon	6/9.5	Bignor	16/25.5	Washington	18.5/29.5
4	Sth Harting*	12.5/20	Washington	12.5/20	Plumpton	20/32
5	Cocking	8/13	Pyecombe	15/24	Alfriston*	18.5/29.5
6	Bignor	9/14.5	Rodmell	14/22.5	Eastbourne*	12.5/20
7	Washington	12.5/20	Alfriston*	8/13		
8	Steyning	7.5/12	Eastbourne*	12.5/20		
9	Pyecombe	9.5/15				
10	Plumpton	5/8				
11	Rodmell	10.5/17				
12	Alfriston*	8/13				
13	Eastbourne*	12.5/20				

* There are no campsites at places marked with an asterisk but alternative accommodation is available

SIDE TRIP TO MOUNT CABURN

The only part of the South Downs that is not covered by the South Downs Way is the isolated hill near Lewes known rather grandly as Mount Caburn. It is something of an anomaly, being the only part of the Downs separated from the main spine of chalk hills. The hill's unique position makes it an excellent vantage point for admiring the rest of the Downs stretched out to the south, as well as the Ouse Valley and the county town of Lewes. The top of the hill is a National Nature Reserve renowned for its butterflies as well as its paragliders.

The hill is best approached from the village of Glynde where there is a railway station. From the station Mount Caburn (152m/498ft) looms above. Head towards the hill by walking up the road for five minutes. Just past the old village smithy (blacksmith), which is still being used, is a junction that marks the centre of Glynde village. Turn left and look for the stile in the hedgerow opposite the village shop. The path to the top of Mount Caburn follows the obvious route through the fields from the stile and takes about 30-45 minutes. The return is by the same route or via a path further to the north which drops through a small copse to emerge on the lane north of Glynde village.

❑ HIGHLIGHTS – THE BEST DAY AND WEEKEND WALKS

There is nothing quite like taking on a long-distance path in one go but sometimes the time needed is just not available.

The following list suggests a number of day and weekend walks covering the best of the South Downs Way, most of which are easily accessible using public transport (see pp41-6). Many walkers come back weeks, months or even years later to walk sections of the path they have missed. Fitter walkers will find that many of the weekend walks suggested here can be completed in a day.

Wide views from Beacon Hill near Exton
© Jim Manthorpe

DAY WALKS

Exton to Buriton
12 miles/19.5km (see pp87-94)
The best of the East Hampshire downland, passing over Old Winchester Hill and its magnificent hill-fort remains and Butser Hill, the highest hill on the Downs, with magnificent views over the Meon Valley and Queen Elizabeth Country Park.

Amberley to Steyning
13 miles/21km (see pp116-130)
Starting in one of the prettiest villages on the Way and ending in one of the most beautiful towns, this

Thatched cottage in East Meon
© Henry Stedman

walk provides extensive views from the spine of the Downs, taking in the famous local landmark of Chanctonbury Ring.

Devil's Dyke to Ditchling Beacon   5 miles/8km (see pp140-2)
Possibly the most spectacular dry valley on the Downs, Devil's Dyke is the magnificent starting point of this short section that continues by climbing over the isolated Newtimber Hill before ending at the beauty spot of Ditchling Beacon.

Kingston-near-Lewes to Southease   5 miles/8km (see pp150-6)
One of the quieter stretches of the Downs with fine views of Mount Caburn on the other side of the Ouse Valley and a little bit of literary history to be had at Rodmell, once the home of Virginia Woolf.

PLANNING YOUR WALK

DAY WALKS
(cont'd from p33)

Exceat to Eastbourne via Cuckmere Haven 9 miles/14.5km (see pp163-71)
Arguably the finest day of walking anywhere between Winchester and Eastbourne, following the rollercoaster tops of the Seven Sisters chalk cliffs to the high point of Beachy Head high above Eastbourne.

On the white cliffs near Beachy Head
© Bryn Thomas

Alfriston to Eastbourne via Jevington
10 miles/16km (see pp172-8)
Not as spectacular as the coastal route to Eastbourne but equally enjoyable, encompassing the beautiful Cuckmere Valley, the ramshackle timber-framed houses of Alfriston and the curious Long Man of Wilmington chalk figure.

WEEKEND WALKS

Buriton to Amberley   23½ miles/38km (see pp98-116)
Stopping off in either Cocking or Midhurst for the night, this section takes in the fine wooded sections close to Buriton and the airy Harting Down on the first day, followed by Bignor Hill with its Roman Road, Stane Street, on the second day.

Amberley to Pyecombe   20½ miles/33km (see pp122-38)
Extensive views and the curious, enchanted Chanctonbury Ring are the highlights of the first day with a wide choice of places to stay in historic Steyning or Bramber with its castle. The second day follows the open top of the Downs all the way to the impressive valley of Devil's Dyke.

Eastbourne circular walk via Alfriston and Cuckmere Haven
19 miles/30.5km (see pp163-78)
If there is one section of the Downs that should be seen more any other it is this wonderful circular walk. Beginning and ending in Eastbourne, the walk combines the coastal and inland routes of the SDW. You'll pass through the beautiful villages of Jevington, Alfriston, Litlington and Westdean as well as walking the entire coastal section from Cuckmere Haven to Eastbourne. This is possibly the most spectacular walking that can be found anywhere in South-East England.

❏ Flint
Flint is a mineral found in bands within chalk and has played a big part in the history of the Downs. When man first found the ability to make tools the folk who lived on the Downs used flakes of flint to make arrowheads and knives. It was also found to be a very useful stone for starting fires. Today flint can be seen in local village architecture, being a very versatile building brick. The traditional Sussex Downs house and barn would not be the same if it were not for flint.

PLANNING YOUR WALK

What to take

Deciding how much to take with you can be difficult. Experienced walkers know that you really should take only the bare essentials but at the same time you need to ensure you have all the equipment necessary to make the trip safe and comfortable.

KEEP IT LIGHT – OR USE A LUGGAGE-CARRYING SERVICE!

Carrying a heavy rucksack really can ruin your enjoyment of a good walk and can also slow you down a great deal, turning an easy seven-mile day into an interminable slog. Be ruthless when you pack and leave behind all those little home comforts that you tell yourself don't weigh that much really. Always pack the essentials, of course, but try to leave behind anything that you think might 'come in handy' but probably won't. This advice is even more pertinent to campers who have the added weight of camping equipment to carry.

HOW TO CARRY IT

The size of the **rucksack** you should take depends on where you are planning to stay and how you are planning to eat. If you are camping and cooking for yourself you will probably need a 65- to 75-litre rucksack which can hold the tent, sleeping bag, cooking equipment and food. Make sure your rucksack has a stiffened back and can be adjusted to fit your own back comfortably. This will make carrying the weight much easier.

Rucksacks are decorated with seemingly pointless straps but if you adjust them correctly it can make a big difference to your personal comfort while walking. Make sure the hip belt and chest belt (if there is one) are fastened tightly as this helps distribute the weight: most of it should be carried on the hips.

When packing the rucksack make sure you have all the things you are likely to need during the day near the top or in the side pockets. This includes a map, water bottle, packed lunch, waterproofs and this guidebook (of course!).

If you are using a luggage-transfer service you will need a small **bum bag** or **day pack** for your camera, guidebook and other essentials for the day.

If you are camping you will need to carry a sleeping bag and a camping stove if planning to self-cater. All the YHA hostels on the Way provide bedding, though not towels, and have cooking facilities; and the only independent hostel on the Way provides both bedding and towels and also has self-catering facilities. A 40- to 60-litre rucksack should therefore be sufficient for either.

If you have gone for the B&B option you will probably find a 30- to 40-litre daypack is more than enough to carry your lunch, clothes, camera and guidebook. If you've booked a self-guided holiday, or are using a luggage-carrying service, (see pp23-6) you can just take a suitcase although a backpack is still better for the beginning and end of your trip where you may have to carry your own luggage.

A good habit to get into is always to put things in the same place in your rucksack and memorise where they are. There is nothing more annoying than pulling everything out of your pack to find that lost banana when you're starving or that camera when there is a butterfly basking briefly on a nearby rock. It's also a good idea to keep everything in **canoe bags**, **waterproof rucksack liners** or strong plastic bags (or binliners). If you don't it's bound to rain.

FOOTWEAR

Boots

Your boots are the single most important item of gear that can affect the enjoyment of your hike. In summer you could get by with a light pair of trail shoes if you're carrying only a small pack, although this is an invitation for wet, cold feet if there is any rain and they don't offer support for your ankles. Some of the terrain can be quite rough and wet so a pair of good walking boots is a safer bet. They must fit well and be properly broken in: it is no good discovering that your boots are slowly murdering your feet two days into a one-week walk.

Socks

The traditional wearing of a thin liner sock under a thicker wool sock is no longer necessary if you choose a high-quality sock specially designed for walking. A high proportion of natural fibres makes them much more comfortable. Three pairs are ample.

Extra footwear

Some walkers like to have a second pair of shoes to wear when not on the trail. Trainers, sport sandals, or flip flops are all suitable as long as they are light.

CLOTHES

Experienced walkers will know the importance of wearing the right clothes. Always expect the worst weather even if the forecast is good. Modern technology in outdoor attire can seem baffling but it basically comes down to the old multi-layer system: a base layer to transport sweat away from your skin; a mid-layer to keep you warm; and an outer layer or 'shell' to protect you from the rain.

Base layer

Cotton absorbs sweat, trapping it next to the skin which will chill you rapidly when you stop exercising. A thin lightweight **thermal top** made from a synthetic material is better as it draws moisture away, keeping you dry. It will be cool if worn on its own in hot weather and warm when worn under other clothes in cooler conditions. A spare would be sensible. Also bring a **shirt** or top for wearing in the evening.

Mid layers

In the summer a woollen jumper or mid-weight polyester **fleece** will suffice. For the rest of the year you will need an extra layer to keep you warm. Both wool and fleece, unlike cotton, have the ability to stay reasonably warm when wet.

Outer layer

A decent **waterproof jacket** is essential year-round and will be much more comfortable (but also more expensive) if it's also 'breathable' to prevent the build up of condensation on the inside. This layer can also be worn to keep the wind off.

Leg wear

Whatever you wear on your legs it should be light, quick-drying and not restricting. Many British walkers find **polyester tracksuit bottoms** comfortable. Poly-cotton or microfibre trousers are excellent. Denim jeans should never be worn; if they get wet they become heavy, cold and bind to your legs. A pair of **shorts** is nice to have on sunny days. Thermal **longjohns** or thick tights are cosy if you're camping but are probably unnecessary even in winter. **Waterproof trousers** are necessary most of the year. In summer a pair of wind-proof and quick-drying trousers is useful in showery weather. **Gaiters** are not really necessary but may come in useful in wet weather when the vegetation around your legs is dripping wet.

Underwear

One or two changes of what you normally wear is fine.

Other clothes

A **warm hat** and **gloves** should always be kept in your rucksack; you never know when you might need them. In summer you should also carry a **sun hat** with you, preferably one which covers the back of your neck. Another useful piece of summer equipment is a **swimsuit**.

TOILETRIES

Take only the minimum: a small bar of **soap** (unless staying in B&Bs) in a plastic container which can also be used instead of shaving cream and for washing clothes; a tiny tube of **toothpaste** and a **toothbrush**; and one roll of **loo paper** in a plastic bag. If you are planning to defecate outdoors you will also need a **lighter** for burning the paper and a lightweight **trowel** for burying the evidence (see p62 for further tips). A **towel** (if camping or staying in a hostel), **razor**, **deodorant**, **tampons/sanitary towels** and a high-factor **sunscreen** should cover most needs.

FIRST-AID KIT

Medical facilities in Britain are excellent so you need only take a small kit to cover common problems and emergencies. A basic kit will contain a pack of **aspirin** or **paracetamol** for treating mild to moderate pain and fever; **plasters/Band Aids** for minor cuts; 'moleskin', 'Compeed' or 'Second skin' for blisters; a **bandage** for holding dressings, splints or limbs in place and for supporting a sprained ankle; an **elastic knee support** for a weak knee; a small selection of different sized **sterile dressings** for wounds; **porous adhesive tape**; **antiseptic wipes**; **antiseptic cream**; **safety pins**; **tweezers** and a small pair of **scissors**. Pack the kit in a waterproof container.

GENERAL ITEMS

Essential

The following should be in everyone's rucksack: a **water bottle/pouch** (holding at least one litre); a **torch** (flashlight) with spare bulb and batteries in case you end up walking after dark; **emergency food** which your body can quickly convert into energy; a **penknife**; a **watch** with an alarm; and a **bag** for packing out any rubbish you accumulate. A **whistle** is also worth taking. It can fit in a pocket and although you are very unlikely to need it you may be grateful of it in the unlikely event of an emergency (see p68).

Reception is generally good for **mobile phones**. Even so, make sure you always have the wherewithal to call from a public phone box in case you have no signal at the crucial moment. Calls to the emergency services (☎ 999, or ☎ 112 from a mobile) are free of charge. Calls cost a minimum of 40p, but increasingly you will need a credit, debit, BT or prepaid card instead.

Useful

Many would list a **camera** as essential but it can be liberating to travel without one once in a while; a **notebook** can be a more accurate way of recording your impressions. Other items include a **book** to pass the time on train journeys; a pair of **sunglasses**; **binoculars** for observing wildlife; **walking poles** to take the strain off your knees and a **vacuum flask** for carrying hot drinks. Although the path is easy to follow a 'Silva' type **compass** is a good idea.

SLEEPING BAG

A sleeping bag is necessary only if you are camping. Clearly you won't need one if you are staying in B&B-style accommodation and the same is true if you are planning on using hostels. Campers should find that a two- to three-season bag will cope but obviously in winter a warmer bag is a good idea. On hot summer nights you could get away with a one-season bag.

CAMPING GEAR

Campers need a decent **tent** (or bivvy bag if you enjoy travelling light) that's able to withstand wet and windy weather; a **sleeping mat**; a **stove** and **fuel** (there is special mention in Part 4 of which shops stock fuel); a **mug**; a **spoon**; a wire/plastic **scrubber** for washing up; and a pan or pot. One pot is fine for two people; some pots come with a lid that can be used as a plate or frying pan.

MONEY

There are not many banks along the Way so you will have to carry most of your money as **cash**. A **debit card** is the easiest way to withdraw money either from banks or cash machines and a debit or **credit card** can be used to pay in most larger shops, restaurants and hotels. A **cheque book** is very useful for walkers with accounts in British banks as a cheque will often be accepted where a card is not, though you should also have a debit card to act as a guarantee.

MAPS

The **hand-drawn maps** in this book cover the trail at a scale of 1:20,000 – plenty of detail and information to keep you on the right track; the **colour maps** at the back of the book are at a smaller scale covering the surrounding area.

To explore even further afield you might be interested in Ordnance Survey maps (☎ 0845-605 0505, 🖳 www.ordnancesurvey.co.uk for map sales and digital downloads). Relevant sheets include OS Landranger maps (pink cover) at a scale of 1:50,000, Nos 185, 197, 198 and 199 (£7.99 each) or OS Explorer Maps (orange cover) at 1:25,000 Nos 119, 120, 121, 122, 123 and 132 (£7.99 each). OS also offers **digital maps** (see box below).

There's also a single-sheet Harveys *South Downs Way Map* (Harvey Maps, £13.95, 🖳 www.harveymaps.co.uk) at a scale of 1:40,000.

A Trailblazer **South Downs Way app** is under development. For more information see the Trailblazer website 🖳 www.trailblazer-guides.com.

Sections of the South Downs Way are now available on **Google Street View**.

RECOMMENDED READING

Many bookshops and most of the tourist information centres along the South Downs Way stock many of the following books.

An excellent read recounting **one person's experience** of his walk is *The South Downs Way* (£7.99) by Martin King.

For **birds** there are plenty of books to choose from including the *Collins Bird Guide* (£18.99) by Lars Svensson et al and the *New Birdwatcher's Pocket Guide to Britain and Europe* (£9.99) by Peter Hayman and Rob Hume. The RSPB's *Pocket Guide to British Birds* (£5.99, Simon Harrap and David Nurney) is also

PLANNING YOUR WALK

❏ **Digital mapping**

There are several software packages on the market today that provide Ordnance Survey maps for a PC or smartphone. The two best known are Memory Map and Anquet. Maps are supplied electronically, on DVD, USB media, or by direct download over the Internet. The maps are then loaded into an application, also available by download, from where you can view them, print them and create routes on them.

The real value of digital maps, though, is the ability to draw a route directly onto the map from your computer or smartphone. The map, or the appropriate sections of it, can then be printed with the route marked on it, so you no longer need the full versions of the OS maps. Additionally, the route can be viewed directly on the smartphone or uploaded to a GPS device. Most modern smartphones have a GPS chip so you will be able to see your position overlaid onto the digital map on your phone. Almost every device with built-in GPS functionality now has some mapping software available for it. One of the most popular manufacturers of dedicated handheld GPS devices is Garmin, who have an extensive range. Prices vary from around £100 to £600.

Smartphones and GPS devices should complement, not replace, the traditional method of navigation (a map and compass) as any electronic device can break or, if nothing else, run out of battery. Remember that the battery life of your phone will be significantly reduced, compared to normal usage, when you are using the built-in GPS and running the screen for long periods. **Stuart Greig**

recommended; birds are identified by their plumage and song. One of the best field guides to **flora** is *The Wildflowers of Britain and Ireland* (£18.99) by Marjorie Blamey et al. Now sadly out of print, the best guidebook specifically aimed at the **wildlife of the region** is *Downland Wildlife – A Naturalist's Year in the North & South Downs* by John S Burton, published by Phillips.

The Field Studies Council (☎ 0845-345 4071, 🖳 www.field-studies-council .org) publishes a series of **identification guides** in the form of laminated sheets

---

❏ SOURCES OF FURTHER INFORMATION

Tourist Information
Tourist Information Centres (TICs) are based in towns throughout Britain; they provide all manner of locally specific information and in most staff provide an accommodation-booking service (see box p19). Some places have **visitor information centres/points** staffed by volunteers who can provide information but not book accommodation; they also generally have limited opening hours. Others are not staffed but brochures about places of interest in the area are available.

The following TICs lie on or near the Way: **Winchester** (☎ 01962-850348, 🖳 www.visitwinchester.co.uk); **Petersfield** (☎ 01730-268829); **Lewes** (☎ 01273-483448, 🖳 www.staylewes.info); **Eastbourne** (☎ 01323-415415, 🖳 www.visiteast bourne.com). **Arundel** (🖳 www.arundel.org.uk) has a visitor information point.

In addition there are some **visitor centres** such as the ones at Queen Elizabeth Country Park (see p92) and Seven Sisters Country Park (see box p166). Visitor centres generally only have information about the actual attraction.

● **Tourism South East** This regional tourist board (🖳 www.visitsoutheasteng land.com) is responsible for the official tourist information centres. Their website has a wealth of information regarding accommodation, things to see and do, and they can keep you informed about upcoming festivals and events.

● **South Downs Society** Supported entirely by donations and subscriptions, this society (🖳 www.SouthDownsSociety.org.uk) has been around since 1923, helping to protect and conserve the Downs which they have divided into 12 distinct areas, each of which is under the care of a volunteer district officer. Their main responsibility is to peruse all planning applications that may affect the Downs. Membership costs £23/32 individual/joint members. They also arrange a programme of strolls and walks, on and around the Downs, throughout the year. Also see p58.

Organisations for walkers
● **Backpackers' Club** (🖳 www.backpackersclub.co.uk) A club aimed at people who are involved or interested in lightweight camping through walking, cycling, skiing and canoeing. They produce a quarterly magazine, provide members with a comprehensive advisory and information service on all aspects of backpacking, organise weekend trips and also publish a farm-pitch directory. Membership is £15/20/8.50/12 per year for an individual/family/anyone under 18 or over 65/retired couple.

● **The Long Distance Walkers' Association** (🖳 www.ldwa.org.uk) Membership includes a journal (*Strider*) three times per year with details of challenge events and local group walks as well as articles on the subject. Information on over 730 paths is presented in their *UK Trailwalkers' Handbook*. Membership is £13 a year.

● **Ramblers** (🖳 www.ramblers.org.uk) A charity that looks after the interests of walkers throughout Britain and promotes walking for health. Annual membership costs £33/44 (individual/joint; concessionary rates are £20/26), and includes their quarterly *Walk* magazine as well as access to their library of walking routes.

(£2.75-3.75 each) showing commonly found birds, trees, flowers etc and including 'Features of the South Downs Way'.

There are also several **field guide apps** for smartphones, including those that can aid in identifying birds from their song as well as by their appearance.

Getting to and from the South Downs Way

It could not be easier to reach the South Downs from London as there are numerous road and rail links not just to Winchester and Eastbourne, the start and finish of the walk, but to many other points along the Way. Most parts of the South Downs Way are no more than 1½-2 hours from the capital. Access from other parts of Britain often involves going via London but there are rail services to Winchester and Southampton via Reading. The rail line running across the south coast goes from Dover to Ashford International, then to Hastings and along the coast to Eastbourne and Brighton; from Brighton there are services to Portsmouth and Southampton.

See below for routes from continental Europe to the south coast of England.

❑ **Getting to Britain**

● **By air** The nearest international airport to Winchester is Southampton Airport (🖳 www.southamptonairport.com) on the south coast. The alternative would be to fly to London's Gatwick (🖳 www.gatwickairport.com) or Heathrow airports (🖳 www.heathrowairport.com), both of which serve destinations worldwide.

Further away but with a direct rail connection to Brighton is Luton Airport

● **From Europe by train** Eurostar (🖳 www.eurostar.com) operates a high-speed passenger service via the Channel Tunnel between Paris/Brussels and London. The Eurostar terminal in London is at St Pancras International station: some services also stop at Ashford International. For information about the various rail services to Britain from the continent contact your national rail service provider or visit 🖳 www.railteam.eu.

● **From Europe by coach** Eurolines (🖳 www.eurolines.com) have a huge network of long-distance coach services connecting over 500 cities in 25 European countries to London. However, these tickets often don't work out that much cheaper than flying the same route with a budget airline which is also far quicker. **Megabus** (🖳 www.megabus.com) is part of the Stagecoach group and it operates low-cost coach services from a number of destinations in Europe to London and other cities. Visit their website for details.

● **From Europe by car** Eurotunnel (🖳 www.eurotunnel.com) operates a shuttle **train** service for vehicles via the Channel Tunnel between Calais and Folkestone, taking an hour between the motorway in France and the motorway in England.

There are many **ferry** routes between France (Caen, Calais, Cherbourg, Dieppe, Dunkerque, Le Havre and St Malo) and the south coast ports of England such as Dover, Newhaven, Poole and Portsmouth. There are also services from Spain (Bilbao and Santander) to Portsmouth. Look at 🖳 www.ferrysavers.com or 🖳 www.direct ferries.com for a full list of companies and services.

P L A N N I N G   Y O U R   W A L K

NATIONAL TRANSPORT

By rail

The two main rail operators for services to locations along the South Downs are Southern (from London Victoria to the south coast) and SouthWest Trains (from London Waterloo stopping at Winchester and Petersfield). Other providers are: Thameslink Railway (from Bedford to Brighton via Luton Airport and St Pancras International) and Cross Country (from the Midlands and calling at

---

❏ USEFUL RAIL SERVICES   [see map p45]

Note: not all stops are listed here, nor are all shown on the map. Check the relevant operator's website for full details.

Southern Trains (☎ 0845-127 2920, 🖳 www.southernrailway.com)
(**Note**: services from London Victoria usually also stop at Clapham Junction, East Croydon and Gatwick Airport)
● London Victoria to Horsham via Three Bridges and Crawley, daily 2/hr
  At Horsham the trains divide:
    to **Bognor Regis** via Christ's Hospital, Billingshurst, Pulborough,
        Amberley (at Houghton Bridge), Arundel, Ford, & Barnham, daily 2/hr
    to **Portsmouth Harbour** via Barnham, Chichester & Havant, daily 1/hr
    to **Southampton Central** via Barnham, Chichester & Havant, daily 1/hr
● London Victoria to Brighton (fast service), daily 2/hr
● London Victoria to Haywards Heath, Mon-Sat 2/hr
  At Haywards Heath the trains divide:
    to **Brighton** via Burgess Hill & Hassocks, daily 1/hr
    to **Littlehampton** via Burgess Hill, Hove, Shoreham & Worthing, daily 1/hr
        (note: the train divides again at Worthing and the other half goes to
        Portsmouth Harbour via Bognor Regis & Chichester, daily 1/hr)
    to **Eastbourne** via Wivelsfield, Lewes, Polegate & Hampden Park, daily 1/hr
    to **Ore** via Plumpton, Lewes, Polegate, Eastbourne & Hastings, daily 1/hr
● Ashford International to Brighton via Hastings, Eastbourne & Lewes, daily 1/hr
  (note: Sunday services also call at Berwick & Glynde)
● Ore to Brighton via Eastbourne, Berwick, Glynde, Lewes & Falmer, Mon-Sat 1/hr
● Portsmouth to Brighton via Havant, Chichester, Barnham & Shoreham, daily 1/hr
● Southampton to Brighton via Havant, Chichester, Barnham & Shoreham, daily 1/hr
● Brighton to Seaford via Lewes & Newhaven, daily 2/hr (stops at Southease 1/hr)

SouthWest Trains (☎ 0345-600 0650, 🖳 www.southwesttrains.co.uk)
● London Waterloo to Weymouth via Clapham Junction, Winchester, Southampton
    Airport, Southampton & Bournemouth, Mon-Sat 2/hr, Sun 1/hr
● London Waterloo to Portsmouth via Petersfield, Mon-Fri 1-2/hr, Sat 2/hr, Sun 1/hr
● London Waterloo to Portsmouth via Woking, Basingstoke & Winchester, daily 1/hr

Thameslink Railway (🖳 www.thameslinkrailway.com)
● Bedford to Brighton via Luton, St Pancras, East Croydon, Gatwick Airport,
    Haywards Heath & Burgess Hill, Mon-Sat 2/hr plus 1/hr from London Bridge
    which also calls at Hassocks & Preston Park, Sun 2/hr though not to Preston Park

Cross Country Trains (☎ 0844 811 0124, 🖳 www.crosscountrytrains.co.uk)
● Birmingham to Bournemouth via Reading, Winchester & Southampton, daily 1/hr

Winchester). See box opposite and map p45 for contact and service details.

Timetables, ticket and fare information can be found on the rail operators' websites or through **National Rail Enquiries** (☎ 08457-484950; 🖳 www.nationalrail.co.uk). The rail operators also sell tickets online; it is worth booking in advance to get the cheapest fares. It may also be worth looking at 🖳 www.thetrainline.com to see if you can get an even cheaper fare.

If you think you may want to book a taxi for when you arrive details of companies are given in Part 4. Alternatively, visit 🖳 www.traintaxi.co.uk for details of taxi companies operating at rail stations throughout England. It is also often possible to book train tickets that include bus travel to your ultimate destination: enquire when you book your train ticket or look at Plus Bus's website (🖳 www.plusbus.info).

By coach

Coach travel is generally cheaper but takes longer than the train. **National Express** is the principal coach (long-distance bus) operator in Britain and has services to a number of destinations on or near the Way.

❑ **USEFUL COACH SERVICES** [see map p45]

National Express (☎ 0871-781 8181, 🖳 www.nationalexpress.com)
Note: not all stops are listed – contact National Express for full details.

024	London Victoria Coach Station (VCS) to **Eastbourne** via Gatwick Airport South Terminal, East Grinstead, Uckfield & Polegate, 1/day
025	London VCS to Brighton via Gatwick Airport South Terminal, daily 1/hr (1/day continues to Worthing and Bognor Regis)
031	London VCS to Portsmouth via **Petersfield**, 1/day
032	London VCS to Southampton via **Winchester**, 8/day
203	Heathrow Airport to Portsmouth via **Winchester** & Southampton, 10/day
315	Helston to **Eastbourne** via Falmouth, Truro, Plymouth, Exeter, Bridport, Dorchester, Weymouth, Poole, Bournemouth, Southampton, Portsmouth, Chichester, **Arundel**, Worthing, Brighton, Newhaven & Seaford, 1/day
539	Birmingham to Bournemouth via Oxford, Newbury & **Winchester**, 1/day

---

By car

The south of England is overrun with dual carriageways and bypasses so there is no shortage of 'A' roads to follow down to the Downs. On holiday weekends, however, be prepared for long tailbacks as everyone heads for the coast. There are main roads from London passing through Winchester, Petersfield, Cocking, Amberley, Arundel, Washington, Pyecombe, Lewes, Brighton and Eastbourne.

By air

Although there are local airports, such as the one at Shoreham, the easiest way to fly to the South-East from other corners of England is to get a flight to Gatwick or Southampton; see box p41. Also see 🖳 www.chooseclimate.org for the true costs of flying.

LOCAL TRANSPORT

Hampshire, West Sussex and East Sussex all have excellent local transport networks which make planning linear day and weekend walks easy.

The public transport map opposite summarises all the useful routes; see the box below for details (though not all stops are listed). For more information contact traveline (🖳 www.travelinesoutheast.org.uk. Where school bus services may be of use to walkers they are mentioned in the relevant place in the route guide. The tourist information centres along the Downs can provide, free of charge, a comprehensive local transport timetable for their particular region.

❏ **LOCAL BUS SERVICES**   **[see map opposite]**

bluestar (☎ 01202-338421, 🖳 www.bluestarbus.co.uk)

1   Southampton to Winchester, Mon-Sat 3/hr, Sun 2/hr

Brighton & Hove Buses (☎ 01273-886200, 🖳 www.buses.co.uk)

2   Rottingdean to Shoreham via Brighton & Hove, Mon-Sat 2/hr, Sun 1/hr;
       Rottingdean to Steyning via Brighton, Upper Beeding & Bramber, daily 1/hr

12/12X (Coaster) Brighton to Eastbourne via Rottingdean, Saltdean, Peacehaven,
       Newhaven, Seaford, Exceat (Seven Sisters Park Centre) & East Dean,
       Mon-Sat 4/hr plus 2/hr Brighton to Seaford (see 13X for Sunday services)

12A   Brighton to Eastbourne: same route as No 12 but also stopping at Birling Gap
       & Beachy Head, Mon-Sat 2/hr

13X   Brighton to Eastbourne via Newhaven, Seaford, Exceat (Seven Sisters Park
       Centre), Birling Gap & Beachy Head, Sat, Sun & bank holidays 1/hr

28   Brighton to Ringmer via Lewes, Mon-Sat 2/hr

29   Brighton to Tunbridge Wells via Lewes, Mon-Sat 2/hr plus 2/hr to Uckfield

77   Brighton to Devil's Dyke, mid Apr-June Mon-Fri 6/day, Sat & Sun every 45
       mins, mid June to end Aug daily 2/hr (open-top bus), Sep-mid Apr Mon-Fri
       6/day, Sat, Sun & bank holidays 1/hr (☎ 01273-292480)

79   Brighton to Ditchling Beacon, Sat, Sun & bank holidays 1/hr

Compass Travel (☎ 01903-690025, 🖳 www.compass-travel.co.uk) (see also p46)

23   Worthing to Horsham via Washington, Sun & bank hols 6/day (see also Metrobus)

74   Storrington to Horsham via West Chiltington, Mon-Sat 2/day

74A   Storrington to Horsham, Mon-Sat 4/day

85   Worthing to Chichester via Arundel, Mon-Sat 3/day

85A   Worthing to Chichester via Arundel & Barnham, Mon-Sat 2/day

99   Chichester to Petworth via Goodwood, East Dean, Charlton, Graffham, Sutton
       & Bignor, Mon-Sat 6/day but only stops if prebooked (☎ 01903-264776)

99A   Chichester to Petworth via Sutton & Bignor, Sun & bank hols 5/day

100   Burgess Hill to Pulborough via Henfield, Upper Beeding, Bramber, Steyning
       Washington & Storrington, Mon-Sat 12/day

123   Newhaven to Lewes via Southease, Rodmell & Kingston-near-Lewes,
       Mon-Sat 7/day

125   ('The Downsman') Lewes to Eastbourne via Glynde, Firle, Charleston,
       Selmeston, Berwick, Alfriston, Wilmington, Polegate & Willingdon,
       Mon-Sat 4/day

126   Seaford to Berwick via Alfriston, Mon-Sat 1/day (see also Cuckmere
       Community Bus)

PLANNING YOUR WALK

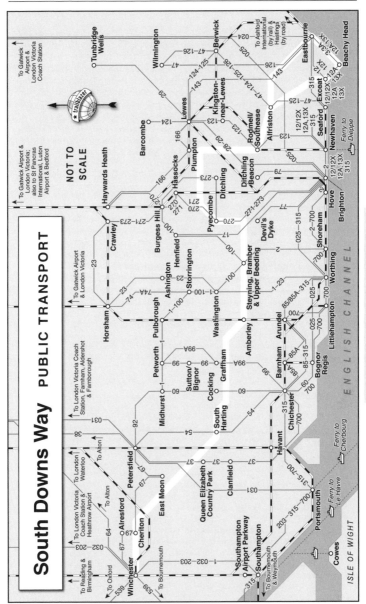

South Downs Way PUBLIC TRANSPORT

NOT TO SCALE

PLANNING YOUR WALK

ENGLISH CHANNEL

ISLE OF WIGHT

❏ LOCAL BUS SERVICES *[cont'd from p44]*

143   Eastbourne to Lewes via Polegate, Hailsham & Ringmer, Mon-Fri 3/day
166   Lewes to Haywards Heath via Plumpton & Wivelsfield, Mon-Fri 6/day

Emsworth & District (☎ 01243-37833, 🖳 emsworthanddistrict.co.uk)
54   Petersfield to Chichester via South Harting & Uppark, Mon-Sat 5/day
92   Midhurst to Petersfield, Mon-Sat 7/day (see Stagecoach for Sun service)

Cuckmere Community Bus (☎ 01323-870920, 🖳 www.cuckmerebuses.org.uk)
Note: Everybody involved in Cuckmere Community Bus (CCB) is a volunteer.
47   Cuckmere Valley Rambler: Berwick Station circular route via Drusillas Zoo
      Park, Alfriston, Seaford, Exceat, Seven Sisters Country Park, Litlington,
      Lullington & Wilmington, late Mar to late Oct Sat, Sun & public hols 1/hr
126   Seaford to Eastbourne via Alfriston, Berwick (Drusillas), Wilmington,
      Polegate & Willingdon, Mon-Sat 2-3/day, Sun & bank hols 4-5/day
CCB also operate some limited-frequency services which stop where it is safe.
  These include: **40** Seaford to Berwick via Exceat, Westdean, Charleston Manor,
  Litlington, Lullington, Wilmington & Alciston, Tue & Fri 1/day; **41** Eastbourne
  circular route via Jevington, Tue & Thur 1/day; **42** Hailsham to Berwick circular
  route via Alciston & Alfriston, Wed 1/day, Fri 1/day though not to Alfriston;
  44 Berwick to Eastbourne via Polegate, Mon 1/day, Tue 2/day plus 1/day Polegate
  to Eastbourne, Thur 2-3/day (services also call at Alciston & Alfriston)

Metrobus (☎ 01293-449191, 🖳 www.metrobus.co.uk)
23   Crawley to Worthing via Horsham, Ashington & Washington,
      Mon-Sat approx 1/hr (Sunday service operated by Compass)
270   East Grinstead to Brighton via Burgess Hill, Hassocks & Pyecombe,
      Mon-Sat approx 1/hr
271   Crawley to Brighton via Burgess Hill, Hassocks & Pyecombe,
      Mon-Sat 6/day, Sun 3/day
273   Crawley to Brighton via Burgess Hill, Ditchling & Pyecombe,
      Mon-Sat 6-7/day

Stagecoach (🖳 www.stagecoachbus.com)
1   Midhurst to Worthing via Petworth, Pulborough, Storrington, Washington &
      Findon, Mon-Sat 1/hr, Sun 6/day
3/3A Foot of Beachy Head to Eastbourne via Meads Village, Mon-Sat 2/hr plus 3/hr
      Meads Village to Eastbourne, Sun 10/day
37   Havant to Petersfield via Waterlooville, Clanfield, Queen Elizabeth Country
      Park, Mon-Sat 12/day, May-Oct Sun 5/day (services connect with No 38)
38   Alton to Petersfield, Mon-Fri 5/day (connects with No 37)
60   Bognor Regis to Midhurst via Chichester, West Dean, Singleton & Cocking,
      Mon-Sat 2/hr plus 2/hr Bognor Regis to Chichester, Sun 1/hr
64   Alton to Winchester, Mon-Sat 1/hr, Sun 5/day
67   Winchester to Petersfield via Alresford, Cheriton, Bramdean, West Meon &
      East Meon, Mon-Sat 5-7/day
92   Midhurst to Petersfield, Sun 6/day (see Emsworth & District for Mon-Sat)
700   (Coastliner; 🖳 www.coastliner700.co.uk) Arundel to Brighton via
      Littlehampton, Goring, Worthing, Shoreham & Hove, Mon-Sat 2/hr, Sun 1/hr
      Littlehampton to Brighton via Goring, Worthing, Shoreham & Hove, Mon-Sat
      4/hr, Sun 2/hr; connecting services (Mon-Sat 3/hr, Sun 2/hr) operate from
      Portsmouth to Chichester via Havant (change bus at Chichester) & Chichester
      to Littlehampton via Bognor Regis (change bus at Littlehampton).

2

THE ENVIRONMENT AND NATURE

Flora and fauna

The South Downs region is essentially a man-made landscape. Centuries of farming have shaped these rolling hills and left a unique habitat for a variety of common and not-so-common species. Left alone the South Downs would revert to scrub and woodland. This may not appear to be a great tragedy. However, the habitat that would be lost is a much scarcer one that provides sanctuary to a variety of endangered species which rely on the unique chalk grassland environment. The Downs are not free of trees either. The plough never reached the steep scarp slope that runs along the northern edge of the Downs. Indeed there is a healthy balance between the open grassland of the high ground and the deciduous beech woodland which can claim to be some of the oldest and most undisturbed woodland in Britain.

Any walker on the Way, however, will notice the precarious relationship between man and the Downs. This corner of England is one of the most populated parts of Europe and the demands on the land have been great. In recent times large chunks of the Downs have been eaten away to be replaced by major roads such as the A3 and M3 and to make way for the expanding south-coast towns such as Brighton. Nevertheless, some good has come out of the race to build homes and roads. More and more people are noticing the value of the South Downs as the area comes under increasing pressure and this has culminated in the award of National Park status. Whether the protection afforded by this status outweighs the increased pressure from ever-greater numbers of tourists is something of a hot debate.

Tourists who are walkers are lucky enough to be travelling at a speed that allows them to appreciate the wildlife around them. Anyone who lives and works in a high-pressure environment – and particularly cities – will find a walk along the top of the Downs to be something of a therapeutic exercise. However, too many people bring the stress of work with them to the countryside, walking as if they have a train to catch. To gain more from a walk on the Downs it is worth allowing yourself the chance to wind down. Look around, not at your feet, walk slowly and take breaks. Quiet and observant walkers are far more likely to notice the plants and maybe the animals of the Downs.

BUTTERFLIES

The Downs are famous for their butterflies. Many of the National Nature Reserves in the area have been set up specifically because of the variety and number of butterflies. One of the most prevalent is the **meadow brown** (*Maniola jurtina*), a very common species, dusty brown in colour with a rusty orange streak and dark, false eyes. They can be seen in meadows all across the Downs. The small **gatekeeper** (*Pyronia tithonus*) likes similar habitat and is also widespread throughout the Downs. They are identified by their deep orange and chocolate-brown markings.

The **peacock** (*Inachis io*) is surely Britain's most beautiful butterfly; it's quite common in this area. The markings on the wings are said to mimic the eyes of an animal to frighten off predators. Also common is the impressive **red admiral** (*Vanessa atalanta*). Owing to climate change it is now starting to overwinter in Britain and appears to be thriving. The **brimstone** (*Gonepteryx rhamni*) is also widespread, though well camouflaged as its wings look very like leaves; the **white admiral** (*Limenitis camilla*), however, is declining in numbers but may still be seen in some woodland sites. Although it has also recently been in decline in other parts of the country, the **small tortoiseshell** (*Aglais urticae*) is still widespread here and also in towns and villages. Other very common butterflies include the **small white** (*Pieris/Artogeia rapae*) and the **large white** (*Pieris brassicae*). Both can travel large distances, some migrating from continental Europe each year.

Along many of the country lanes and tracks the **speckled wood** (*Pararge aegeria*) can be seen basking on hedgerows. It is a small dark butterfly with a few white spots and six small false eyes at the rear.

There are several butterflies that are synonymous with chalk downland, notably the butterflies known as blues. The **holly blue** (*Celastrina argiolus*) and **chalkhill blue** (*Polyommatus/Lysandra coridon*) are both similar in appearance, being very small and pale blue in colour, although the chalkhill blue has a dark strip on the edge of each wing. The **common blue** (*Polyommatus icarus*) is even smaller and as the name suggests is the most common of the blues. The underside of its wings is a dusty brown colour with small orange and white spots.

A rare downland butterfly is the **Duke of Burgundy fritillary** (*Hamearis lucina*) which you may be lucky enough to see on Beacon Hill. It has pale orange spots on small dark wings. Another rarity that relies on chalk grassland is the **silver spotted skipper** (*Hesperia comma*), a diminutive yellow butterfly with small white flashes on the undersides of the wings.

Finally, the **brown argus** (*Aricia agestis*), a small dark butterfly with distinctive orange spots along the edges of each wing, is another that is restricted to chalk grassland; it can sometimes be seen flying close to the ground.

FLOWERS

Many of the flowering meadows that once covered large stretches of downland farmland have been destroyed by modern farming techniques. However, in

Peacock
Inachis io

Small Tortoiseshell
Aglais urticae

Common Blue
Polyommatus icarus

Brimstone
*Gonepteryx
rhamni*

Chalkhill Blue
Polyommatus/Lysandra coridon

Painted Lady
Cynthia cadui

Small Garden/Cabbage White
Pieris/Artogeia rapae

Red Admiral
Vanessa atalanta

Meadow
brown
Maniola jurtina

Large Garden/
Cabbage White
Pieris brassicae

White Admiral
Limenitis camilla

Common Dog Violet
Viola riviniana

Common Centaury
Centaurium erythraea

Honeysuckle
Lonicera periclymemum

Wild marjoram
Origanum vulgare

Germander Speedwell
Veronica chamaedrys

Herb-Robert
Geranium robertianum

Lousewort
Pedicularis sylvatica

Self-heal
Prunella vulgaris

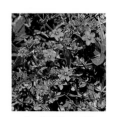

Scarlet Pimpernel
Anagallis arvensis

Viper's Bugloss
Echium vulgare

Ramsons (Wild Garlic)
Allium ursinum

Bluebell
Hyacinthoides non-scripta

Dog Rose
Rosa canina

Meadow Buttercup
Ranunculis acris

Gorse
Ulex europaeus

Tormentil
Potentilla erecta

Birdsfoot-trefoil
Lotus corniculatus

Ox-eye Daisy
Leucanthemum vulgare

St John's Wort
Hypericum perforatum

Primrose
Primula vulgaris

Cowslip
Primula veris

Common Ragwort
Senecio jacobaea

Red Admiral butterfly (*Vanessa atalanta*) on
Hemp Agrimony (*Eupatorium cannabinum*)

Foxglove
Digitalis purpurea

Early Purple Orchid
Orchis mascula

Pyramidal Orchid
Anacamptis pyramidalis

Bell Heather
Erica cinerea

Heather (Ling)
Calluna vulgaris

Common Poppy
Papaver rhoeas

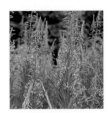

Rosebay Willowherb
Epilobium angustifolium

Common Vetch
Vicia sativa

Forget-me-not
Myosotis arvensis

Rowan (tree)
Sorbus aucuparia

Old Man's Beard
Clematis vitalba

Red Campion
Silene dioica

places, efforts are being made to revive these by encouraging farmers to employ more flower-friendly methods.

Meadows

The dominant grass found in fields all over the Downs is the appropriately named **sheep's fescue** (*Festuca ovina*) which was cultivated specifically for pastureland and is the grass of choice for downland sheep.

Of far greater interest are the likes of the **common poppy** (*Papaver rhoeas*) with its spectacular deep red petals. They often colonise arable fields and path edges, preferring well-disturbed soil. Entire fields turn red in the flowering season in late summer.

Earlier in the season walkers are likely to come across the **cowslip** (*Primula veris*) and its head of pale yellow flowers. The flowers flop down in small bunches earning the plant the old nickname 'bunch of keys'.

Perhaps one of the most beautiful of the downland flowers is the **round headed rampion** (*Phyteuma orbiculare*). Its striking dark blue flowers have earned it the local name 'The Pride of Sussex'.

The tiny yellow flower of **tormentil** (*Potentilla tormentilla*) can be seen hugging the ground in short grassland. It gets its name from an age when it was used as a medicinal remedy for diarrhoea and haemorrhoids: the taste is so foul that it tormented whoever took it.

Another tiny flower that can also be found close to the ground is the **scarlet pimpernel** (*Anagallis avensis*), a member of the primrose family. The flowers are just 5mm in diameter but stand out from their grassy background thanks to their light red colour.

Many people assume orchids to be so rare as to be nearly impossible to find. In truth there are several fairly common species that may readily be seen flowering on the Downs, usually around mid-summer. These include the **early purple orchid** (*Orchis mascula*) which can be seen in rough grassland. It stands about 10-15cm tall and has an elongated head of pinky-purple flowers.

There are of course some species that do fit the rare orchid label including the **fly orchid** (*Ophrys insectifera*) with flowers resembling small insects. These cleverly designed flowers attract wasps which pick up the pollen and take it on to the next insect-shaped flower they see. Another orchid with the same tactic is the **bee orchid** (*Ophrys apifera*) whose flowers are shaped like, well, bees.

Apart from the orchids, one of the most endangered and also one of the most striking flowering plants that may be seen, particularly on the Downs above Eastbourne, is **pheasant's-eye** (*Adonis annua*) with its blood red petals and large seed head.

In overgrown areas thorny **gorse** (*Ulex europeous*) bushes brighten up the summer with their small yellow flowers that burst open from February until June, filling the air with a coconut-like scent.

Woodland and hedgerows

There are several flowering plants associated with open woods and woodland edges. In May the pink flowers of the slightly inaccurately named **red campion**

(*Silene dioica*) come into view along woodland edges and at the foot of hedgerows while deeper into the woods the floor becomes covered with **blue-bells** (*Hyacinthoides non-scripta*) in the early spring. Other common woodland flowering plants include the **wood anemone** (*Anemone nemorosa*) with its round white flowers which cover forest floors in a similar way to bluebells. A more isolated flower, although sometimes seen growing in small groups, is the cheerful yellow **primrose** (*Primula vulgaris*).

Bramble (*Rubus fruticosus*) is a common woodland and hedgerow species with small sharp thorns. It spreads rapidly, engulfing everything in its path. In its favour, blackberries appear on the branches in the autumn to provide sustenance for hungry birds and greedy walkers.

In hedgerows and along woodland edges you'll see the distinctive feathery climber, **old man's beard** (*Clematis vitalba*), also known as traveller's joy. The feathery part of the plant is actually the fruit.

The **foxglove** (*Digitalis purpurea*) is a very tall and graceful plant with white or purple trumpet-like flowers. It is commonly spotted along hedgerows, roadside verges and in shady woodland. Other fairly common woodland species that are just as comfortable on hedgebanks include the **forget-me-not** (*Myosotis arvensis*) which has very small blue flowers and **cow parsley** (*Anthriscus sylvestris*), a tall plant with a head of white flowers.

Perhaps the most unusual and to some eyes the ugliest of plants, found in dark corners of beech woodland, is the **bird's nest orchid** (*Neottia nidus-avis*), so-called because of its nest-like root system that intertwines across the ground.

TREES

Over the last few hundred years the once-extensive forest cover in southern England has been fragmented into a patchwork of copses and coppiced woodland. Trees were felled for fuel and for shipbuilding and, in the case of the South Downs, to clear land for agricultural needs. In more recent times many of the hedgerows that helped create the familiar patchwork landscape have been grubbed up to create much larger fields.

Nevertheless, there are parts of the Downs that have survived the threat from axe and chainsaw. The north-facing scarp slope was, and still is, too steep for clearing and too inaccessible for ploughing. Consequently, this is where most of the trees are found. Although there are still areas of semi-natural or ancient mixed woodland, much of the remaining woodland has been coppiced, an old method of promoting growth of more numerous and narrower trunks by cutting a tree at its base. Coppicing was common in hazel stands and the resulting product used in constructing fences and making furniture.

Although coppicing is no longer widespread it is still practised in some parts by enthusiasts of old woodland crafts and also by conservationists who recognise that coppiced woodland can be beneficial to certain species.

Most of the woodland the walker will encounter on the Downs is mixed deciduous, made up largely of beech and ash but there are many other species to look out for.

THE ENVIRONMENT AND NATURE

Tree species

The **beech** (*Fagus sylvatica*) with its thick, silvery trunk is one of the most attractive native trees. It can grow to a height of 40 metres with the high canopies blocking out much of the light. As a result the floors of beech woodlands tend to be fairly bare of vegetation. They favour well-drained soil, hence their liking for the steep scarp slope. In autumn the colours of the turning leaves can be quite spectacular. One species that does survive the shady floor of beech woodland is the distinctive **common holly** (*Ilex aquifolium*) with its dark waxy leaves which have sharp points. Holly varies in size, usually growing as a sprawling bush on the woodland floor or in hedgerows but also as a tree when established in more isolated locations.

Famous for its longevity, lasting for well over a thousand years in some cases, the **common yew** (*Taxus baccata*) is abundant in churchyards but there are also natural stands on the scarp slope and among beech woodland. The dark glossy needles are quite distinctive as is the flaky red bark of the often gnarled and twisted old trunks and branches. Do not be tempted to eat the bright red berries; they're poisonous. Another tree with red berries is the **hawthorn** (*Crataegus monogyna*). It has small leaves and is usually found in hedgerows but can also grow as a small tree. In early autumn the berries provide food for woodland birds and are particularly popular with blackbirds.

MAMMALS

The well-drained soil of chalk downland is ideal habitat for the **badger** (*Meles meles*), a sociable animal with a distinctive black-and-white-striped muzzle. Badgers live in family groups in large underground 'setts'. They are rarely spotted since they tend to emerge after dark to hunt for worms in the fields. Sadly, they are more commonly seen dead on the road: after hedgehogs they are the most inept at crossing roads.

The **fox** (*Vulpes vulpes*) is another common mammal on the Downs. Although they prefer to come out at night they are not exclusively nocturnal; particularly in summer they may be out in broad daylight in some of the quieter corners of the hills though the best time to spot a fox is at dusk when you might see one trotting along a field or woodland edge.

The **rabbit** (*Oryctolagus cuniculus*) is seemingly everywhere on the Downs. The well-drained, steep grassland is ideal for their warrens.

The **grey squirrel** (*Sciurus carolinensis*) was introduced from North America at the end of the 19th century. Its outstanding success in colonising Britain is very much to the detriment of other native species including the red squirrel. Greys are bigger and stockier than reds and to many people the reds, with their tufted ears, bushy tails and small beady eyes, are the far more attractive of the two. Sadly there are no red squirrels anywhere on the Downs.

The **roe deer** (*Capreolus capreolus*) is a small, native species of deer that tends to hide in woodland. They can sometimes be seen, alone or in pairs, on field edges or clearings in the forest but you are more likely to hear the sharp dog-like bark made when they smell you coming.

At dusk **bats** can be seen hunting for moths and flying insects along hedgerows, over rivers and around street lamps. All 17 species in Britain are protected by law. The commonest, and smallest, species is the **pipistrelle** (*Pipistrellus pipistrellus*). Although it is only about 4cm long it can eat up to 3000 insects in one night. You may also be lucky enough to see the slighter larger **Daubenton's** bat (*Myotis daubentonii*) hunting for mosquitoes over rivers and ponds.

If the Downs were made for any one species it is probably the **brown hare** (*Lepus europaeus*) which, if you are observant, can be seen racing across the fields on the hilltops. Hares are bigger than rabbits, with longer hind legs and ears, and are far more graceful than their prolific little cousins. Some other small but fairly common species to keep an eye out for include the carnivorous **stoat** (*Mustela erminea*), its smaller cousin the **weasel** (*Mustela nivalis*), the **hedgehog** (*Erinaceus europaeus*) and a number of species of **voles**, **mice** and **shrews**.

REPTILES

The **adder** (*Vipera berus*) is the only poisonous snake in Britain. It is easily recognised by the distinctive zig-zag markings down its back and a diamond shape on the back of its head. On summer days adders bask in sunny spots such as on a warm rock or in the middle of a path so watch your step. Adders tend to move out of the way quickly but should you be unlucky enough to inadvertently step on one and get bitten sit still and send someone else for help. Their venom is designed to kill small mammals, not humans. A bite is unlikely to be fatal to an adult but *is* serious enough to warrant immediate medical attention, especially in the case of children. Nevertheless, the likelihood of being bitten is minuscule. Walkers are far more likely to frighten the adder away once it senses your footsteps.

The **grass snake** (*Natrix natrix*), an adept swimmer, is a much longer, slimmer snake with a yellow collar around the neck. It's non-venomous but does emit a foul stench should you attempt to pick one up. It's much better for you and the snake to leave it in peace.

The **common lizard** (*Lacerta/Zootoca vivipara*) is a harmless creature which can often be seen basking in the sun on rocks and stone walls. About 15cm long, it is generally brown with patterns of spots or stripes. However, you are far more likely to hear them scuttling away through the undergrowth as you approach.

A curious beast, looking like a slippery eel or small snake, is the **slow worm** (*Anguis fragilis*) which despite the name is neither a worm nor indeed an eel or snake but a legless lizard. Usually a glossy grey or copper colour, they can be seen on woodland floors and in grassland. They are completely harmless and usually slip away into the leaf litter when they hear footsteps.

BIRDS

The chalk grassland of the Downs is ideal for a variety of bird species but the grassy hillsides are not the only habitat on the Downs. There are many woodland species in the beech forests on the steep scarp slope, freshwater species on the rivers and sea birds by Cuckmere Haven and the Seven Sisters' cliffs. The following list gives just a few of the birds that may be seen while walking on the Downs.

Scrubland and chalk grassland

One of the most attractive birds the Downs walker might spot, usually seen feeding on open arable farmland, is the **lapwing** (*Vanellus vanellus*), also known as the pee-wit. It has long legs, a short bill and a distinc-tive long head crest. Sadly, this attractive bird is declining in numbers. The name comes from its lilting flight, frequently changing direction with its large rounded wings. It is also identified by a white belly, black and white head, black throat patch and distinctive dark green wings.

LAPWING/PEEWIT
L: 320MM/12.5"

Towards dusk **barn owls** (*Tyto alba*) hunt for voles along field and wood-land edges. To see a barn owl, with its ghostly white plumage, is a real treat but their dwindling numbers make such a sighting increasingly rare.

The colourful little **stonechat** (*Saxicola rubicola*) with its deep orange breast and black head is among the more com-monly sighted of Downland birds. They are easily iden-tified by their habit of flitting from the top of one bush to another, only pausing to call out across the fields. The stonechat's call sounds much like two stones being struck together, hence the name stonechat.

The **yellowhammer** (*Emberiza citrinella*), also known as the yellow bunting, can sometimes be seen perched on the top of gorse bushes. Most field guides to birds along with most old romantic country folk claim that the distinctive

STONECHAT
L: 135MM/5.25"

song of the yellowhammer sounds like 'a little bit of bread and no cheese'. At a push they are right but the yellowhammer is certainly no talking parrot.

The call of the **skylark** (*Alauda arvensis*) can probably be considered the sound of the Downs. This small, buff-coloured, ground-nesting lark is usually heard but not often seen. The characteristic flight pattern, rising steadily upwards on rapid wingbeats whilst twittering relentlessly, is what makes the skylark such a distinctive little bird. However, the skylark is difficult to see against the blue sky but if you look careful-ly you might just spot one way up high.

Woodland

A common raptor that is often heard before it's seen is the **buzzard** (*Buteo buteo*), a large broad-winged bird of prey which looks much like a small eagle. It

SKYLARK
L: 185MM/7.25"

THE ENVIRONMENT AND NATURE

is dark brown in appearance but slightly paler on the underside of the wings. It has a distinctive mewing call and can be spotted soaring ever higher on the air thermals or sometimes perched on the top of fenceposts. Buzzards are less common towards the eastern end of the Downs where the woodland cover is not so great. They are far easier to spot above the dense woodland on the West Sussex Downs and around the Meon Valley in Hampshire.

The **kestrel** *(Falco tinnunculus)*, a small falcon, is much smaller than the buzzard and is far more prevalent. It hovers expertly in a fixed spot above grassland and roadside verges, even in the strongest of winds, hunting for mice and voles.

Similar in size and appearance but rarely seen is the **hobby** *(Falco subbuteo)* which appears in the summer months, often on the margins of woodlands.

The **green woodpecker** *(Picus viridis)* is not all green, sporting a bright red and black head. They are sometimes spotted clinging to a vertical tree trunk or feeding on the ground in open fields. The most common view, however, is as the bird flies away when disturbed. The undulating flight pattern is characterised by rapid wing beats as the bird rises followed by a pause when the bird slowly drops. This is accompanied by a loud laughing call that has earned the bird its old English name of yaffle.

WOODCOCK
L: 330mm/13"

The **woodcock** *(Scolopax rusticola)*, with its long straight beak and plump body, is common in damp woodland where it can lie hidden thanks to its leafy brown plumage. It is most easily sighted in spring at dusk and dawn. This is when the males perform their courtship flight, known as 'roding', which involves two distinct calls, one a low grunting noise, the other a sharp 'k-wik k-wik' call.

❑ **Geology**

It helps to examine the geology of the region as a whole in order to understand how the South Downs reached their present-day form. South-East England is made up of three bands of rock and sediment, the deepest layer being sandstone, the one above clay and the top layer chalk. Over time these three layers were pushed up, probably due to tectonic plate movements, with Africa nudging into Europe. Through the ensuing millennia the soft chalk was eroded through weathering, exposing first the clay and then the more resistant sandstone. The North and South Downs are all that remains of the chalk that lies over the deeper clay and sandstone layers. They are still being eroded today.

One interesting feature of the Downs is the lack of streams. Chalk is highly permeable so streams flow only very briefly during periods of very heavy rainfall. It is worth remembering this when walking on a hot day.

THE ENVIRONMENT AND NATURE

Conservation of the South Downs

Ever since the Industrial Revolution and the rapid development over the last 200 years the English countryside has been put under a great deal of strain. The South Downs were once wooded hills, home to wolves, wild boar and other species that have long since departed. The need to feed an increasing population led to much of the countryside being cleared and ploughed. The result of this is the landscape we see today, although the traditional patchwork pattern of fields and hedgerows has been replaced in some parts of the Downs by much larger fields, the hedgerows having been torn out.

The South Downs is, then, a man-made landscape: even the woodland has been coppiced and the meadows ploughed at one time or another. This is not necessarily a bad thing, however. The resulting habitat is a rare one that provides an essential niche for endangered species, most notably the butterflies for which the Downs are famous.

Although the Downs, positioned in a populous corner of England, continue to be put under pressure from road and housing projects, the increasing awareness of the value of our natural (or perhaps semi-natural) heritage has resulted in greater efforts in the conservation of the Downs. There are several groups, on both a local and national scale and on both a voluntary and government basis, who help protect the species, habitats and buildings of the Downs. They also help visitors to get the most out of their trip to the countryside whilst at the same time trying to ease the pressure brought by the increase in tourist numbers.

Now that the South Downs have finally been granted National Park status (see p56) the effort to conserve the area should become less of a struggle owing to the increased environmental protection and financial benefits that the National Park designation brings.

❑ **Dew ponds**
The chalk soil of the Downs is highly permeable so there is rarely any standing or free-flowing water available for livestock. To combat the problem farmers have, since prehistoric times, constructed dew ponds. These small, circular ponds are designed to collect and retain water for the sheep and cattle that graze the dry hilltops. Despite their name, dew accounts for very little of the moisture that collects in these man-made bowls; most of it is rainwater. The water is prevented from filtering through the chalk thanks to a base layer of straw and clay, although modern-day dew ponds usually have a layer of concrete instead.

Many dew ponds are hundreds of years old and in a state of disrepair, being overgrown and barely recognisable as ponds. However, in recent years many have been restored, either because of their historic interest or simply to be used again for their original purpose. Good examples of dew ponds can be seen near Chanctonbury Ring and also between Southease and Alfriston.

THE ENVIRONMENT AND NATURE

❏ **How the South Downs became a National Park**

The South Downs almost became one of the first designated national parks back in the 1950s but the proposal was rejected on the grounds that the area did not offer sufficient recreational possibilities for the public. This seems rather surprising today when you consider the number of walkers, cyclists, horse-riders and paragliders who use the hills. National Park status is not just about providing an area of fun for outdoor enthusiasts, however. It is about protecting the area from harmful development such as road building, a real problem in the South-East, and preserving the natural and cultural heritage of the area.

In 1999 the Department for the Environment proposed that the Countryside Agency, now part of Natural England, designate the South Downs a National Park. A Designation Order was published in late 2002 and in November 2003 a public inquiry began, to hear the views of those likely to be affected by the change. In 2006 a report was passed to the Secretary of State. After several more delays and legal wrangles, in 2009 it finally was announced that the South Downs would receive National Park status, and the newly appointed South Downs National Park Authority (🖥 www.south downs.gov.uk) officially assumed responsibility for it on 1st April 2011.

Although at 1648 sq km it is not the largest in area (that distinction going to the Lake District National Park at 2292 sq km), being only an hour from London it encompasses several large towns including Petersfield and Lewes, and is by far the most densely populated of all the National Parks, with around 108,000 residents.

GOVERNMENT AGENCIES AND SCHEMES

Natural England

Natural England (🖥 www.gov.uk/government/organisations/natural-england; regional offices: Winchester ☎ 0300-060 2514; Worthing ☎ 0300-060 0300) is the single government body responsible for identifying, establishing and managing National Parks, Areas of Outstanding Natural Beauty, National Nature Reserves, Sites of Special Scientific Interest, and Special Areas of Conservation.

The highest level of landscape protection is the designation of land as a **National Park** which recognises the national importance of an area in terms of landscape, biodiversity and as a recreational resource. This designation does not signify national ownership and they are not uninhabited wildernesses, making conservation a knife-edged balance between protecting the environment and the rights and livelihoods of those living in the park. In April 2011 the South Downs became England's ninth National Park, and its most densely populated (see box above). Some 85% of the land within the South Downs National Park is agricultural, so this balancing act is particularly critical here.

The next level of protection within the National Park includes **National Nature Reserves (NNRs)** and **Sites of Special Scientific Interest (SSSIs)**. The **NNRs** along the course of the South Downs Way (SDW) include: Beacon Hill (see p85), just before the village of Exton; Old Winchester Hill (see p86), just after Exton; Butser Hill (see p91) several miles further along the path and Lullington Heath (p175). **SSSIs** range in size from little pockets protecting wild flower meadows, important nesting sites or special geological features, to vast swathes of upland, moorland and wetland. They are a particularly important

❑ **National Trails**
The South Downs Way is one of 15 National Trails (⌨ www.nationaltrail.co.uk) in England and Wales. These are Britain's flagship long-distance paths which grew out of the post-war desire to protect the country's special places, a movement which also gave birth to National Parks and AONBs. The Pennine Way was the first to be created.

National Trails in England are designated and largely funded by Natural England and are managed on the ground by a National Trail Officer. They co-ordinate the maintenance work undertaken by the local highway authority and landowners to ensure that the trail is kept to nationally agreed standards.

designation as they have some legal standing. They are managed in partnership with the owners and occupiers of the land who must give written notice before initiating any operations likely to damage the site and who cannot proceed without consent from Natural England. SSSIs along the SDW include: Cheesefoot Head (see p81), Butser Hill (see p91), Heyshott Down (see p106), Chanctonbury Hill (see p128) and Seaford to Beachy Head (see p170). **Special Areas of Conservation** (SACs) are designated by the European Union's Habitats Directive and provide an extra tier of protection to the areas that they cover. Along the SDW Butser Hill NNR and SSSI is also a SAC. See Natural England's website for further information about all of these.

CAMPAIGNING AND CONSERVATION ORGANISATIONS

The **National Trust** (NT; ⌨ www.nationaltrust.org.uk) is a charity which aims to protect, through ownership, threatened coastline, countryside, historic houses, castles, gardens and archaeological remains for everyone to enjoy. It manages large sections of the Downs including an area of chalk grassland on the Seven Sisters between the hamlet of Crowlink and Birling Gap (see p168), Devil's Dyke (see p139), Harting Down (see p101), and Newtimber Hill (see p139). It also owns various properties on the Way, such as Monk's House (see p154) in Rodmell and the Alfriston Clergy House (see box p160), its first-ever property, bought in 1896; both are open to the public.

The **Wildfowl & Wetlands Trust** (WWT; ⌨ www.wwt.org.uk) is the biggest conservation organisation for wetlands in the UK; their centre at

❑ **Other statutory bodies**
• **Department for Environment, Food and Rural Affairs** (⌨ www.defra.gov.uk) Government ministry responsible for sustainable development in the countryside.
• **English Heritage** (Historic Buildings and Monuments Commission for England; ⌨ www.english-heritage.org.uk) Organisation whose central aim is to ensure that the historic environment of England is properly maintained. Bramber Castle (see p132) is one of the properties it manages.
• **County councils: Hampshire** (⌨ www.hants.gov.uk); **East Sussex** (⌨ www.eastsussex.gov.uk); **West Sussex** (⌨ www.westsussex.gov.uk)

THE ENVIRONMENT AND NATURE

Arundel (⌨ www.wwt.org.uk/wetland-centres/arundel; see p119) is well-known and very popular with visitors year-round.

The **Wildlife Trust** (⌨ www.wildlifetrusts.org) undertakes projects to improve conditions for wildlife and promote public awareness of it as well as acquiring land for nature reserves to protect particular species and habitats. The Sussex Wildlife Trust (⌨ www.sussexwildlifetrust.org.uk) manages the Amberley Wild Brooks network of ponds and marshland along with Ditchling Beacon and Malling Down, Lewes. The Hampshire and Isle of Wight Wildlife Trust (⌨ www.hwt.org.uk) manages St Catherine's Hill, Winchester.

The **Royal Society for the Protection of Birds** (RSPB; ⌨ www.rspb.org .uk) was the pioneer of voluntary conservation bodies and although it doesn't have any reserves directly on the South Downs Way, there is one near Pulborough, a couple of miles north of Storrington. The wet grassy meadows here attract ducks, geese, swans and wading birds.

Butterfly Conservation (⌨ butterfly-conservation.org) was formed to prevent the decline in the number of butterflies and moths. The two branches relevant to the SDW are Hampshire and the Isle of Wight (⌨ www.hantsiow-but terflies.org.uk) and Sussex (⌨ www.sussex-butterflies.org.uk). Sites along the SDW where butterflies are likely to be found include Beachy Head and Malling Down.

There are also smaller conservation groups such as the **Murray Downland Trust** (⌨ murraydownlandtrust.blogspot.co.uk) which manages five reserves (Heyshott Escarpment, Heyshott Down, Buriton, Under Beacon, and The Devil's Jumps) in West Sussex and East Hampshire. The Trust's main objective is to 'rescue and enhance neglected areas of unimproved chalk downland' but it also looks after some ancient monuments in the area such as the Bronze Age archaeological site (see p108). Access to the Trust's sites is permitted except when the area should be left undisturbed for conservation reasons. The trust relies on human volunteers to help clear the land in its care but sheep are often brought in during the winter months to eat the scrub that threatens the grassland.

The South Downs Society (⌨ www.southdownssociety.org.uk) campaigns specifically for the conservation and enhancement of the landscape of the national park. The Society describes itself as operating as a 'critical friend' of the South Downs National Park Authority. They have divided the Downs from Winchester to Eastbourne into areas, each looked after by a volunteer District Officer whose main task is to look at planning applications in the area and respond accordingly. In 2012 they were in discussion with a commercial energy provider to minimise the impact of a huge offshore wind farm that is to be built by 2018 on a site within view of the South Downs National Park. All power cables will be underground and they will also bury existing overhead power lines as well, by way of compensation for the disruption resulting from the cabling work.

MINIMUM IMPACT & OUTDOOR SAFETY

Minimum impact walking

Walk as if you are kissing the Earth with your feet
Thich Nhat Hanh *Peace is every step*

The popularity of the 'Great Outdoors' as an escape route from the chaos of modern living has experienced something of a boom over the last decade or so. It is therefore important to be aware of the pressures that each of us as visitors to the countryside exert upon the land. The South Downs are particularly vulnerable, situated as they are in the most populous corner of the British Isles. Thousands of people explore the network of trails that criss-cross these historic chalk hills.

Minimum impact walking is all about a common-sense approach to exploring the countryside, being mindful and respectful of the wildlife and those who live and work on the land. Those who appreciate the countryside will already be aware of the importance of safeguarding it. Simple measures such as not dropping litter, keeping dogs on leads to avoid scaring sheep and leaving gates as you find them will already be second nature to anyone who regularly visits the countryside. However, there are several other measures that are not quite so well known and are worth repeating here.

ECONOMIC IMPACT

Rural businesses and communities in Britain have been hit hard in recent years by a seemingly endless series of crises. In addition, they have to compete with the omnipresence of chain supermarkets that are now so common in towns across Britain. Faced with such competition local businesses struggle to survive. Visitors to the countryside can help these local businesses by 'buying locally'. It benefits the local economy as well as the consumer.

Buy local

Look and ask for local produce to buy and eat. Not only does this cut down on the amount of pollution and congestion that the transportation of food creates, so-called 'food miles', but also ensures that you are supporting local farmers and producers – the very people who have moulded the countryside you have come to see and who are in the best position to protect it. If you can find local food which is also organic so much the better.

Support local businesses

It's a fact of life that money spent at local level – perhaps in a market, or at the greengrocer, or in an independent pub – has a far greater impact for good on that community than the equivalent spent in a branch of a national chain store or restaurant. While no-one would advocate that walkers should boycott the larger supermarkets, which after all do provide local employment, it's worth remembering that businesses in rural communities rely heavily on visitors for their very existence. If we want to keep these shops and post offices, we need to use them. The more money that circulates locally and is spent on local labour and materials, the greater the impact on the local economy and the more power the community has to effect the changes it wants to see.

Encourage local cultural traditions and skills

No two parts of the countryside look the same. Buildings, food, skills and language evolve out of the landscape and are moulded over hundreds of years to suit the locality. Discovering these cultural differences is part of the pleasure of walking in new places. Visitors' enthusiasm for local traditions and skills brings awareness and pride, nurturing a sense of place; an increasingly important role in a world where economic globalisation continues to undermine the very things that provide security and a feeling of belonging.

ENVIRONMENTAL IMPACT

By choosing a walking holiday you are already minimising your impact on the environment. Your interaction with the countryside and its inhabitants, whether they be plant, animal or human, can bring benefits to all. The following are some ideas on how you can go a few steps further in helping to minimise your impact on the natural environment while walking the South Downs Way.

Use public transport whenever possible

Both Sussex and Hampshire are blessed with an excellent public transport system (see pp44-6). There are various bus routes which drop off and pick up passengers at convenient start and finish points for day walks along the Downs and there are many buses linking the Way with nearby towns and villages. There are also plenty of bus and train links to get the walker to the Downs in the first place, making a car quite unnecessary.

Never leave litter

Leaving litter shows a total disrespect for the natural world and others coming after you. As well as being unsightly, litter kills wildlife, pollutes the environment and can be dangerous to farm animals. Please take your rubbish with you so you can dispose of it in a bin in the next village. It would be very helpful if you could pick up litter left by other people, too.

● **Is it OK if it's biodegradable?** No. Apple cores, banana skins, orange peel and the like are an eyesore, encourage flies, ants and wasps and ruin a picnic spot for others. They also promote a higher population of scavengers such as carrion crows and magpies, an explosion of which can have a detrimental effect on rarer bird species.

Those who use the excuse that orange peel is natural and biodegradable are simply fishing for an excuse to clear their conscience. Biodegradable? Yes, but surprisingly slowly. Natural? The South Downs have never been known for banana plantations or orange groves.

● **The lasting impact of litter** A piece of orange peel left on the ground takes six months to decompose; silver foil 18 months; a plastic bag 10 years; clothes 15 years; and an aluminium can 85 years.

Erosion
● **Stay on the main trail** The effect of your footsteps may seem minuscule but when they are multiplied by several thousand walkers each year they become rather more significant. Avoid taking shortcuts, widening the trail or taking more than one path; your boots will be followed by many others. This is particularly pertinent on the South Downs where there is such a huge volume of visitors.
● **Consider walking out of season** Unfortunately, most people prefer to walk in the spring and summer which is exactly the time of year when the vegetation is trying to grow. Walking on the South Downs in the autumn and winter can be just as enjoyable as in the high season and eases the burden on the land during the busy summer months. The quieter season also gives the walker a greater chance of a peaceful walk away from the crowds and there are fewer people competing for accommodation.

Respect all wildlife, plants and trees
If you come across wildlife keep your distance and don't watch for too long. Your presence can cause considerable stress, particularly if the adults are with young or in winter when the weather is harsh and food is scarce.

Young animals are rarely abandoned. If you come across young birds keep away so that their mother can return. Never pick flowers, leave them for others to enjoy too and try to avoid breaking branches off or damaging trees in any way.

The code of the outdoor loo
As more and more people discover the joys of the outdoors, issues like toilet business rapidly gain importance. How many of us have shaken our heads at the sight of toilet paper strewn beside the path or, even worse, someone's dump left in full view? In some parts of the world where visitor pressure is higher than in Britain walkers and climbers are required to pack out their excrement. This could soon be necessary here. Human excrement is not only offensive to our senses but, more importantly, can infect water sources.

● **Where to go** Wherever possible **use a toilet**. Public toilets are marked on the trail maps in this guide and you will also find facilities in pubs, cafés and campsites along the Way.

If you do have to go outdoors choose a site at least **30 metres away from running water** and 200 metres from any high-use areas such as hostels and beaches, or from any sites of historic or archaeological interest. Carry a small trowel and dig a small hole about 15cm (6") deep in which to bury your excrement. It decomposes quicker when in contact with the top layer of soil or leaf mould. Use a stick to stir loose soil into your deposit as well, as this speeds up decomposition even more. Do not squash it under rocks as this slows down the composting process. If you have to use rocks to cover it make sure they are not in contact with your faeces.

● **Toilet paper and tampons** Toilet paper takes a long time to decompose whether buried or not. It is easily dug up by animals and may then blow into water sources or onto the path. The best method for dealing with it is to **pack it out**. Put the used paper inside a paper bag which you then place inside a biodegradable bag. Then simply empty the contents of the paper bag at the next toilet you come across and throw the bag away. You should also pack out **tampons** and **sanitary towels** in a similar way; they take years to decompose and will be dug up and scattered about by animals.

Wild camping

There is very little opportunity for wild camping along the length of the Downs. Most of the land is private farmland and much of this is arable cropland. If the urge to camp away from an organised site is too much to resist always ask the landowner first. If the opportunity for wild camping is there take it. Camping in such an independent way is an altogether more fulfilling experience than camping on a designated site.

Living in the outdoors without any facilities allows the walker to briefly live in a simple and sustainable way in which everyday activities from cooking and eating to personal hygiene suddenly take on greater importance. Remember that by camping off the beaten track you accept added responsibilities. By taking on board the following suggestions for minimising your impact the whole experience of wild camping will be a far more satisfying one.

● **Be discreet** Camp alone or in small groups and spend only one night in each place. Pitch your tent late in the day and move off as early in the morning as you can.

● **Never light a fire** The deep burn caused by camp fires, no matter how small, seriously damages the turf and can take years to recover. Cook on a camp stove instead.

● **Don't use soap or detergent** There is no need to use soap; even biodegradable soaps and detergents pollute streams. You won't be away from a shower for more than a couple of days. Wash up without detergent; use a plastic or metal scourer, or failing that some bracken or grass.

● **Leave no trace** Enjoy the skill of moving on without leaving any sign of having been there. Make a final check of your campsite before heading off; pick up any litter that you or anyone else has left, so leaving the place in a better state than you found it.

ACCESS

The south-east corner of England is the most populated area of the British Isles and is criss-crossed by some of the busiest roads in the country. Thankfully, there are also countless public footpaths and rights of way for the large local population and visitors alike. But what happens if you want to explore some of the local woodland or tramp across a meadow? Most of the land on the South Downs is agricultural land and, unless you are on a right of way, it's off limits. However, the 'Right to Roam' legislation (see below) has opened up some previously restricted land to walkers.

Rights of way
As a designated National Trail (see box p57) the South Downs Way is a public right of way – this is either a footpath, a bridleway or a byway; the South Downs Way is made up of all three.

Rights of way are theoretically established because the owner has dedicated them to public use. However, very few rights of way are formally dedicated in this way. If the public has been using a path without interference for 20 years or more the law assumes the owner has intended to dedicate it as a right of way. If a path has been unused for 20 years it does not cease to exist; the guiding principle is 'once a highway, always a highway'.

On a public right of way you have the right to 'pass and repass along the way' which includes stopping to rest or admire the view or to consume refreshments. You can also take with you a 'natural accompaniment' which includes a dog but obviously could also be a horse on bridleways and byways. All 'natural accompaniments' must be kept under close control.

Farmers and land managers must ensure that paths are not blocked by crops or other vegetation, or otherwise obstructed, and the route is identifiable and the surface is restored soon after cultivation. If crops are growing over the path you have every right to walk or ride through them, following the line of the right of way as closely as possible. If you find a path blocked or impassable you should report it to the appropriate highway authority. Highway authorities are responsible for maintaining public rights of way. Along the South Downs Way the highway authorities are Hampshire County Council, East Sussex County Council and West Sussex County Council (see box p57). The councils are also the surveying authority with responsibility for maintaining the official definitive map of public rights of way.

Right to roam
For many years groups such as the **Ramblers** (see box p40) and the **British Mountaineering Council** (🖳 www.thebmc.co.uk) campaigned for new and

wider access legislation. This finally bore fruit in the form of the Countryside & Rights of Way Act of November 2000, colloquially known as the CRoW Act or 'Right to Roam'. It came into full effect on 31 October 2005 and gave access for 'recreation on foot' to mountain, moor, heath, down and registered common land in England and Wales. In essence it allows walkers the freedom to roam responsibly away from footpaths, without being accused of trespass, on about four million acres of open, uncultivated land. The areas of access land open to walkers are shown on new edition OS Explorer maps.

'Right to Roam' does not mean free access to wander over farmland, woodland or private gardens and much of the true chalk grassland of the South Downs has long since been ploughed up. Along with this, most of that which remains is already annexed as national and local nature reserves where access is relatively unrestricted anyway, so the results of the CRoW Act on the South Downs Way might not be quite as liberating as expected.

For those who wish to get off the beaten track and away from the crowds there are plenty of lesser-known rights of way. Follow any of these and you are likely to spend the whole day alone, which is not an easy thing to do in this part of England. However, if you want to leave the path entirely and beat your own trail through the woods and fields always check with local landowners.

Those who do exercise their 'right to roam' should remember that this added freedom comes with the responsibility to respect the immediate environment. This is particularly pertinent on the South Downs where most of the land is worked by farmers and is the home to a variety of wildlife. Always keep this in mind and try to avoid disturbing domestic and wild animals.

THE COUNTRYSIDE CODE

The Countryside Code, originally described in the 1950s as the Country Code, was revised and relaunched in 2004, in part because of the changes brought about by the CRoW Act (see above); it was updated again in 2012. The Code seems like commonsense but sadly some people still appear to have no understanding of how to treat the countryside they walk in.

An expanded version of the 2012 Code, launched under the logo 'Respect, Protect and Enjoy', is given below:

Respect other people
● **Consider the local community and other people enjoying the outdoors** Access to the countryside depends on being sensitive to the needs and wishes of those who live and work there. Being courteous and friendly to those you meet will ensure a healthy future for all based on partnership and co-operation.
● **Make no unnecessary noise** Enjoy the peace and solitude of the outdoors by staying in small groups and acting unobtrusively.
● **Leave gates and property as you find them** Normally a farmer leaves gates closed to keep livestock in but may sometimes leave them open to allow livestock access to food or water.

Protect the natural environment
● **Leave no trace of your visit and take your litter home** 'Pack it in, pack it out'. Litter is not only ugly but can be harmful to wildlife. Small mammals often become trapped in discarded cans and bottles. Many walkers think that orange peel and banana skins do not count as litter (see p61). Even biodegradable foodstuffs attract common scavenging species such as crows and gulls to the detriment of less-dominant species.

● **Keep your dog under control** Across farmland dogs should be kept on a lead. During lambing time they should not be taken with you at all (see box below).

● **Keep to paths across farmland unless wider access is available** Stick to the official path across arable or pasture land. Minimise erosion by not cutting corners or widening the path.

● **Use gates and stiles to cross fences, hedges and walls** If you have to climb over a gate because you can't open it always do so at the hinged end.

● **Leave livestock, crops and machinery alone** Help farmers by not interfering with their means of livelihood.

● **Guard against all risk of fire** Accidental fire is a great fear of farmers and foresters. Never make a camp fire and take matches and cigarette butts out with you to dispose of safely.

● **Help keep all water clean** Leaving litter and going to the toilet near a water source can pollute people's water supplies. See pp61-2 for advice.

● **Protect wildlife, plants and trees** Care for and respect all wildlife you come across along the Way. Don't pick plants, break trees or scare wild animals. If you come across young birds that appear to have been abandoned leave them alone.

● **Take special care on country roads** Drivers often go dangerously fast on narrow winding lanes. To be as safe as possible, walk facing the oncoming traffic and carry a torch or wear highly visible clothing when it's getting dark.

Enjoy the outdoors
● **Plan ahead and be prepared** You're responsible for your own safety: follow the guidelines on pp66-8.

● **Follow advice and local signs** In some areas there may be temporary diversions in place – particularly in forestry sections, for logging purposes. Take notice of these and other local trail advice.

❑ **Lambing**
Most of the South Downs Way passes through private farmland, some of which is pasture for sheep. Lambing takes place from mid-March to mid-May when dogs should not be taken along the path. Even a dog secured on a lead is liable to disturb a pregnant ewe. If you should see a lamb or ewe that appears to be in distress contact the nearest farmer.

Outdoor safety and health

AVOIDANCE OF HAZARDS

Walking does not come much more hazard-free than on the South Downs; however, these low southern hills should be given as much respect as their loftier counterparts. Good preparation is just as important here as it is on the northern mountains.

The following common-sense advice should ensure that those out for a day walk as well as those embarking on the whole route enjoy a safe walk. Always make sure you have **suitable clothes** to keep you warm and dry, whatever the conditions, as well as a spare change of inner clothes. Every rucksack should have inside it a compass, torch, whistle and simple first-aid kit (see p38). However, you may not use your compass as the trail is easy to follow. A whistle is also unlikely to be used due to the close proximity of people and villages. The **emergency signal** is six blasts on the whistle or six flashes with a torch.

Take more **food** than you expect to eat. High-energy snacks such as chocolate, fruit, biscuits and nuts are useful for those last few gruelling miles each day. With the Downs being made of permeable chalk there is a distinct lack of running water so make sure you have at least a one-litre **water bottle** or **pouch** that can be refilled when the opportunity arises.

You need to drink plenty of water when walking; 3-4 litres per day depending on the weather. There are a few drinking water taps placed conveniently along the path. These are marked on the maps in Part 4. If you start to feel tired, lethargic or get a headache it may be that you are not drinking enough. Thirst is not a good indicator of when to drink; stop and have a drink every hour or two. A good indicator of whether you are drinking enough is the colour of your urine – the lighter the better. If you are not needing to urinate much and your urine is dark yellow you may need to increase your fluid intake.

It is a good idea to be aware of where you are throughout the day. **Check your location** on the map regularly. Getting lost on the Downs is unlikely to be a major cause for concern but it can turn a pleasant day's walk into a stressful trudge back in the dark, praying that the pub chef has not gone home. If you do get lost it is unlikely to be long before someone passes by who does know their Bottoms from their Downs.

If you are walking alone you must appreciate and be prepared for the increased risk. It is always a good idea to leave word with somebody about where you are going; you can always ring ahead to book accommodation and let them know you are walking alone and what time you expect to arrive. Don't forget to contact whoever you have left word with to let them know you've arrived safely. Carrying a mobile phone can be useful though you cannot rely on getting good reception.

Be aware that as much of the South Downs Way is on a chalk ridge high above the surrounding countryside, there may be a steep climb down to, and back up from, the adjacent towns and villages.

To ensure you have a safe trip it is well worth following this advice:

● Keep to the path – avoid steep sections of the escarpment and old quarries
● Be aware of the increased possibility of slipping over in wet or icy weather, especially where the chalk is exposed
● Wear strong sturdy boots with good ankle supports and a good grip; in very dry stable weather trainers or sandals are fine
● Be extra vigilant with children
● In an emergency dial ☎ 999.

MINIMUM IMPACT & OUTDOOR SAFETY

FOOTCARE

Caring for your feet is vital; you're not going to get far if they are out of action. Wash and dry them properly at the end of the day, change your socks every few days and if it is warm enough take your boots and socks off when you stop for lunch to allow your feet to dry out in the sun.

It is important to 'break in' new boots before embarking on a long walk. Make sure the boots are comfortable and try to avoid getting them wet on the inside. If you feel any 'hot spots' stop immediately and apply a few strips of zinc oxide tape and leave them on until the area is pain free or the tape starts to come off. If you have left it too late and a blister has developed you should surround it with 'moleskin' or any other blister treatment to protect it from abrasion. Popping it can lead to infection. If the skin is broken keep the area clean with antiseptic and cover with a non-adhesive dressing material held in place with tape.

SUNBURN

It can happen, even in England and even on overcast days. The only surefire way to avoid it is to stay wrapped up but that's not really an option. What you must do, therefore, is to smother yourself in sunscreen (with a minimum factor of 15) and apply it regularly throughout the day. Don't forget your lips, nose, the back of your neck and even under your chin to protect you against rays reflected from the ground.

HYPOTHERMIA

Also known as exposure, this occurs when the body can't generate enough heat to maintain its normal temperature, usually as a result of being wet, cold, unprotected from the wind, tired and hungry. The risk of hypothermia while walking on the Downs is extremely small. However, it is worth being aware of the dangers. Hypothermia is easily avoided by wearing suitable clothing, carrying and eating enough food and drink, being aware of the weather conditions and checking the morale of your companions.

Early signs to watch for are feeling cold and tired with involuntary shivering. Find some shelter as soon as possible and warm the victim up with a hot drink and some chocolate or other high-energy food. If possible give them another warm layer of clothing and allow them to rest until feeling better.

If allowed to worsen, strange behaviour, slurring of speech and poor co-ordination will become apparent and the victim can quickly progress into unconsciousness, followed by coma and death. In the unlikely event of a severe case of hypothermia, quickly get the victim out of wind and rain, improvising a shelter if necessary. Rapid restoration of bodily warmth is essential and best achieved by bare-skin contact: someone should get into the same sleeping bag as the patient, both having stripped to their underwear with any spare clothing under or over them to build up heat. Send urgently for help.

HYPERTHERMIA

Hyperthermia occurs when the body generates too much heat, eg heat exhaustion and heatstroke. Not an ailment that you would normally associate with the south of England, heatstroke is a serious problem nonetheless. Symptoms of **heat exhaustion** include thirst, fatigue, giddiness, a rapid pulse, raised body temperature, low urine output and, if not treated, delirium and finally a coma. The best cure is to drink plenty of water.

Heatstroke is another matter altogether, and even more serious. A high body temperature and an absence of sweating are early indications, followed by symptoms similar to hypothermia (see p67) such as a lack of co-ordination and convulsions. Coma and death will follow if treatment is not given instantly. Sponge the victim down, wrap them in wet towels, fan them, and get help immediately.

WEATHER FORECASTS

The South Downs is one of the driest parts of what is a notoriously wet island. However, the weather can still change from blazing sunshine to a stormy wet gale in the space of a day. The wind, in particular, can be surprisingly severe along the top of the Downs. Couple this with rain and a nice walk can turn into a damp battle against the elements. For detailed local weather outlooks online log on to 🖳 www.bbc.co.uk/weather, or 🖳 www.metoffice.gov.uk.

DEALING WITH AN ACCIDENT

● Use basic first aid to treat the injury to the best of your ability.
● Try to attract the attention of anybody else who may be in the area. The emergency signal is six blasts on a whistle, or six flashes with a torch.
● If possible leave someone with the casualty while others go to get help. If there are only two people, you have a dilemma. If you decide to get help leave all spare clothing and food with the casualty.
● Telephone ☎ 999 and ask for the emergency services. They will assist in both offshore and onshore incidents. Be sure you know exactly where you are before you call. Report the exact position of the casualty and their condition.

Using this guide

This route guide has been divided according to logical start and stop points. However, these are not intended to be strict daily stages since people walk at different speeds and have different interests. The maps can be used to plan how far to walk each day but note that these are walking times only (see box below).

The **route summaries** describe the trail between significant places and are written as if walking the path from west to east. To enable you to plan your own itinerary **practical information** is presented clearly on the trail maps. This includes walking times for both directions, places to stay, camp and eat, as well as shops where you can buy supplies. Further service **details** are given in the text under the entry for each place.

For **map profiles** see the colour pages at the end of the book. For an overview of this information see itineraries on pp28-34 and the village and town facilities table on pp30-1.

See overleaf for the cumulative **distance chart**.

TRAIL MAPS

Scale and walking times [see map key, p191]

The trail maps are to a scale of 1:20,000 (1cm = 200m; 3¹/₈ inches = one mile). Walking times are given along the side of each map and the arrow shows the direction to which the time refers. Black triangles indicate the points between which the times have been taken. **See note below on walking times**.

The time-bars are a tool and are not there to judge your walking ability. There are so many variables that affect walking speed, from the weather conditions to how many beers you drank the previous evening. After the first hour or two of walking you will see how your speed relates to the timings on the maps.

❏ **Important note – walking times**
Unless otherwise specified, **all times in this book refer only to the time spent walking**. You will need to add 20-30% to allow for rests, photography, checking the map, drinking water etc. When planning the day's hike count on 5-7 hours' actual walking.

	START Winchester	Chilcomb	(Cheriton +1.5)	Exton	(East Meon + 1)	(Buriton + 0.5)	(South Harting + 0.5)	(Cocking + 0.5)	(Heyshott + 0.5)	(Graffham + 1)	(Sutton/Bignor + 1)	(Bury + 1)	Houghton Bridge	Amberley	(Storrington + 1.5)	(Washington + 0.5)	(Steyning/Bramber/Upper Beeding + 1)
START Winchester	0																
Chilcomb	2																
(Cheriton +1.5)	6½	4½															
Exton	12	10	5½														
(East Meon + 1)	17	15	10½	5													
(Buriton + 0.5)	24½	22½	18	12½	7½												
(Sth Harting + 0.5)	28	26	21½	16	11	3½											
(Cocking + 0.5)	35	33	28½	23	18	10½	7										
(Heyshott + 0.5)	37	35	30½	25	20	12½	9	2									
(Graffham + 1)	38½	36½	32	26½	21½	14	10½	3½	1½								
(Sutton/Bignor + 1)	42½	40½	36	30½	25½	18	14½	7½	5½	4							
(Bury + 1)	45	43	38½	33	28	20½	17	10	8	6½	2½						
Houghton Bridge	46	44	39½	34	29	21½	18	11	9	7½	3½	1					
Amberley	47½	45½	41	35½	30½	23	19½	12½	10½	9	5	2½	1½				
(Storrington + 1.5)	50½	48½	44	38½	33½	26	22½	15½	13½	12	8	5½	4½	3			
(Washington + 0.5)	53½	51½	47	41½	36½	29	25½	18½	16½	15	11	8½	7½	6	3		
(Steyning/U Bd + 1)	57½	55½	51	45½	40½	33	29½	22½	20½	19	15	12½	11½	10	7	4	
(Fulking + 0.5)	64	62	57½	52	47	39½	36	29	27	25½	21½	19	18	16½	13½	10½	6½
(Poynings + 0.5)	66	64	59½	54	49	41½	38	31	29	27½	23½	21	20	18½	15½	12½	8½
Pyecombe	68	66	61½	56	51	43½	40	33	31	29½	25½	23	22	20½	17½	14½	10½
(Clayton + 0.5)	69	67	62½	57	52	44½	41	34	32	30½	26½	24	23	21½	18½	15½	11½
(Ditchling + 1.5)	70½	68½	64	58½	53½	46	42½	35½	33½	32	28	25½	24½	23	20	17	13
(Plumpton + 0.5)	72½	70½	66	60½	55½	48	44½	37½	35½	34	30	27½	26½	25	22	19	15
(Lewes + 3)	73½	71½	67	61½	56½	49	45½	38½	36½	35	31	28½	27½	26	23	20	16
(Kingston + 1)	78½	76½	72	66½	61½	54	50½	43½	41½	40	36	33½	32½	31	28	25	21
Rodmell/Southease	82½	80½	76	70½	65½	58	54½	47½	45½	44	40	37½	36½	35	32	29	25
(West Firle + 1)	86	84	79½	74	69	61½	58	51	49	47½	43½	41	40	38½	35½	32½	28½
(Alciston/Bwk + 1)	88½	86½	82	76½	71½	64	60½	53½	51½	50	46	43½	42½	41	38	35	31
Alfriston	90½	88½	84	78½	73½	66	62½	55½	53½	52	48	45½	44½	43	40	37	33
[via AR] Jevington*	93	91	86½	81	76	68½	65	58	56	54½	50½	48	47	45½	42½	39½	35½
[via AR] End (E + 1)*	97	95	90½	85	80	72½	69	62	60	58½	54½	52	51	49½	46½	43½	39½
Littlington	91½	89½	85	79½	74½	67	63½	56½	54½	53	49	46½	45½	44	41	38	34
Exceat/Seven Sstrs	93	91	86½	81	76	68½	65	58	56	54½	50½	48	47	45½	42½	39½	35½
Birling Gap	96	94	89½	84	79	71½	68	61	59	57½	53½	51	50	48½	45½	42½	38½
Beachy Head	99	97	92½	87	82	74½	71	64	62	60½	56½	54	53	51½	48½	45½	41½
END (Eastbrn + 1)	100	98	93½	88	83	75½	72	65	63	61½	57½	55	54	52½	49½	46½	42½

* ALTERNATIVE (INLAND) ROUTE FROM ALFRISTON

ROUTE GUIDE AND MAPS

ROUTE GUIDE AND MAPS

South Downs Way
DISTANCE CHART

Winchester to Eastbourne

miles (approx) – 1 mile = 1.6km

Note: Where a place name is shown in (brackets) on this chart the distance to the turnoff to this place is shown. Add the (+) number in the brackets to calculate the total distance to that place. Most villages lie below the South Downs.

(Fulking + 0.5)	(Poynings + 0.5)	Pyecombe	(Clayton + 0.5)	(Ditchling + 1.5)	(Plumpton + 0.5)	(Lewes + 3)	(Kingston near Lewes + 1)	Rodmell/Southease	(West Firle + 1)	(Alciston/Berwick + 1)	Alfriston	[via inland route*] Jevington	[via inland route*] End (Eastbourne + 1)	Littlington	Exceat/Seven Sisters	Birling Gap	Beachy Head	END (Eastbourne + 1)
2																		
4	2																	
5	3	1																
6½	4½	2½	1½															
8½	6½	4½	3½	2														
9½	7½	5½	4½	3	1													
14½	12½	10½	9½	8	6	5												
18½	16½	14½	13½	12	10	9	4											
22	20	18	17	15½	13½	12½	7½	3½										
24½	22½	20½	19½	18	16	15	10	6	2½									
26½	24½	22½	21½	20	18	17	12	8	4½	2								
29	*27*	*25*	*24*	*22½*	*20½*	*19½*	*14½*	*10½*	*7*	*4½*	*2½*							
33	*31*	*29*	*28*	*26½*	*24½*	*23½*	*18½*	*14½*	*11*	*8½*	*6½*	*4*						
27½	25½	23½	22½	21	19	18	13	9	5½	3	1							
29	27	25	24	22½	20½	19½	14½	10½	7	4½	2½			1½				
32	30	28	27	25½	23½	22½	17½	13½	10	7½	5½			4½	3			
35	33	31	30	28½	26½	25½	20½	16½	13	10½	8½			7½	6	3		
36	34	32	31	29½	27½	26½	21½	17½	14	11½	9½			8½	7	4	1	

Up or down?

The trail is shown as a dashed line. An arrow across the trail indicates the gradient; two arrows show that it's steep. Note that the *arrow points uphill*, the opposite of what OS maps use on steep roads. A good way to remember our style is: '**front-pointing** on crampons **up** a steep slope' and 'open arms – Julie Andrews-style – **spreading out** to unfold the view **down** below'. If, for example, you are walking from A (at 80m) to B (at 200m) and the trail between the two is short and steep it would be shown thus: A— — — >> — — – B. Reversed arrow heads indicate downward gradient.

Accommodation

Apart from in large towns where some selection of places has been necessary, almost every place to stay that is within easy reach of the trail is marked. Details of each place are given in the accompanying text.

The number of **rooms** of each type is stated, ie: **S** = Single, **T** = Twin room, **D** = Double room, **Tr** = Triple room and **Qd** = Quad. Note that most of the triple/quad rooms have a double bed and one/two single beds (or bunk beds); thus for a group of three or four, two people would have to share the double bed but it also means the room can be used as a double or twin. See also p19.

Rates quoted for B&B-style accommodation are **per person (pp) based on two people sharing a room** for a one-night stay; rates are usually discounted for longer stays. Where a **single room (sgl)** is available the rate for that is quoted if different from the rate per person. The rate for **single occupancy (sgl occ)** of a double/twin may be higher, and the per person rate for three/four sharing a triple/quad may be lower. Unless specified, rates are for bed and breakfast. At some places the only option is a **room rate**; this will be the same whether one or two people (or more if permissible) use the room.

The accommodation will either have **en suite** (bath or shower) facilities in the room or **private**, or **shared, facilities** (in either case this may be a bathroom or shower room just outside the bedroom).

The text also mentions whether the premises have: **wi-fi (WI-FI)**; if a bath (●) is available either in an en suite room or in a separate bathroom – for those who prefer a relaxed soak at the end of the day; if **packed lunches** (Ⓛ) can be prepared subject to prior arrangement; and if **dogs** (🐾 – see also pp186-7) are welcome in at least one room (often places only have one room suitable for dogs), or at campsites, subject to prior arrangement, and any associated charges and requirements – some places make an additional charge while others may require a deposit which is refundable if the dog doesn't make a mess.

If arranged in advance many B&B proprietors are happy to collect walkers from the nearest point on the trail and deliver them back again next morning; they may also be happy to transfer your **luggage** to your next accommodation place on the map. Some may make a charge for either or both of these services. Check the details at the time of booking.

GPS waypoints

The numbered GPS waypoints refer to the list on pp183-6.

Other features

Features are marked on the map when pertinent to navigation. In order to avoid cluttering the maps and making them unusable not all features have been marked each time they occur.

❏ The Legend of St Swithun

St Swithun, once bishop of Winchester, died in 862AD. Before his death he asked to be buried outside the Old Minster and was duly interred in accordance with his wishes. St Swithun, however, had not counted upon the wishes of Bishop Aethelwold who on 15 July 971 decided to extend the Minster. The expansion plans required the temporary opening of St Swithun's grave before he was carefully re-interred within the new Minster's walls. On the day of the re-interment it began to rain and did not stop for forty days. To this day the legend says that if it rains on St Swithun's Day it will rain for the next forty days. Some would say this is not unusual for England in July.

WINCHESTER   MAP 1, p77

Winchester is a city steeped in history. The area was settled as long ago as 450BC when the nearby **St Catherine's Hill** was inhabited by a Celtic tribe. After the Roman occupation came the Dark Ages of 400-600AD during which time it is believed that **King Arthur** reigned from here. Many romantics today believe the city to be the site of legendary Camelot.

Things brightened up after the Dark Ages when in 871 **King Alfred the Great** (849-899) made the city the capital of Saxon England. He has probably had the greatest influence on the city so it is not surprising that a **bronze statue** of him, constructed in 1901, stands in the Broadway. **St Swithun** (see box above) is also inextricably linked with Winchester.

In 1066 **William the Conqueror** arrived in Hastings and made his way to Winchester where he duly took charge and ordered the building of the castle. Soon after, in 1079, work began on the cathedral.

Other famous people who have links with the city include **Winston Churchill** and **Eisenhower** who reviewed their troops at Peninsula Barracks the day before D-Day. Those with more tenuous associations include **John Keats** who was inspired to pen *Ode to Autumn* while wandering around the water meadows here in 1819.

The city has had a long and sometimes turbulent history but it is well worth spending an afternoon or the whole day exploring the compact city's many sights.

What to see and do

Winchester Cathedral (☎ 01962-857200, 🖳 www.winchester-cathedral.org.uk; Mon-Sat 9.30am-5pm, Sun 12.30am-3pm, £7.50) stands elegantly in parkland in the

This gravestone by Winchester Cathedral recommends drinking strong beer when hot and so avoid the fate of Thomas Thetcher. 'Small' beer was weak beer in which the alcohol content was not high enough to kill off any water-borne infections.

city centre. The spectacular nave is said to be the longest Gothic cathedral nave in the world. The best time to visit the cathedral is during the Sunday morning service when the choir can be heard.

The cathedral has witnessed many a historic event: **Henry III** was baptised here in 1207 and it was also the scene of the marriage of **Mary Tudor** to **Philip of Spain** in 1554. In more recent history it became the final resting place in 1817 of **Jane Austen** (see box below). Her grave and memorial is in the north aisle of the cathedral.

Tours include Cathedral Tours (Mon-Sat hourly between 10am and 3pm), which includes a look at the twelfth-century Winchester Bible; Tower Tours (Jun-Aug Mon-Sat 2.15pm plus Sat 11.30am, Sep-May Sat 11.30am & 2.15pm, Wed 2.15pm; £6) and Crypt Tours (Mon-Sat 10.30am, 12.30pm & 2.30pm).

Even though the cathedral is the centrepiece of the city there are other equally fascinating places such as the remains of **Wolvesey Castle** (Apr-Sep daily 10am-5pm; free), the palace (residence) for the bishops of Winchester until about the 1680s.

On College St, not far from Wolvesey Castle, is the house where **Jane Austen** died. (It's the yellow building next to the college although be aware that this is a private residence so don't peer through the windows).

Also near the cathedral is the **City of Winchester Museum** (☎ 01962-863064, 🖳 www.winchester.gov.uk/museums; Apr-Oct Mon-Sat 10am-5pm, Sun noon-5pm, Nov-Mar Tue-Sat 10am-4pm, Sun noon-4pm, admission free). The museum traces the history of the city from the Romans to the Victorians and most things in between.

The Round Table in the Great Hall

Some of the exhibits in Winchester's museums can be viewed online at 🖳 www .winchestermuseumcollections.org.uk.

Next to **Westgate**, one of two city gates, is the **Great Hall** (☎ 01962-846476, 🖳 www3.hants.gov.uk/greathall, Castle Ave; daily 10am-5pm, free but donations of £3 are welcome; tours are available on request), the only surviving part of Winchester Castle. Here, on the west wall, hangs, so legend has it, *the* table around which King Arthur and his Knights of the Round Table sat. Carbon dating has quashed that particular story, however, and the table is actually a few hundred years too young to have been used by Arthur, having

ROUTE GUIDE AND MAPS

❑ **Jane Austen**
Jane Austen, born near Basingstoke in Hampshire in 1775, is one of the most important English novelists, having written such classics as *Pride and Prejudice*, *Persuasion* and *Northanger Abbey*. In 1816 she began writing *Sanditon* but in the same year she contracted Addison's disease and the novel was never completed. As her condition worsened she moved to a house in Winchester where she spent the last few weeks of her life, dying at the age of 41 on 18 July 1817.

been constructed around the end of the 13th century; but it's still a mightily impressive disc of oak, weighing over a ton and elaborately painted during the time of Henry VIII with a beautiful Tudor rose. The Great Hall is also famous for the trial of **Sir Walter Raleigh** for treason in 1603.

In the heart of the city is **City Mill** (☎ 01962-870057, 🖳 www.nationaltrust.org .uk/winchestercitymill; Feb half term to end of Nov, daily 10am-5pm; Dec 10.30am-4pm, other times Fri-Mon 11am-4pm, closed 23-31 Dec; admission £4/£4.40 with gift aid; NT and Wildlife Trust members free), a working water mill sitting astride the River Itchen. It's also now the official **'Gateway' to the South Downs National Park** and doubles as an information centre for the park. Although there has been a mill on this site for centuries the present building dates from 1743. On most Saturdays and Sundays (11am-4pm) visitors can watch demonstrations of flour milling. Call to check the details if you are interested in seeing this.

It is possible to visit **Winchester College** (☎ 01962-621209, 🖳 www.win chestercollege.co.uk; one-hour tours, Mon, Wed, Fri & Sat 10.15am, noon, 2.15pm & 3.30pm, Tue & Thur 10.45am & noon, Sun 2.15pm & 3.30pm, year-round except Christmas and New Year; admission £7) which was founded in 1382 by William of Wykeham, then Bishop of Winchester, and is said to be the oldest continuously running school in the country. Originally it was home to 70 pupils but it now has more than 700. Amongst the buildings included in the tour are the 14th-century chapel, the College Hall, the 17th-century schoolroom and the medieval cloister.

Services

The **tourist information centre** (TIC; ☎ 01962-840500, 🖳 www.visitwinchester .co.uk; May-Sep Mon-Sat 10am-5pm, Sun & bank holiday Mon 11am-4pm, Oct-Apr Mon-Sat 10am-5pm) is on the ground floor of the Guildhall on High St; they have two free internet access terminals for visitors. For **information on the South Downs National Park** see City Mill above.

On the pedestrianised High St there are countless **banks** and **cash machines** while the main **post office** (Mon-Sat 9am-5.30pm) is now housed in the local branch of WH Smith at the top of the High St.

There are several **supermarkets** – the biggest, Sainsbury's, adjoins **Brooks Shopping Centre** on Middle Brook St – and also farmers' markets (see box p22).

Last-minute hiking equipment (including blister kits) can be found in any of the **outdoor shops**, including Millets and Blacks, which are situated on the High St. **Lloyds Pharmacy** (Mon, Wed-Fri 8.45am-5.30pm, Tues & Sat 9am-5pm) is near the TIC at 155 High St.

There's free **internet access** at the TIC and also inside the Discovery Centre (Mon-Fri 9am-7pm, Sat 9am-5pm, Sun 10am-4pm) on Jewry St.

Public transport

[See the public transport map and table, pp44-6] There are **train** services to Winchester from London Waterloo (SouthWest Trains) and from Southampton and Portsmouth. Cross Country Trains run services between Bournemouth and Birmingham via Reading and Winchester. The **railway station** is about five minutes' walk from the city centre on Station Rd.

National Express **coach** services between London and Southampton; Heathrow Airport and Portsmouth; and between Birmingham and Bournemouth call at the **bus station** opposite the TIC.

From Southampton you should take bluestar's No 1 **bus** while for Petersfield and the villages in between take Stagecoach's No 67. Stagecoach's No 64 (from Alton) also calls here.

Where to stay

Being a popular tourist destination, Winchester is blessed with plenty of guesthouses and hotels. However, the demand on accommodation throughout the year is such that **booking well in advance** is strongly recommended to avoid a night on the park bench by the cathedral.

Close to the city centre and offering the chance to stay in a traditional old inn is

Westgate Hotel (☎ 01962-820222, 🖳 wghguy@yahoo.co.uk; 6D en suite, 1D/1T share bathroom, 1Qd private bathroom; ☕; WI-FI; 🐕; Ⓛ) at 2 Romsey Rd. B&B costs £35-45pp (sgl occ full room rate; from £100 for four sharing).

Slightly further out is ***5 Clifton Terrace*** (☎ 01962-890053, 🖳 cliftonterrace@hotmail.co.uk; 1Qd/1D, both with private facilities; ☕; WI-FI) with B&B for £40-45pp, or £75-85 if you're on your own (£130 for up to four sharing).

Cathedral Cottage (☎ 01962-878975, 🖳 www.cathedralcottagebandb.co.uk; 1D en suite, WI-FI; Ⓛ), at 19 Colebrook St, is just a stone's throw from the cathedral with a cosy room from £42.50pp (sgl occ full room rate) overlooking a pretty cottage garden, in which you can have your English or continental breakfast served. Occasionally during term-time they also have another room available for £55-60.

Nearby at 10 Colebrook Place is the delightful ***Wolvesey View*** (☎ 01962-852082, 🖳 www.wintonian.co.uk; 1S/1D/1Tr; ☕ shared bathroom; WI-FI) where welcoming host John offers B&B from £43pp (sgl/sgl occ £48-58; three sharing about £110). The house used to belong to Sir Alec Guinness.

In a beautiful Queen Anne house at the top of St John's St, is ***St John's Croft*** (☎ 01962-859976, 🖳 www.st-johns-croft.co.uk; 2D or T/1Qd, ☕ shared bathroom; WI-FI) with B& 'Aga-cooked'-B from £45pp sharing or £55 single occupancy. There are comfortable good-sized rooms with views over Winchester.

A short distance up Magdalen Hill at Nos 5-9 is ***Magdalen House*** (☎ 01962-869634, 🖳 www.magdalen-house.co.uk; 1D/1T/1Tr, private shower room; WI-FI) charging from £35pp, single occupancy from £55. The breakfast room gives you a good view over Winchester while you eat the generous 'light' breakfast (included) or the full fry up (an extra £5).

Another good bet is ***53a Parchment Street*** (☎ 01962-849962, 1D en suite; WI-FI), a terraced townhouse on a quiet street yet close to the hubbub of the centre. B&B costs £40pp (sgl occ £70).

Winchester Royal (☎ 01962-840840, 🖳 www.sjhotels.co.uk/winchester; 43D/28T/3 suites, all en suite; ☕; WI-FI) is on St Peter St. This 16th-century townhouse was once a bishop's residence then a convent but now offers luxurious hotel accommodation with four-poster beds in some of the rooms. Rates vary but expect to pay £50-100pp (sgl occ from £129), often less if booking more than a week in advance: check their website for special offers.

Further from the bustling centre are several affordable guesthouses in a Victorian part of town: ***5 Compton Road*** (☎ 01962-869199, 🖳 www.winchesterbedandbreakfast.net; 2D or T, shared bathroom; ☕; WI-FI; 🐕; Ⓛ) with B&B from £32.50pp (sgl occ £45). They serve cereals, fruit and toast for breakfast, and have drying facilities. Subject to a £15 charge, and a two-night booking, they can collect walkers from Exton and take them back the next day.

The comfortable and popular ***Giffard House*** (☎ 01962-852628, 🖳 www.giffardhotel.co.uk; 4S/1T/1D or T/7D all en suite; ☕; WI-FI; Ⓛ) with B&B for £51.50-57.50pp (sgl from £78, sgl occ £89-107) is at 50 Christchurch Rd.

At 75 Kingsgate St is ***The Wykeham Arms*** (☎ 01962-853834, 🖳 wykehamarmswinchester.co.uk; 2S/10D/2T, all en suite; ☕ in most rooms; 🐕 £7.50; WI-FI), a cosy inn with quality rooms priced from £57.50 to £101pp (sgl/sgl occ £93-99). It's named after William of Wykeham who founded Winchester College.

Sounding as attractive as its associated restaurant (The Black Rat), ***The Black Hole*** (☎ 01962-807010, 🖳 www.theblackholebb.co.uk; 10D, ☕; WI-FI; 🐕) charges from £50pp for its luxurious 'cells'.

Where to eat and drink

For a coffee or snack there are several cafés on the High St including the upmarket French chain ***Maison Blanc*** with seating outside and the more interesting ***Chococo*** nearby. As the name suggests they specialise in all things chocolate (classic hot chocolate is £2.50) but also serve soup.

For sausage rolls and other quick eats, there's ***Greggs Bakery*** (☎ 01962-813580;

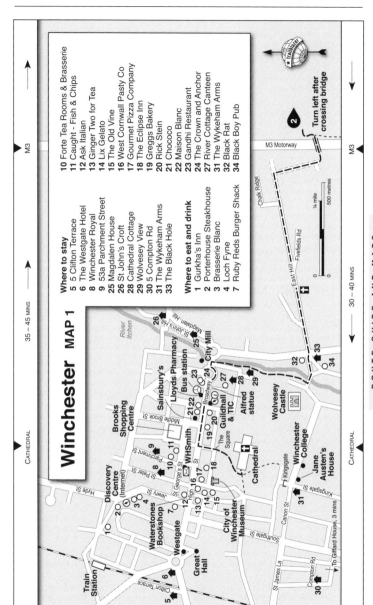

Winchester MAP 1

Where to stay
5 5 Clifton Terrace
6 The Westgate Hotel
8 Winchester Royal
9 53a Parchment Street
25 Magdalen House
26 St John's Croft
28 Cathedral Cottage
29 Wolvesey View
30 5 Compton Rd
31 The Wykeham Arms
33 The Black Hole

Where to eat and drink
1 Gurkha's Inn
2 Porterhouse Steakhouse
3 Brasserie Blanc
4 Loch Fyne
7 Ruby Reds Burger Shack

10 Forte Tea Rooms & Brasserie
11 Caught - Fish & Chips
12 Ask Italian
13 Ginger Two for Tea
14 Lix Gelato
15 The Old Vine
16 West Cornwall Pasty Co
17 Gourmet Pizza Company
18 The Eclipse Inn
19 Greggs Bakery
20 Rick Stein
21 Chococo
22 Maison Blanc
23 Gandhi Restaurant
24 The Crown and Anchor
27 River Cottage Canteen
31 The Wykeham Arms
32 Black Rat
34 Black Boy Pub

M3 · CATHEDRAL · 35 – 45 MINS · M3 · M3

Discovery Centre (Internet)
Waterstones Bookshop
Westgate
Train Station
Clifton Terrace
Great Hall
Brooks Shopping Centre
Sainsbury's
River Itchen
Lloyds Pharmacy
Bus station
City Mill
Magdalen Hill
St John's Hill
Hyde St
St Peter St
Parchment St
Jewry St
St George's St
High St
Middle Brook St
Broadway
WHSmith
The Square
The Guildhall & TIC
Alfred statue
City of Winchester Museum
Cathedral
Kingsgate
Jane Austen's House
Winchester College
Kingsgate St
Canon St
Southgate St
St James La
Compton Rd
To Giffard House, 3 mins
Wolvesey Castle
Chalk Ridge
East Hill
Fivefields Rd
M3 Motorway
Turn left after crossing bridge

CATHEDRAL · 30 – 40 MINS

¼ mile
0 · 500 metres

Mon-Sat 8am-6pm, Sun 9.30am-4.30pm), further up the High St. There's also *West Cornwall Pasty Co* (Mon-Sat 8.30am-6pm, Sun 9.15am-5pm), with pasties from £3.95. There's a good chippy on St George's St *Caught – Fish & Chips* open daily noon-2.30pm and 4.30-9pm (to 8.30pm on Mon).

For teas and light lunches the *Forte Tea Rooms & Brasserie* (Mon-Fri 9am-5pm, Sat 9am-5.30pm, Sun when the farmers' market is on), 78 Parchment St, is popular, traditional and recommended. A cream tea for two is £6. Another highly recommended place for teas and light lunches is *Ginger Two for Tea* (☎ 01962-877733; Mon-Fri 7.30am-6pm, Sat 8.30am-6pm & Sun 8.30am-5pm) at 28 St Thomas St. Has a great selection of teas, coffees, tempting cakes, salads, sandwiches and paninis. Almost opposite and run by the same people is *Lix Gelato* offering a mouthwatering range of frozen yoghurts and ice cream.

For something Italian you could try *Ask* (☎ 01962-849464; Sun-Thur 11am-10pm, Fri & Sat 11am-11pm) on the High St; they have a large range of pizzas and pasta dishes. There's also the *Gourmet Pizza Company* (☎ 01962-842553; Mon-Sat 11am-11pm, Sun 11am-10.30pm) which is consistently recommended.

There are numerous places to eat lining Jewry St. *Ruby Reds Burger Shack* (5 Jewry St; daily 9am to late) does burgers from £6.50, burritos from £7.20, and pancake breakfasts as well as cocktails, beers and shakes. Further up Jewry St at No 24 is *Porterhouse Steakhouse* (☎ 01962-810532; Sun-Thur noon-10.30pm, Fri & Sat noon-11pm) with high-quality steaks from £11.95. Almost next door is a branch of the seafood chain *Loch Fyne* (☎ 01962-872930; Sun-Thur 9am-10pm, Fri & Sat 9am-10.30pm).

Spicier food can be found at the stylishly refurbished *Gandhi Restaurant* (☎ 01962-863940; daily noon-2.30pm & 5.30-11.30pm) near the roundabout at the bottom of Broadway; typical tandoori dishes start at £8.45. For more subcontinental fare though with a Himalayan twist there's *Gurkha's Inn* (☎ 01962-842843; daily noon-2.30pm & 5.30-11pm, to 11.30pm at

weekends), a busy Nepalese restaurant and takeaway at 17 City Rd.

There are numerous pubs to choose from. One of the most attractive and historic is at 25 The Square: *The Eclipse Inn* (☎ 01962-865676; food Mon-Fri noon-2.30pm, Sat & Sun noon-3pm). It's a tiny whitewashed, timber-framed house which once served as a 16th-century rectory and is rumoured to be haunted. Another good traditional pub is *The Black Boy* (☎ 01962-861754; food Mon-Fri noon-2pm & 7-9pm; Sat noon-2.30pm & 7-9pm; Sun noon-3pm) at 1 Wharf Hill. Near the TIC, *The Crown and Anchor* (☎ 01962-620849; food Tue-Sat noon-8pm, Sun & Mon noon-4pm) is basic with cheap pub grub to eat as you watch Sky Sports on TV.

In Minster St, *The Old Vine* (☎ 01962-854616; food Mon-Fri noon-2.30pm & 6.30-9.30pm, Sat noon-3pm & 6.30-9.30pm, Sun noon-3pm & 6.30-9pm), another refurbished old pub that offers a traditional ploughman's lunch for £5.95, handmade pork pie with salad for £8.95 and more substantial dishes from £11.50.

The Wykeham Arms (see Where to stay: Mon-Sat noon-3pm, Sun noon-3.30pm; daily 6-9.30pm) serves top-class fare with an à la carte menu (main dishes around £16) and using local produce.

For some top-notch food that's great value there's a branch of the famous French chef Raymond Blanc's *Brasserie Blanc* (☎ 01962-810870, 🖳 brasserieblanc.com/location/winchester; food Mon-Sat 8.30am-9.45pm, Sun 9.30am-8.45pm). There are set lunches from £11.95 (Mon-Sat) and dinners from £14.45.

River Cottage Canteen (☎ 01962-457747, 🖳 www.rivercottage.net; lunch daily noon-3pm, to 4pm Sun; dinner Tue-Sat 6.30-10.30pm), in Abbey Mill Gardens, is part of TV chef Hugh Fearnley-Whittingstall's River Cottage chain. There are sharing boards from £11.75 and main dishes are £10.95-16.95. It's good value and very busy.

There are two other pricey places vying for the title of best restaurant in Winchester. *Rick Stein* (☎ 01962-353535, 🖳 www.rickstein.com; Mon-Fri noon-3pm

& 6-10pm; Sat & Sun noon-10pm) is another TV chef to open here with this seafood restaurant, which was his first outside Cornwall. Fruits de Mer are £40; the cheapest deals are the set lunches at £19.95/24.95 for 2/3 courses.

The *Black Rat* (☎ 01962-844465, 🖳 www.theblackrat.co.uk; daily 7-9.15pm and noon-2.15pm at weekends) is at 88 Chesil St. They were awarded a Michelin star in 2011. Expect to spend around £40-50pp for a really memorable evening meal.

The route guide

WINCHESTER TO EXTON   MAPS 1-7

These **12 miles (19.5km, 4¼-5¾hrs)** begin at the cathedral in the centre of Winchester. The route takes you from the cathedral grounds, along the main shopping street, past the statue of King Alfred then down beside the River Itchen. It does not take long for the South Downs Way to leave the city and enter the rolling East Hampshire countryside but first you must cross the M3.

On crossing the bridge spanning the noisy motorway spare a thought for the remains of **Twyford Down**. This once beautiful hill a few miles to the south was, despite vociferous demonstrations, ruthlessly sliced in two as part of a highly controversial road improvement scheme in the early 1990s.

Once away from the noise of the road the path crosses a field before arriving at **Chilcomb** (see below). The church aside, there's little in the way of shops or services to keep you in Chilcomb so once you have admired the thatched cottages head on up the lane for the gradual but steady ascent to **Cheesefoot Head** (Map 3) where there are great views to the north over the Itchen Valley.

If you're going to **Cheriton** (35-45 mins, see below), take the path in the corner of the field (see Map 4, p83) rather than following the busy A272.

CHILCOMB   MAP 2, p80

Chilcomb is the first of several beautiful Hampshire villages passed through on the way to Sussex. In fact Chilcomb is one of the older settlements, with a **church** (off the path to the south) that pre-dates Winchester Cathedral.

Campers will find pitches for £4.50-6.50pp in a two-person tent at *Morn Hill Caravan Club Site* (☎ 01962-869877; camping June-Sep; 🐾 if on a leash). To get there turn left where the path hits the junction of lanes just before Chilcomb. Follow the lane up to the busy A31 then follow this road as far as the big roundabout a mile further east. They have limited space for tent pitches so booking is highly recommended.

There's also a B&B, *Complyns* (☎ 01962-861600, 🖳 www.complyns.co.uk; 1D/1T, 🛏 shared bathroom; WI-FI; Ⓛ), a 17th-century former farmhouse, which charges £32.50pp (sgl occ from £40). They have a boiler house where you can dry clothes.

CHERITON   MAP 4a, p82

On hot sunny days the locals can be seen paddling in the clear waters of the tiny River Itchen, which bubbles out of the chalk about a mile south of Cheriton and runs straight through the village passing beautiful thatched houses and the village green.   *(cont'd on p82)*

ROUTE GUIDE AND MAPS

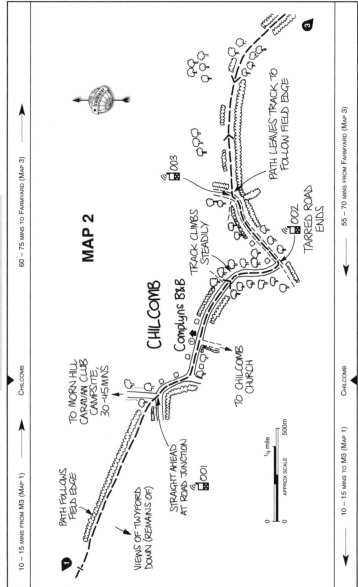

10 – 15 MINS FROM M3 (MAP 1)　　　CHILCOMB　　　60 – 75 MINS TO FARMYARD (MAP 3)

1

PATH FOLLOWS FIELD EDGE

VIEWS OF TWYFORD DOWN (REMAINS OF)

STRAIGHT AHEAD AT ROAD JUNCTION

001

TO MORN HILL CARAVAN CLUB CAMPSITE, 30-45MINS

MAP 2

CHILCOMB

Complyns B&B

TO CHILCOMB CHURCH

TRACK CLIMBS STEADILY

002

TARRED ROAD ENDS

003

PATH LEAVES TRACK TO FOLLOW FIELD EDGE

3

¼ mile

500m

APPROX SCALE

10 – 15 MINS TO M3 (MAP 1)　　　CHILCOMB　　　55 – 70 MINS FROM FARMYARD (MAP 3)

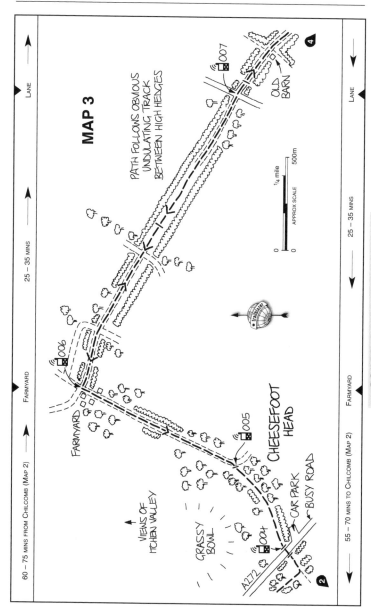

MAP 3

PATH FOLLOWS OBVIOUS UNDULATING TRACK BETWEEN HIGH HEDGES

007

OLD BARN

006

005

CHEESEFOOT HEAD

004

CAR PARK

BUSY ROAD

A272

GRASSY BOWL

VIEWS OF ITCHEN VALLEY

FARMYARD

APPROX SCALE

¼ mile   500m

60 – 75 MINS FROM CHILCOMB (MAP 2)   FARMYARD   25 – 35 MINS   LANE

55 – 70 MINS TO CHILCOMB (MAP 2)   FARMYARD   25 – 35 MINS   LANE

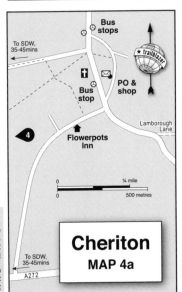

Cheriton

MAP 4a

To SDW, 35-45mins

A272

Those who do make the visit should bear in mind that it was not always such a peaceful and charming spot. In 1644, during the English Civil War, the Battle of Cheriton took place just to the east of the village, off Lamborough Lane. The clash between the Parliamentarians and the Royalists resulted in the deaths of 2000 men with the Parliamentarians coming out on top. To this day it is claimed that 'Lamborough Lane ran with the blood of the slain'.

In the centre of the village is a very useful combined **shop, newsagent, off-licence and post office** (☎ 01962-771251; Mon-Sat 7am-6pm, Sun 7.30am-1pm) that is open long hours but note that the post office part opens only on Monday (1.30-4.30pm) and Thursday (9am to noon).

The charming *Flower Pots Inn* (☎ 01962-771318, 🖳 www.flowerpots.f2s .com; 2T both en suite; ✿; ①) on the outskirts of the village has its own brewery; their Flowerpots Bitter is definitely worth a taste. As well as the beer they have a decent bar menu (food daily noon-1.45pm, Mon-Sat 6-8.45pm, except Bank Hol Mon, but these hours depend on demand) and B&B from £42.50pp (sgl occ from £49). Note the pub is closed 2.30-6pm (Sun 3-7pm).

Stagecoach **bus** No 67 passes through Cheriton on its way between Winchester and Petersfield and stops in the centre of the village, next to the church. For more information see the public transport map and table, pp44-6.

(*cont'd from p79*) The village is about 35-45 minutes from the South Downs Way so unfortunately, unless you are planning on staying the night here, you are likely to miss Cheriton's quaint charms. There are two routes (see Map 4, opposite); the cross country route is better than following the busy A272.

The route continues along leafy country lanes and tracks through a typically English landscape of patchwork fields, hedgerows and pockets of woodland. Along this section is *The Milbury's* (Map 5, p84; ☎ 01962-771248; food daily noon-2pm, Mon-Fri 6.30-9pm, Sat 6-9pm), an ideal lunch stop. A filled baguette and chips is £5.95; steak and kidney pudding costs £11.95. They also do **B&B** (2D/1T all en suite; WI-FI; ✆) for £35pp. It's worth dropping in just for a drink (though the pub is closed 3-6pm in winter) and to admire the 250-year-old **indoor treadmill** and 300ft-deep (92m) well lit all the way to the bottom.

If you're staying at *Dean Farmhouse* (Map 5, p84; ☎ 01962-771286; 🖳 www.warrdeanfarm.co.uk; 2D/1T en suite/private bathroom; £40pp with substantial continental breakfast; WI-FI; ✆; ①) take the next road north to Kilmeston.

The highlight of this stage appears rather unexpectedly at the top of **Beacon Hill** (Map 6, p85), a National Nature Reserve and the first real taste of steep downland scenery. The view over the Meon Valley to Old Winchester Hill is a fine reward for the day's effort. (*cont'd on p87*)

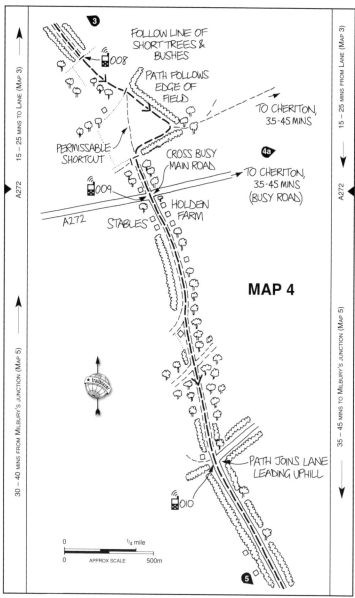

3

FOLLOW LINE OF
SHORT TREES &
BUSHES

PATH FOLLOWS
EDGE OF
FIELD

008

TO CHERITON,
35-45 MINS

PERMISSABLE
SHORTCUT

CROSS BUSY
MAIN ROAD

4a

009

TO CHERITON,
35-45 MINS
(BUSY ROAD)

A272

HOLDEN
FARM

STABLES

MAP 4

15 – 25 MINS TO LANE (MAP 3)

A272

30 – 40 MINS FROM MILBURY'S JUNCTION (MAP 5)

15 – 25 MINS FROM LANE (MAP 3)

A272

35 – 45 MINS TO MILBURY'S JUNCTION (MAP 5)

ROUTE GUIDE AND MAPS

★ trailblazer

PATH JOINS LANE
LEADING UPHILL

010

0   ¼ mile
0   500m
APPROX SCALE

5

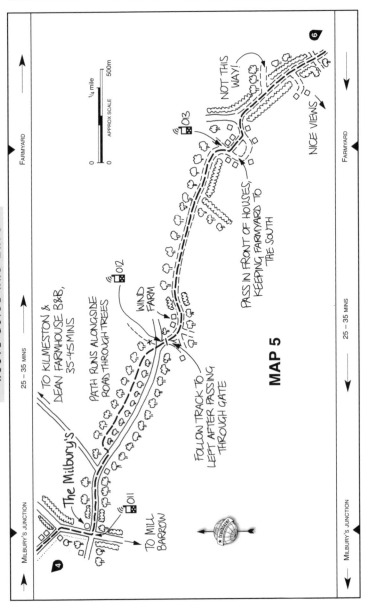

MAP 5

FARMYARD

25 – 35 MINS

MILBURY'S JUNCTION

TO KILMESTON &
DEAN FARMHOUSE B&B,
35-45 MINS

PATH RUNS ALONGSIDE
ROAD THROUGH TREES

The Milbury's

TO MILL BARROW

FOLLOW TRACK TO
LEFT AFTER PASSING
THROUGH GATE

WIND FARM

PASS IN FRONT OF HOUSES,
KEEPING FARMYARD TO
THE SOUTH

NOT THIS
WAY!

NICE VIEWS

¼ mile

500m

APPROX SCALE

trailblazer

MAP 6

NATIONAL NATURE RESERVE

BEACON HILL

▢ 014

△ TRIG POINT

☼ TUMULUS

EXTON BEACON

STEEP DROP THROUGH FIELD WITH VIEWS OVER EXTON

PUNCH BOWL

LOOK OUT FOR STILE BY ROADSIDE

▢ 015

▢ 016

PATH CROSSES A NUMBER OF FIELDS

★ trailblazer

0 ¼ mile

0 APPROX SCALE 500m

7

ROUTE GUIDE AND MAPS

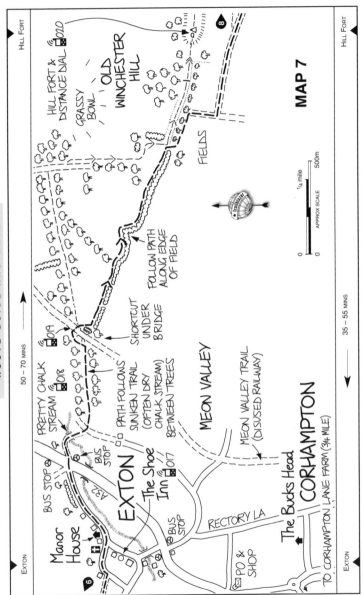

MAP 7

Hill Fort
EXTON

Hill Fort
EXTON

HILL FORT & DISTANCE DIAL 🔲🔲 D20

GRASSY BOWL

OLD WINCHESTER HILL

🔲🔲 D20

FIELDS

FOLLOW PATH ALONG EDGE OF FIELD

SHORTCUT UNDER BRIDGE

🔲🔲 D19

PRETTY CHALK STREAM 🔲🔲 D18

PATH FOLLOWS SUNKEN TRAIL (OFTEN DRY CHALK STREAM) BETWEEN TREES

MEON VALLEY

MEON VALLEY TRAIL (DISUSED RAILWAY)

BUS STOP

The Shoe Inn 🔲🔲 D17

EXTON

BUS STOP

Manor House

BUS STOP

A32

The Bucks Head CORHAMPTON

RECTORY LA

PO & SHOP

TO CORHAMPTON LANE FARM (¾ MILE)

50 – 70 MINS

35 – 55 MINS

¼ mile

500m

0

0

APPROX SCALE

(*cont'd from p82*) **Beacon Hill** is one of a number of hills in southern England where beacons or bonfires were lit to warn of invasions, most notably in the 16th century because of the Spanish Armada and more recently in June 2012 as part of the celebrations for the Queen's Diamond Jubilee.

There have been plans to change the course of the South Downs Way across the Meon Valley ongoing for many years but for now the trail goes through the pretty village of **Exton** – and all the better for it.

EXTON   MAP 7

The Meon valley is known for its natural beauty and also for the Meon villages, all of which claim to be the prettiest in the area. Exton is the smallest of them, if you discount the adjoining hamlets of Meonstoke and Corhampton, and dates back to at least 940AD when it was first mentioned in official documents. It also merited an entry in the Domesday Book of 1086, described as a hamlet of one church and two mills.

Manor House (☎ 01489-877529, 🖳 www.extonbedandbreakfast.com; 2D both en suite, 🍴; Ⓛ) offers B&B for £55pp sharing. Minimum two-night stay at weekends.

The Shoe Inn (☎ 01489-877526, 🖳 www.theshoeexton.co.uk; food Mon-Fri noon-2.15pm & 6-9pm, Sat & Sun noon-3pm & 6-9pm, Sun to 8.30pm in winter) is a friendly village pub with real ales and good food though it's closed 3-6pm during the week. The menu may include slow-cooked belly of pork (£14.95) and haddock in beer batter (£8.50); they always have a vegan option (around £13.95). Booking is advised. The pub's name derives from the building next door which used to be the village cobbler's. There's a nice beer garden across the road and on hot days they now even open an ice-cream 'shack' here.

CORHAMPTON   MAP 7

A short distance south of Exton, Corhampton is useful for its shop and two good places to stay, one of them a pub. If you do stay down here note that there's a shortcut back to the South Downs Way following the disused railway track.

Meonstoke Village Store (Mon-Sat 5.30am-7pm, Sun 7am-4pm) incorporates the **Post Office** (Mon-Fri 9am-5.30pm, Sat 9am-12.30pm) and is 500m south of Exton. There's a good range of local produce.

The Bucks Head (☎ 01489-877313, 🖳 www.thebuckshead.co.uk; food Mon-Sat noon-3pm & 5.30-9pm, Sun noon-3pm) is another welcoming pub and they also offer B&B (2T/3D all en suite, 🍴; WI-FI; Ⓛ) for £40pp (£65 single occupancy).

About a mile down Corhampton Lane (off Map 7) is *Corhampton Lane Farm* (☎ 01489-878755, 🖳 www.corhamptonlane farm.co.uk; 2Tr both with private facilities, 🍴; WI-FI; 🐾 £5; Ⓛ) with **B&B** for £37.50pp (sgl occ £50, three sharing £90). Luggage transfer and lifts to and from the village/pub by arrangement. They also offer laundry facilities. Often recommended: 'best B&B on the whole trip' said one reader! **Campers** (£5 per pitch) can use the toilet, kitchen and wash basin in the barn.

EXTON TO BURITON   MAPS 7-12

This fine stretch of the Way covering **12½ miles (20km, 4½-6hrs)** takes the walker beside **Old Winchester Hill** (Map 7, opposite), a typical downland hill of chalk grassland and steep ancient woodland and a National Nature Reserve. The top of the hill boasts one of the finest Iron Age hill-fort sites in the south. The old earthworks clearly mark the outline of the fort and a display board has an artist's impression of how it once would have looked when the earthy banks were lined with the wooden stakes that formed the walls of the fort. It is clear why it was positioned here since the views in all directions are spectacular, stretching as far as the Isle of Wight on a clear day. Presumably the soldiers of the time also appreciated the views for the strategic advantage it gave them.

Right on the SDW, shortly before the turn-off to **East Meon**, is *Meon Springs* (Map 8; ☎ 01730-823134, 🖳 www.meonsprings.com), a fly-fishing base where you can pick up refreshments (bacon & egg rolls 8am-noon; baguettes and snacks till about 7pm in summer; bar open in licensing hours) and bike spares, fill your water bottles and **camp** (£10pp; 🐾) if you have a tent. There's a toilet and washing facilities but no showers. Campers can just turn up but occasionally they are fully booked so check the calendar on their website before you go. Just over half a mile to the south of here is *Combe House, Bed in a Shed* (Map 8; ☎ 01730-823541, 🖳 www.southdownsbnb.com; 1D or T en suite; WI-FI; ●; Ⓛ) with B&B in a self-contained annex for £50pp sharing.

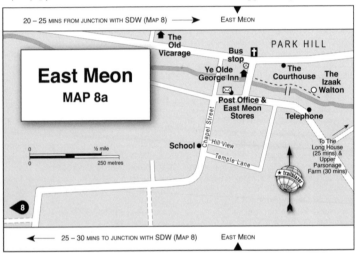

20 – 25 MINS FROM JUNCTION WITH SDW (MAP 8) ⟶ EAST MEON

The Old Vicarage

Bus stop

PARK HILL

Ye Olde George Inn

The Courthouse

The Izaak Walton

Post Office & East Meon Stores

East Meon

MAP 8a

Chapel Street

Telephone

School ● Hill View

Temple Lane

To The Long House (25 mins) & Upper Parsonage Farm (30 mins)

★ trailblazer

0   ½ mile
0   250 metres

8

⟵ 25 – 30 MINS TO JUNCTION WITH SDW (MAP 8)   EAST MEON

ROUTE GUIDE AND MAPS

EAST MEON   MAP 8a

East Meon is only a half-hour detour from the official path and is well worth the effort for a lunch stop or overnight stay. There are records of a settlement here as far back as 400AD and the whole area was once a royal estate belonging to King Alfred. Anyone visiting the village should take a look at the 900-year-old **church** at the foot of the hill where you can also admire the 14th-century **courthouse**, once part of a monastery.

The **post office** (Mon-Fri 9am-5pm, Sat 9am-noon) and **East Meon Stores** (Mon-Fri 7am-6pm, Sat 7am-5pm, Sun 8am-1pm) are on the High St. The Stores are surprisingly well stocked.

Stagecoach **bus** No 67 stops here on the Winchester–Petersfield route; see pp44-6.

Where to stay and eat

In the centre of the village, *Ye Olde George Inn* (☎ 01730-823481, 🖳 www.yeoldegeorgeinn.net; 3D/2D or T, all en suite; ●; 🐾; WI-FI; Ⓛ; food Mon-Sat noon-2.30pm & 6.30-9.30pm, Sun noon-3pm & 6.30-8.30pm: book ahead at weekends) has B&B for £45-55pp (sgl occ from £65).

The Old Vicarage (☎ 01730-823560, 🖳 www.bandb-east-meon.co.uk; 2D/1T, private bathrooms; ●; 🐾; WI-FI; Ⓛ) offers comfortable B&B from £40pp. With notice they can pick up and collect from the Way.

The Long House (☎ 01730-823239, 🖳 www.thelonghouseeastmeon.co.uk; 2D en suite/1D or T adjacent bathroom; ●; WI-FI; 🐾; Ⓛ) lies just round the corner from the end of Frogmore Lane, about a mile from the

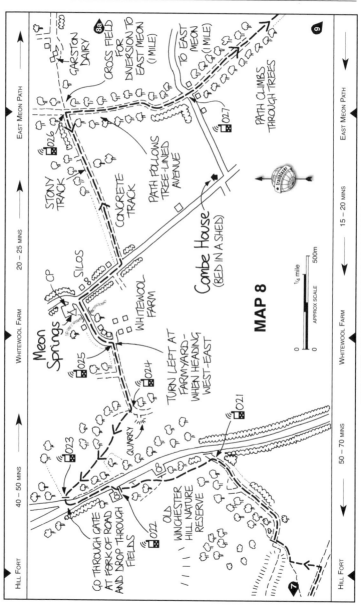

MAP 8

village on the Ramsdean road. B&B in this friendly place with possibly the world's most powerful shower is from £42.50pp, or from £45pp in an en suite room (sgl occ £50). About 300m south of here *Upper Parsonage Farm* (Map 9; ☎ 01730-823490, 🖳 www.upperparsonagefarm.co.uk; 3D, en suite; ✿; 🐾; WI-FI; Ⓛ) is a 1400-acre farm with B&B from £47.50pp for two sharing.

You can also **camp** (toilets/showers available) here for £10 and they have a restored shepherd's hut for £80 per night (sleeps two in a double bed). *The Izaak Walton* (☎ 01730-823252, 🖳 www.izaakwalton.biz; food: Tue-Sat noon-2pm & 7-8.30pm, Sun roast noon-4pm, food served till 6.30pm) is a freehouse pub named after the famous local angler. Also open bank hol Mondays.

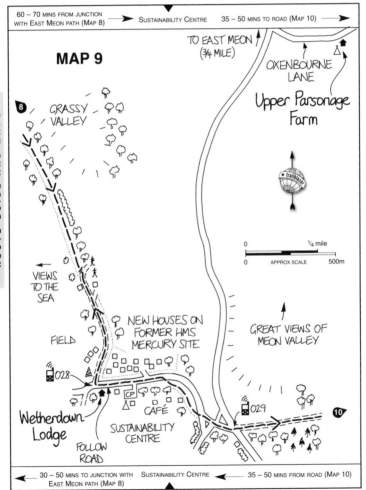

MAP 9

TO EAST MEON (¾ MILE)

OXENBOURNE LANE

Upper Parsonage Farm

GRASSY VALLEY

★ trailblazer

0 ¼ mile
0 APPROX SCALE 500m

VIEWS TO THE SEA

GREAT VIEWS OF MEON VALLEY

FIELD

NEW HOUSES ON FORMER HMS MERCURY SITE

028

029

Wetherdown Lodge

CP

CAFÉ

SUSTAINABILITY CENTRE

FOLLOW ROAD

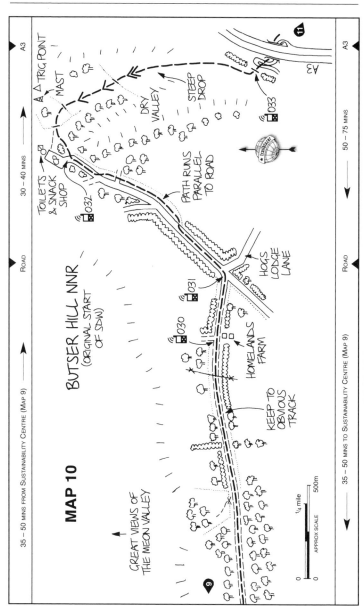

MAP 10

35 – 50 MINS FROM SUSTAINABILITY CENTRE (MAP 9) ──▶

ROAD ▶

30 – 40 MINS ──▶

A3 ▶

GREAT VIEWS OF THE MEON VALLEY

BUTSER HILL NNR
(ORIGINAL START OF SDW)

TRIG POINT

MAST

TOILETS & SNACK SHOP

032

031

030

HOMELANDS FARM

KEEP TO OBVIOUS TRACK

HOGS LODGE LANE

PATH RUNS PARALLEL TO ROAD

DRY VALLEY

STEEP DROP

033

A3

¼ mile
APPROX SCALE
500m
0

35 – 50 MINS TO SUSTAINABILITY CENTRE (MAP 9) ──▶

ROAD ▶

50 – 75 MINS ──▶

A3 ▶

After the turn off to East Meon there is a tough pull up the slope for about two miles to the **Sustainability Centre** (Map 9, p90) and *Wetherdown Lodge* (☎ 01730-823549, 🖳 www.sustainability-centre.org; 2T/9Tr, one room sleeping up to six; 🛏; WI-FI), which is part of the centre. As you'd expect, everything is environmentally friendly and they use renewable energy. The rate is £33 for one person in a room and then £20pp; this includes a continental breakfast. Online booking is now available through their website; booking in general is recommended as sometimes the hostel is booked for sole occupancy use. **Campers** (£10-12pp; 🐾 on lead £1) may appreciate the fact that they allow camp fires (£6 for firewood & kindling).They also have two **tipis** (tepees) each sleeping 5/8 people (£22pp) and three **yurts** each sleeping 2-4 people (bedding provided for up to two people; £33pp; two-night and two-person bookings only at the weekend). The (solar) shower block is open Apr to Oct; running water and compost toilets are available all year. The hostel has self-catering facilities but there is also the on-site *Beech Café* (☎ 01730-823755; daily 10am-4pm, Nov-Feb/Mar to 3pm) which can provide packed lunches if booked in advance.

It is around here that the true line of the Downs begins, stretching east as a high-level ridge, interrupted only by a few river valleys, all the way to Beachy Head near Eastbourne.

The Way continues along the broad ridge with fine views over the Meon valley to the north culminating in the highest point of the South Downs at Butser Hill (270m). **Butser Hill** (see Map 10, p91) is another National Nature Reserve, earning its status for its fine chalk grassland. It is home to over thirty species of butterfly including the tiny, difficult-to-spot but exquisite Chalkhill blue (see opposite p48). It was also the original starting point for the South Downs Way before it was decided to extend the path all the way to Winchester. The only blot on the landscape here is the car park at the top of the hill and the less-than-attractive A3 dual carriageway that slices through the lower flanks. Once past the din of racing traffic the path climbs steadily back to the top of

---

❏ **Queen Elizabeth Country Park**

The South Downs Way cuts right through the heart of this vast protected area which includes the chalk downland of Butser Hill. To the east of the hill the park is dominated by one of the largest expanses of unbroken woodland cover in the South-East, comprising both ancient broadleaved wood and beech and conifer plantations.

The park (open all the time) is popular with daytrippers and picnickers largely thanks to its proximity to the main A3 road. The **Visitor Centre** (Map 11; ☎ 023-9259 5040, 🖳 www3.hants.gov.uk/qecp; Mar-Oct daily 10am-5.30pm, Nov-mid Dec & early Jan-Feb daily 10am-4.30pm) can provide maps and guides to the park. The centre houses a **shop** and **café** offering a selection of cakes and snacks.

Stagecoach's No 37 (Havant to Petersfield) **bus** stops on the A3 most of the time but on Sundays (May-Oct) goes to the visitor centre. The northbound stop lies just beyond the slip road under the A3 (the slip road needs to be used with care). Access to the park from the stop on the south side is no problem. Either way make sure you let the driver know you want to stop here and also if you are waiting at the bus stop make sure you can be seen. See the public transport map and table pp44-6.

the downland escarpment above Buriton, passing through the **Queen Elizabeth Country Park** (Map 11), a magnificent natural mixed woodland that covers the rolling Downs for miles around, just as it has done through the centuries. If the accommodation in **Buriton** (p94) is booked up you could head into the old market town of **Petersfield** (p94), where there are several more places.

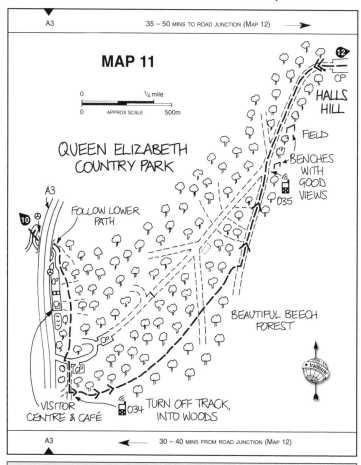

A3   35 – 50 MINS TO ROAD JUNCTION (MAP 12) ➞

MAP 11

0   ¼ mile
0   APPROX SCALE   500m

12
CP
HALLS HILL

QUEEN ELIZABETH COUNTRY PARK

FIELD

BENCHES WITH GOOD VIEWS

035

A3

10

FOLLOW LOWER PATH

CP

BEAUTIFUL BEECH FOREST

★ trailblazer

VISITOR CENTRE & CAFÉ

034 TURN OFF TRACK, INTO WOODS

A3   ⟵ 30 – 40 MINS FROM ROAD JUNCTION (MAP 12)

ROUTE GUIDE AND MAPS

❑ **Important note – walking times**
Unless otherwise specified, **all times in this book refer only to the time spent walking**. You will need to add 20-30% to allow for rests, photography, checking the map, drinking water etc.

BURITON   MAP 12

Buriton is yet another pretty village commanding an enviable position at the foot of the wooded downland escarpment.

The **Church of St Mary** by the duck pond is of particular interest as the interior dates back to the 12th century.

Where to stay and eat

Perfectly placed just below the Way, *Toads Alley* (☎ 01730-263880; 🖥 www.toads alley.co.uk; 1D/1T, ☛; Ⓛ) is an attractive 15th-century cottage with B&B from £37.50/42.50pp for shared/private bathroom. Single occupancy is from £60.

A good accommodation choice if you can face the 1½-mile walk up the lane is *Nursted Farm* (☎ 01730-264278; 🖥 www .nurstedfarm.co.uk; 1Tr/1T en suite, 1T with private bathroom, ☛; Ⓛ). It is a magnificent old farmhouse with B&B from £35pp (no sgl occ rate). There is plenty of wildlife to spot in the garden and the owner has lived there all his life so he knows a thing or two about the area.

The Five Bells (☎ 01730-263584, 🖥 www.fivebells-buriton.co.uk; bar daily 11am-11pm; food Mon-Sat noon-2pm & 7-9pm, Sun noon-4pm) is a great pub with friendly staff and excellent food (standard pub fare with main dishes for around £8.95).

The old Maple Inn will reopen soon as *The Village Inn* (☎ 01730-267275; 17D, ☛). It's owned by a company that runs weddings (🖥 www.manorhouseburiton.co. uk) so they may not have accommodation for walkers at weekends in summer. Unless you're getting married, of course...

PETERSFIELD   MAP 12a, p97

This market town still retains charm, despite attempts to turn it into something bland and modern with supermarkets and a small shopping arcade.

Petersfield Museum (☎ 01730-262601, 🖥 www.petersfieldmuseum.co.uk; Mar-Dec Tue-Sat 10am-4pm; £2), behind The Square, has old newspaper cuttings, photos and antique maps of the local area.

Tucked down an alley to the right of St Peter's Church in The Square is the **Flora Twort Gallery** (☎ 01730-260756; Mar-Dec Tue-Sat 10am-4pm; £2) which exhibits paintings by Flora Twort as well as historic costumes from the Bedales collection.

An oasis of calm amongst the bustle is afforded by **Petersfield Physic Garden** (open daily, admission free), reached via an alley off the High St. It features many of the characteristics and plant varieties of a 17th -century town garden with herbs, topiary and an orchard and plenty of benches to relax on with your takeaway lunch.

Services

The **Tourist Information Centre** (☎ 01730-268829; Mon-Sat 9am-5pm) is in the library; alternatively look at 🖥 www .visitpetersfield.com. The **library** (☎ 0300-555 1387) is open Mon-Sat 9am-5pm, though to 7pm on Wed & Fri. There are two good bookshops: **Waterstones** and **One Tree Books** which also has a café. The **post office** (Mon-Fri 9am-5.30pm, Sat 9am-12.30pm) is on the edge of The Square.

On the High St there are various **banks** with ATMs, as well as a branch of the **camping shop** Millets (Mon-Sat 9am-5.30pm, Sun 10am-4pm), while round the corner, on Swan St, is a **pharmacy** (Mon-Fri 9am-5.30pm, Sat 9am-5pm).

On the High St is a Boots and an M&S Foodstore, while just off it is a large Waitrose **supermarket**. There's a Tesco in the south of the town and also a **farmers' market** in The Square on the first Sunday of every month (10am-2pm).

Public transport

[See the public transport map & table, pp44-6] SouthWest operates **trains** from here to both London Waterloo and Portsmouth. National Express's London to Portsmouth No 31 **coach** service also calls here.

Buses leave from the town centre. The most useful services are: Emsworth & District's No 54 (to Chichester) and their No 92 (to Midhurst Mon-Sat), and Stagecoach's No 67 (to Winchester), their No 37 (to Havant), No 38 (to Alton) and No 92 Sunday service (to Midhurst).

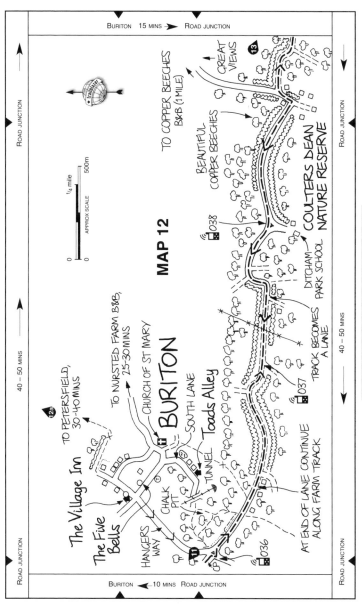

Where to stay

Tucked away behind a high hedge at 4 Heath Rd, pretty little 16th-century *Border Cottage* (☎ 01730-263179, 🖥 www.border cottage.co.uk; 1D or T en suite; WI-FI; Ⓛ) offers B&B from £32.50pp (sgl occ £50) with a continental breakfast served in your room; if you prefer the thought of a cooked breakfast a room-only rate (£25pp; sgl occ £40) is available and they can suggest places for you to go to.

At the end of Sheep St, *1 The Spain* (☎ 01730-263261, 🖥 www.1thespain.com; 1D private bathroom ➾; 1D/1T en suite; WI-FI; 🐾 for a small additional charge; Ⓛ) is a well-kept 18th-century townhouse with B&B from £40pp (sgl occ from £50).

Just west of the railway station, *80 Rushes Rd B&B* (☎ 01730-261638, 🖥 www.rushes-road.co.uk; 1D or T private bathroom ➾; WI-FI; Ⓛ) is run by a friendly tour guide. B&B is £35pp (sgl occ £50).

Closest to the Way at No 64A The Causeway, *Causeway Guest House* (☎ 01730-262924, 🖥 www.petersfieldbedand breakfast.co.uk; 2S/1D/1Tr; ➾; WI-FI; Ⓛ) offers B&B from £35pp.

The Good Intent (☎01730-263838; 🖥 www.goodintentpetersfield.co.uk; 1D/1Tr en suite; 1D private bathroom; ➾; WI-FI) offers B&B for £40pp (sgl occ £60).

The Old Drum (☎ 01730-300544; 🖥 www.theolddrum.co.uk) is currently undergoing renovations but will reopen in mid-2015 with five letting rooms.

JSW (☎ 01730-262030; 🖥 jswrestau rant.com; 4D, all en suite; ➾; WI-FI; Wed-Sun only) offers B&B for £47.50-60pp (sgl occ £80-105) though during the week there may be special rates if you also book one of their tasting menus (see Where to eat).

Where to eat and drink

Petersfield is replete with eating places. For takeaway lunch ingredients try the popular *Heidi's Swiss Patisserie* (☎ 01730-231889; shop Mon-Sat 8.30am-5pm, coffee lounge to 4pm), or for a tasty pasty head for *Greggs Bakery* (☎ 01730-263450; Mon-Sat 7am-5pm) on Chapel St.

On the town square there's a *Caffè Nero* (☎ 01730-261783; Mon-Sat 7.30am-6pm, Sun 8.30am-5pm). They also serve a variety of light lunches.

The excellent *Monoloco* (☎ 01730-266119, 🖥 www.monolo.co; Mon-Sat, 9am-4pm & 6-11pm) began as a popular café and now opens in the evenings as a steakhouse: you cook your own steak at the table on hot lava stones. It's good value: the lunch dishes are all £8.

One of the best places to eat here is *Annie Jones* (☎ 01730-262728, 🖥 www.anniejones.co.uk). Their patisserie and coffee bar is open Tue-Sun 10am-3.30pm (to 5pm on Sat); the garden bar and tapas bar open Tue-Thur noon-2.45pm & 6-9.30pm, Fri-Sat noon-2pm & 6-10pm, Sun noon-2pm. The tapas – eg calamari rings with lemon mayo (£5) – is very good.

Reopening soon, *The Old Drum* (see Where to stay; food: Mon-Sat noon-2pm & 6.30-9.30pm, Sun noon-3pm) is a 300-year-old freehouse, recommended for a drink or a meal.

The Square Brewery (☎ 01730-264291, 🖥 www.thesquarebrewery.com; food Mon-Fri 10am-4pm, Sat-Sun 10am-5pm, evenings only on Wed & Thur 6-9pm) is a popular local pub with live music on Wed and Sat evenings. On The Square, *The George* (☎ 01730-233343, 🖥 www.the georgepetersfield.co.uk; food daily 9am-3pm & 6-9pm) is an upmarket pub and restaurant under new management.

The Good Intent (see Where to stay; food: Mon-Sat noon-2.30pm & 6.30-9.30pm, Sun noon-2.30pm) serves standard pub grub such as sausages and mash (£10).

Recommended by several readers, *Fez* (☎ 01730-231266, 🖥 www.fezpetersfield .com; daily noon-10pm) is a Turkish restaurant and meze bar at 39b Chapel St. A mid-week three-course menu is £16.95.

For cheap eats there's *Nicky's Fish & Chips* (☎ 01730-262188; Mon-Sat 11.30am-2pm & 5-10pm). On Lavant St are several other options, including *Seafare Fish and Chip Shop* (☎ 01730-265702; Tue-Sat 11.30am-2pm, Mon-Thur 5-10pm, Fri & Sat 4.30-10pm), the Chinese rivals *Peking* (☎ 01730-233323; Mon-Thur 5-10.30pm, Fri & Sat 5-11.15pm, Sun 5.30-10pm) and the superior *Hong Kong House* (☎ 01730-

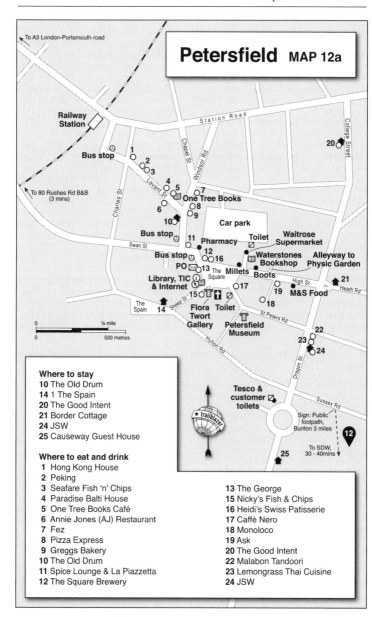

Petersfield MAP 12a

To A3 London-Portsmouth road

Railway Station

Bus stop

Station Road

College Street

20

To 80 Rushes Rd B&B (3 mins)

Charles St

Lavant St

Chapel St

Windsor Rd

1
2
3
4 5
7 One Tree Books
6
8
9
10
Car park

Bus stop
11 Pharmacy
Toilet
Waitrose Supermarket

Swan St

Bus stop
12
16
PO 13 The Square
Millets
Waterstones Bookshop
Alleyway to Physic Garden

Library, TIC & Internet
15
Boots
High St
21
Heath Rd

The Spain
14
Sheep St
17
19 M&S Food

Flora Twort Gallery
Toilet
18
St Peters Rd

Petersfield Museum
22
23
24

Rylton Rd

Dragon St

0 ¼ mile
0 500 metres

★ trailblazer

Tesco & customer toilets

Sign: Public footpath, Buriton 3 miles

12

25

Sussex Rd

To SDW, 30 - 40mins

Where to stay
10 The Old Drum
14 1 The Spain
20 The Good Intent
21 Border Cottage
24 JSW
25 Causeway Guest House

Where to eat and drink
1 Hong Kong House
2 Peking
3 Seafare Fish 'n' Chips
4 Paradise Balti House
5 One Tree Books Café
6 Annie Jones (AJ) Restaurant
7 Fez
8 Pizza Express
9 Greggs Bakery
10 The Old Drum
11 Spice Lounge & La Piazzetta
12 The Square Brewery

13 The George
15 Nicky's Fish & Chips
16 Heidi's Swiss Patisserie
17 Caffè Nero
18 Monoloco
19 Ask
20 The Good Intent
22 Malabon Tandoori
23 Lemongrass Thai Cuisine
24 JSW

ROUTE GUIDE AND MAPS

265256; Tue-Thur & Sun 5-11pm, Fri & Sat noon-2pm & 5pm-midnight).

Going more upmarket, at 23 Lavant St, *Paradise Balti* (☎ 01730-265162, 🖳 www.paradise-restaurant.com; Sun-Thur noon-2.30pm & 5.30-11.30pm, Fri 5.30pm-midnight, Sat noon-2.30pm & 5.30pm-midnight) is a smart Indian restaurant. *Spice Lounge* (☎ 01730-303303, 🖳 www.spice loungepetersfield.co.uk; Mon-Sat noon-2.30pm & 5.30-11.30pm, Sun noon-10pm) is another Indian restaurant, on the High St. Sharing the same building is the popular *La Piazzetta* (☎ 01730-260006; daily noon-2pm & 5.30-10pm), with pizzas from £7.

Other options for Italian food include the chains *Pizza Express* (☎ 01730-710357; Mon-Tue 11.30am-10.30pm, Wed-Sun 11.30am-11pm) on Chapel St or, along the High St, there's *Ask* (☎ 01730-231113; Mon-Thur noon-11pm, Fri & Sat noon-11.30pm, Sun noon-10pm).

For a more upmarket dining experience, book a table at Michelin-starred chef Jake Watkins' small, swish and exclusive *JSW* (see Where to stay: Wed-Sun noon-1.30pm & 7-9.30pm). A two-course set menu costs £25 at lunch (Wed-Fri only), though there is an á la carte menu too. If you really want to splash out they have tasting menus; their five-course menu is £45 at lunch and £55 in the evening.

In the same vicinity at 16-18 Dragon St is the restaurant-cum-takeaway *Lemongrass Thai Cuisine* (☎ 01730-267077, 🖳 www.lmpetersfield.co.uk; daily noon-2.30pm & 5.30-10.45pm with dishes such as Thai green curry for £8.95, while next door at No 14 *Malabon Tandoori* (☎ 01730-268352, 🖳 www.malabonrestaurant .co.uk; daily noon-2.30pm & 6-11.30pm) serves Indian & Bangladeshi meals to eat-in or take away and has a vast menu with mains starting from £6.50.

BURITON TO COCKING   MAPS 12-16

The route from Buriton follows tracks and lanes along the top of the South Downs escarpment for **10½ miles (17km, 3¾-4¾hrs)**. It is very wooded before reaching South Harting (Map 13) so although the views are limited there is plenty of beautiful shady woodland to enjoy.

About ten minutes south of the Way where it crosses the B2146 is **Uppark House**.

❏ Uppark House

Uppark House (off Map 13, opposite; ☎ 01730-825857, 🖳 www.nationaltrust.org.uk/ uppark; house open daily Mar to late Oct 12.30-4.30pm; gardens and café open year round 10am-5pm) is a magnificent 17th-century country home perched high on a hill with extensive views across the Downs and beyond. The Georgian interior and gardens can be toured for just £10; visiting the garden costs £6.

One of the most remarkable things about Uppark is the near-perfect restoration of the building after it was all but gutted by a rampant fire in 1989.

Emsworth & District's No 54 bus service calls here (see pp44-6).

SOUTH HARTING   MAP 13

From the top of Harting Down the village of South Harting with its distinctive church steeple is clearly visible and looks very inviting.

It's not a long walk to the village from the Way but you do have to climb back up the hill through the woods on the return.

The **Church of St Mary & St Gabriel** is interesting and contains an impressive statue of the Archangel Gabriel, by sculptor Philip Jackson, suspended from the ceiling. The village stocks are still by the path outside the church.

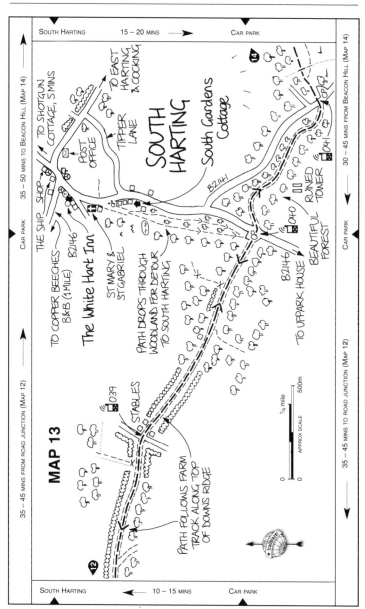

SOUTH HARTING   15 – 20 MINS ⟶   CAR PARK

TO SHOTGUN COTTAGE, 5 MINS

TO EAST HARTING & COCKING

TIPPER LANE

POST OFFICE

SOUTH HARTING

South Gardens Cottage

B2141

14

35 – 50 MINS TO BEACON HILL (MAP 14)

30 – 45 MINS FROM BEACON HILL (MAP 14)

CAR PARK

THE SHIP SHOP

TO COPPER BEECHES B&B (1 MILE)

B2146

The White Hart Inn

ST MARY & ST GABRIEL

PATH DROPS THROUGH WOODLAND FOR DETOUR TO SOUTH HARTING

RUINED TOWER

BEAUTIFUL FOREST

B2146

TO UPPARK HOUSE

CAR PARK

35 – 45 MINS FROM ROAD JUNCTION (MAP 12)

35 – 45 MINS TO ROAD JUNCTION (MAP 12)

CAR PARK

MAP 13

STABLES

039

PATH FOLLOWS FARM TRACK ALONG TOP OF DOWNS RIDGE

12

¼ mile

APPROX SCALE

0   500m

SOUTH HARTING   ⟵ 10 – 15 MINS   CAR PARK

ROUTE GUIDE AND MAPS

Services

The **post office** (Mon, Tue, Thur & Fri 9am-1pm & 2-5.30pm, Wed 9am-1pm only, Sat 9am-12.30pm) is on The Square and there is an excellent village **shop** (☎ 01730-825219; Mon-Fri 7am-7pm, Sat 7.30am-1pm, Sun 8am-1pm), on North Lane, which sells a wide variety of provisions as well as hot pies and pasties, wine and beer. It's owned and run by the villagers and does cashback if you need some money.

Emsworth & District's No 54 **bus** service calls here en route between Petersfield and Chichester; see the public transport map and table, pp44-6.

Where to stay

The most beautiful B&B in the village is the spectacular old timber-framed, thatched 16th-century *South Gardens Cottage* (☎ 01730-825040, 🖳 julia@randjhomes.plus .com; 1D en suite, ☛; 1D private shower facilities), with a garden that's ablaze with flowers in the summer. B&B costs from £36pp (from £40pp in the en suite room; sgl occ negotiable).

Visit South Harting church to see Philip Jackson's statue of the Archangel Gabriel

Up North Lane, *Shotgun Cottage* (☎ 01730-826878, 🖳 qejoy@hotmail.com; 1D or T/1Tr private facilities; ☛; 🐾; WI-FI) charges from £40pp (sgl occ £40-50; three sharing from £110). One of the rooms in the house is en suite, the other has a private bathroom. To reach the cottage turn right into Pays Farm, which is on the right-hand side of the road. Further north up North Lane, just over a mile from South Harting, is *The Severals B&B* (☎ 01730-821720, 🖳 www.theseverals.co.uk; 1S private bathroom/ 1D en suite; ☛; WI-FI; Ⓛ). The hospitable owners charge £45pp (sgl £50, sgl occ £70) They will collect/return walkers to the SDW. Highly recommended by readers.

The upmarket *White Hart* (☎ 01730-825124, 🖳 www.the-whitehart.co.uk; 4D/ 1T/1Qd en suite; ☛; WI-FI) now offers B&B for £35-60pp (four sharing £95-135, sgl occ £70).

Just over a mile west of South Harting along the Petersfield road (B2146) and directly accessible from the South Downs Way (See Map 12, p95), is *Copper Beeches* (☎ 01730-826662, 🖳 www.copperbeeches .net; 1D/1Tr en suite; ☛; WI-FI; 🐾; Ⓛ) with B&B from £35pp (sgl occ £50 or £70 at weekends).

Where to eat and drink

The *White Hart* (see Where to stay; 🐾; food Mon-Sat noon-2.30pm & 6-9pm, Sun noon-3.30pm & 6.30-8.30pm) boasts an excellent chef. There are imaginative bar snacks (salt & pepper squid, chilli jam, £5.95) as well as full meals.

After South Harting the trees begin to thin out as the Way passes over **Harting Down**. The views open up over the patchwork fields below and the path climbs even higher onto **Beacon Hill** (Map 14).

There then follows another wooded section, the **Monkton Estate**, where it's worth listening out for peacocks before the path continues through the pastureland of **Cocking Down** down to the main road leading to Cocking. There is an interpretation board (see Map 16, p105) in the car park there.

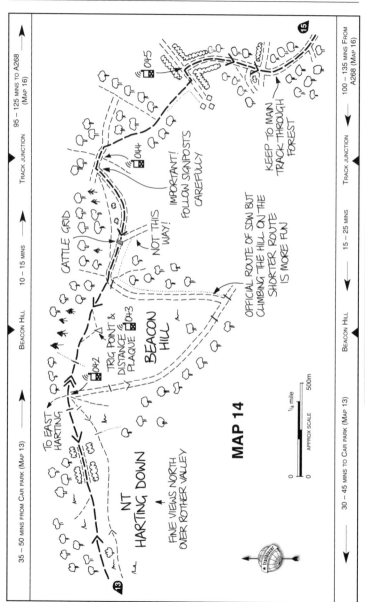

95 – 125 MINS TO A268 (MAP 16)

☞ 045

TRACK JUNCTION

10 – 15 MINS

☞ 044

IMPORTANT! FOLLOW SIGNPOSTS CAREFULLY

KEEP TO MAIN TRACK THROUGH FOREST

100 – 135 MINS FROM A268 (MAP 16)

TRACK JUNCTION

CATTLE GRID

NOT THIS WAY!

OFFICIAL ROUTE OF SDW BUT CLIMBING THE HILL ON THE SHORTER ROUTE IS MORE FUN

BEACON HILL

15 – 25 MINS

TRIG POINT & DISTANCE PLAQUE ☞ 043

☞ 042

BEACON HILL

BEACON HILL

To EAST HARTING

MAP 14

¼ mile

500m

APPROX SCALE

0

0

NT HARTING DOWN

FINE VIEWS NORTH OVER ROTHER VALLEY

35 – 50 MINS FROM CAR PARK (MAP 13)

30 – 45 MINS TO CAR PARK (MAP 13)

13

15

ROUTE GUIDE AND MAPS

❑ **Glorious Goodwood – not so glorious for walkers**
Goodwood (🖳 www.goodwood.co.uk), near Singleton, has long been associated with country pursuits such as horse-racing and shooting but is also host to sports such as flying and motor racing. The Festival of Speed, held every July, celebrates the history of motor sport and is one of many events held here around the year. Whilst these are probably not of interest to walkers of the South Downs Way, the relevance is that accommodation in the area is often booked up months in advance so it is probably worth checking the dates for events (see the Goodwood website) before you set off.

Compass Travel's No 99 bus service calls here if prebooked (see pp44-6).

COCKING — MAP 16, p105

Cocking is pleasant enough but the busy main road that slices the village in two has rather taken the soul out of the place despite one or two pretty old cottages. The consolation is that it is not too far from the Way. It is best reached by ignoring the obvious route down the busy main road and continuing, instead, to the farm buildings ten minutes east of this road and following the farm track north down the hill to the village.

Services

The **shop/post office** (☎ 01730-817867, 🖳 www.cockingstores.co.uk; shop summer Mon-Fri 7am-6.30pm, Sat 7am-6pm, Sun 8am-4pm; winter Sat to 4pm, Sun to 1pm; post office Mon-Fri 9am-5pm, Sat 9am-noon) is on the corner of the main road with Mill Lane. They sell hot drinks and sandwiches – which you can eat on one of their benches outside.

The **bus stop** is on the main road and Stagecoach's No 60 passes through regularly on its route between Chichester and Midhurst; see the public transport map p44-6.

Where to stay, eat and drink

The most convenient place to stay is ***Hilltop Cottages*** (☎ 01730-814156; 1T private bathroom; ☕; Ⓛ), part of Manor Farm, and right on the Way; it offers B&B from £30pp (sgl occ £40). They also offer basic **camping** (Easter to end Oct) at £5/8 for one/two people in a tent with access to toilet facilities; campers can have breakfast (order in advance). They have a **farm shop** (Fri-Sun 11am-4pm) selling eggs, home-made sausages as well as sandwiches, drinks, snacks and ice cream.

There is always a warm welcome for walkers at ***Moonlight Cottage Tea Rooms*** (☎ 01730-813336, 🖳 www.moonlightcottage.co.uk; 1D or T en suite, 1S/1T/1D share bathroom; ☕; 🐕; WI-FI; Ⓛ) with **B&B** for £37.50-45pp (sgl/sgl occ £55/70). Evening meals are available if booked in advance and contact them for details of their luggage-transfer service. If you arrive wet and dirty for a small charge they will be happy to wash and dry your clothes. They now also have a **bunkhouse** (4 beds; £20pp inc bedding & towels, breakfast £8pp) with washing facilities, toilets and basic self-catering facilities (kettle, fridge & microwave); booking is essential. As the name suggests, there is a **tea room** here too: they are open for light lunches and afternoon teas (Mar-Oct Fri-Sun & Bank Hol Mons 10am-5.30pm).

Directly opposite and owned by the same people, the 16th-century ***Malthouse*** (see Moonlight Cottage for contact details; 1T/1Tr en suite; 1Tr private bathroom; ☕; WI-FI; Ⓛ) offers B&B for £45-47.50pp (sgl occ £70; three sharing room rate plus £35). Meals are eaten at Moonlight. **Camping** (£10pp, £18pp inc breakfast; shower/toilet facilities) is available in their garden.

On Bell Lane there's ***Downsfold*** (☎ 01730-814376, 🖳 www.downsfold.co.uk; 1D/1T, shared bathroom ☕; WI-FI; Mar-Oct), with B&B from £40pp (sgl occ £45).

B&B at ***The Bluebell Inn*** (☎ 01730-810200, 🖳 www.thebluebellinnatcocking.co.uk; 3D en suite, 1D/1T share facilities; WI-FI; Ⓛ) costs £42.50-62.50pp (sgl occ £60-90). Food is served daily (daily noon-2.30pm & 6-9pm) and they have a bar menu as well as an à la carte menu.

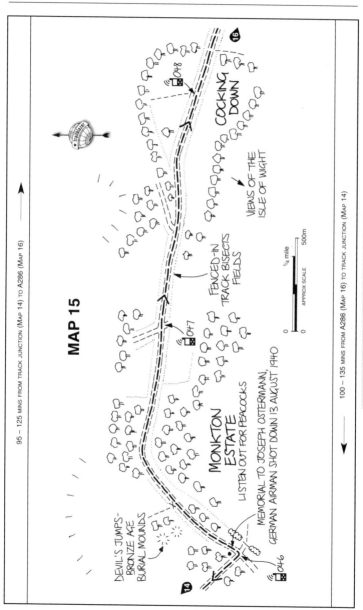

MAP 15

DEVIL'S JUMPS-
BRONZE AGE
BURIAL MOUNDS

MONKTON
ESTATE

LISTEN OUT FOR PEACOCKS

MEMORIAL TO JOSEPH OSTERMANN,
GERMAN AIRMAN SHOT DOWN 13 AUGUST 1940

046

047

FENCED-IN
TRACK BISECTS
FIELDS

COCKING DOWN

VIEWS OF THE
ISLE OF WIGHT

048

¼ mile

APPROX SCALE   500m

MIDHURST   **off MAP 16, p105**

If everywhere in Cocking (see p102) is booked up you can take Stagecoach's No 60 **bus** (see public transport map and table pp44-6) to Midhurst about two to three miles to the north where there is a wider choice of accommodation including the friendly *Pear Tree Cottage* (☎ 01730-817216, 🖳 www.peartreecottagebandbmidhurst.co.uk; 1Tr/2D plus 4ft sofa bed, all en suite, WI-FI) on Lamberts Lane. B&B costs from £40pp (£55-65pp during Goodwood; sgl occ from £50, full rate at times; three sharing from £100). The rooms are self contained, can sleep three people, and have a fridge, microwave, toaster and kettle. The owner leaves the ingredients for a continental breakfast in the room the night before.

Just outside Elsted and almost equidistant between Midhurst and South Harting (just over three miles from each) is *The Elsted Inn* (☎ 01730-813662, 🖳 www.theelstedinn.com; 2T/2D en suite; 🐾; WI-FI in the bar; 🐕; Ⓛ), a well-run, popular pub. The friendly owners will collect walkers staying with them from the Way and take them back next morning.

Failing those have a look at 🖳 www.visitmidhurst.com for additional suggestions.

Midhurst has a good range of eating places, a Tesco Express, NatWest and Barclays banks and other services should you find yourself here.

COCKING TO AMBERLEY   MAPS 16-22

It is **11½ miles (18.5km, 3¾-5¼hrs)** from the Cocking turnoff to the Amberley turnoff. From the main road south of Cocking the Way follows a chalk lane, climbing steadily through fields to rejoin the high escarpment. There is a water tap by the farm buildings (see Map 16). Just after that you will notice that the window frames on the cottages here, including Hilltop Cottages (see p102), are painted yellow; this shows they are part of the Cowdray Estate (see box below).

The track here used to be bordered on one side by dense woodland and on the other by a high hedge so the view was somewhat obscured in parts but the former South Downs Joint Committee and Graffham Down Trust created a wildlife corridor in order to link up two rich grassland sites – Heyshott Down (Map 17) and Graffham Down (Map 18). **Heyshott Down** is one of the nature reserves in this area which is managed by the Murray Downland Trust (see p58) – making it easier for a lot of the flora and fauna here to survive. The best view is probably from the trig point (Map 17), about 50m off the path.

❏ The two Cowdray Gold Cups

The Cowdray Estate is probably best known for the Polo Club and the polo matches (both national and international) held there during the year; the main event is the Gold Cup which is held in July.

The second Gold Cup refers to the colour of the paint seen on the window frames and doors of cottages and buildings that are part of the estate, particularly around Midhurst. The 'cowardy custard' yellow, as some locals call it, was first used on the cottages by the 2nd Viscount Cowdray who was a Liberal MP (yellow being the colour particularly associated with the Liberal Party), thus it was a good way of promoting the Liberal party. The paint was made specially for the Viscount and was originally called Cowdray Gold but is now known as Gold Cup, though it is not exactly the same shade as the original colour.

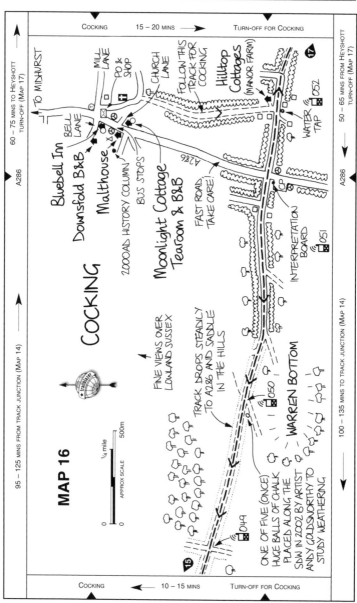

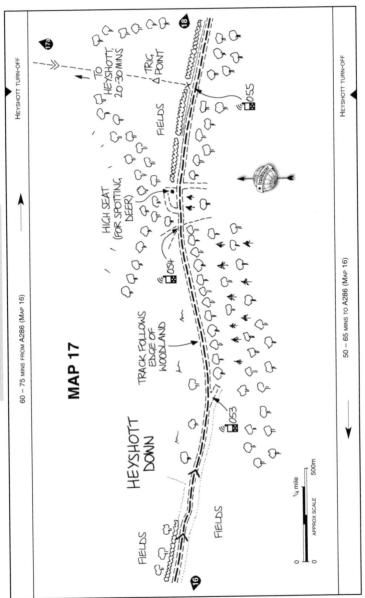

MAP 17

HEYSHOTT DOWN

FIELDS

FIELDS

FIELDS

TRACK FOLLOWS EDGE OF WOODLAND

HIGH SEAT (FOR SPOTTING DEER)

TRIG POINT

TO HEYSHOTT, 20-30 MINS

FIELDS

053

054

055

16

18

17a

HEYSHOTT TURN-OFF

HEYSHOTT TURN-OFF

60 – 75 MINS FROM A286 (MAP 16)

50 – 65 MINS TO A286 (MAP 16)

¼ mile

500m

APPROX SCALE

0

0

HEYSHOTT MAP 17a

Now that the two B&Bs here have closed there's just a pub to justify the steep and sometimes muddy descent from the Way.

A little way to the west of the village is *The Unicorn Inn* (☎ 01730-813486, 🖥 www.unicorn-inn-heyshott.co.uk; bar generally Tue-Sat 11am-11pm, Sun noon-4pm; food Tue-Sat noon-2pm & 6-9.30pm, Sun noon-2.30pm), a smart country pub with excellent food. Main dishes, which include ale-battered cod with chips and peas, start from £10.95 but the great views across the hay meadows to the Downs escarpment are free. The pub is closed on Sunday evenings and all day on Mondays except at lunchtime May to September.

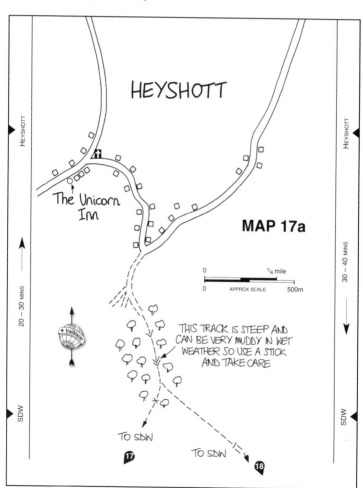

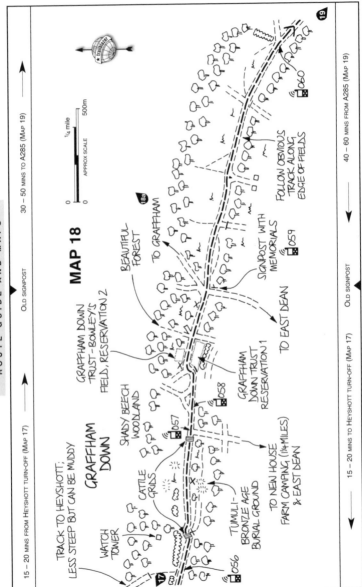

MAP 18

15 – 20 MINS FROM HEYSHOTT TURN-OFF (MAP 17)

OLD SIGNPOST

30 – 50 MINS TO A285 (MAP 19)

40 – 60 MINS FROM A285 (MAP 19)

OLD SIGNPOST

15 – 20 MINS TO HEYSHOTT TURN-OFF (MAP 17)

TRACK TO HEYSHOTT;
LESS STEEP BUT CAN BE MUDDY

WATCH
TOWER

GRAFFHAM
DOWN

CATTLE
GRIDS

SHADY BEECH
WOODLAND

GRAFFHAM DOWN
TRUST-BONLEY'S
FIELD, RESERVATION 2

BEAUTIFUL
FOREST

TO GRAFFHAM

TUMULI-
BRONZE AGE
BURIAL GROUND

TO NEW HOUSE
FARM CAMPING (1¼ MILES)
& EAST DEAN

GRAFFHAM
DOWN TRUST
RESERVATION 1

TO EAST DEAN

SIGNPOST WITH
MEMORIALS

FOLLOW OBVIOUS
TRACK ALONG
EDGE OF FIELDS

APPROX SCALE
0 — 500m
0 — ¼ mile

056
057
058
059
060

> ❏ **Tumuli**
> All along the crest of the Downs are numerous burial mounds known as tumuli. These
> are in the region of 4000 to 4500 years old. Some are overgrown or are not particu-
> larly distinct but many are surprisingly well preserved. A glance at an Ordnance
> Survey map of the area will indicate exactly where they are. Next time you stop for
> lunch on that nice grassy hump just remember you may be sitting on the grave of
> someone who has been dead for 4500 years.

The path then continues past a **Bronze Age burial ground** (Map 18) with
tumuli clearly visible among the tussocks of grass. Shortly after is the turn south
to *New House Farm Camping* (off Map 18; ☎ 01243-811685; 🖥 www.nhfcamp
ing.com; 🐾; £5 per pitch and £5pp) 1¼ miles from the Way and on the edge of
East Dean. It's a basic place with portaloos and a cold water tap but no showers.

The track continues on through a mixture of woodland and grassland, passing the turn-off for **Graffham**.

GRAFFHAM   MAP 18a, p110

There is little to see in Graffham but it has
a lazy, peaceful air about it, being well
away from any major roads.

There's a very well-stocked **shop**
(Mon-Fri 7am-7pm, Sat 8am-5pm) where
you can also get hot drinks and snacks, next
to the village hall. The **post office** is next
door. Compass Travel's No 99 **bus service**
calls here if booked in advance (see pp44-
6). On school days you can use their No
412 service from Midhurst, mid afternoon.

B&B can be found on Selham Rd at
Brook Barn (☎ 01798-867356, 🖥 www
.brookbarn-graffham.co.uk; 1D en suite;
▼; 🐾 £5; WI-FI) from £45pp (sgl occ £60-
80). A camp bed can be put in the room for
a third (and indeed fourth; £30pp) person.
Dogs (and horses!) are welcome, too.

The Foresters Arms (☎ 01798-867202,
🖥 www.forestersgraffham.com; 2D/1T en
suite; 🐾 in bar only; WI-FI in main building) has comfortable, well-equipped rooms
and charges £47.50-62.50pp (sgl occ full
room rate) including a continental breakfast; a full English for £5pp is available if
requested in advance. They do food Wed-

Sat noon-2.30pm & 6-9pm & Sun noon-
3pm & 6-9pm). They have good real ales
on tap.

Campers should head up the road for
about a mile to the *Graffham Camping &
Caravanning Club Site* (☎ 01798-867476,
🖥 www.campingandcaravanningclub.co.uk;
end Mar to early Nov; limited WI-FI; 🐾 on
leads) where a pitch is £9.35pp in high season including use of shower facilities.

There are two good pubs serving **food**:
the first, *The White Horse* (☎ 01798-
867331, 🖥 whitehorsegraffham.com; food
Mon-Sat noon-2.30pm & 6-9pm, Sun
noon-3.30pm) is just outside the village
close to the Downs. It's a friendly place
with some interesting real ales (it's a free
house), a quiet garden and spectacular
views onto the hills. It's open all day at
weekends but is closed 3-5.30pm weekdays
and on Mondays January to March. B&B is
offered at *Willow Barns* (☎ 01798-867493,
🖥 willowbarns.co.uk; 4D/2D or T, all en
suite; ▼), which is right behind the pub;
they charge £50-60pp (sgl occ full room
rate). There is a minimum two-night booking policy at weekends in summer.

After the Graffham turn-off the Way eventually drops down across pasture
to the A285 main road (Map 19). Compass's No 99 **bus** service calls here if
booked in advance; see public transport map and table, pp44-6.

Climbing back up towards Bignor Hill the views open out spectacularly to
the south. The rather outlandish-looking tent structure visible by the coast is the
Butlins holiday complex at Bognor Regis. *(cont'd on p113)*

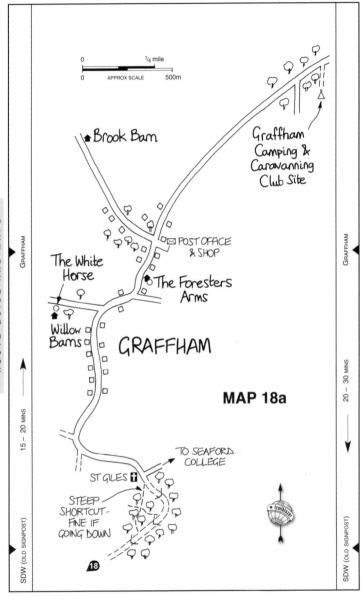

ROUTE GUIDE AND MAPS

GRAFFHAM

GRAFFHAM

15 – 20 MINS

20 – 30 MINS

SDW (OLD SIGNPOST)

SDW (OLD SIGNPOST)

Brook Barn

Graffham Camping & Caravanning Club Site

POST OFFICE & SHOP

The White Horse

The Foresters Arms

Willow Barns

GRAFFHAM

MAP 18a

TO SEAFORD COLLEGE

ST GILES

STEEP SHORTCUT- FINE IF GOING DOWN

18

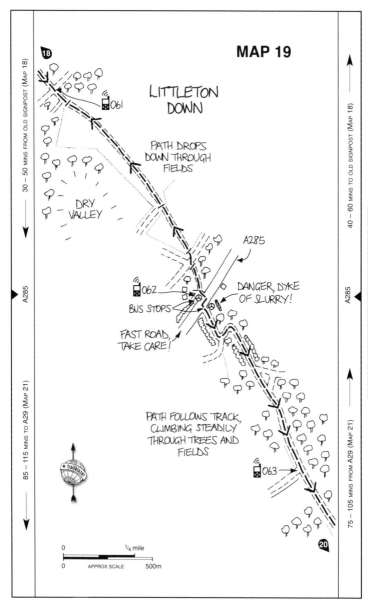

MAP 19

18

LITTLETON DOWN

061

30 – 50 MINS FROM OLD SIGNPOST (MAP 18)

40 – 60 MINS TO OLD SIGNPOST (MAP 18)

PATH DROPS DOWN THROUGH FIELDS

DRY VALLEY

A285

062

BUS STOPS

DANGER, DYKE OF SLURRY!

FAST ROAD, TAKE CARE!

A285

A285

PATH FOLLOWS TRACK, CLIMBING STEADILY THROUGH TREES AND FIELDS

063

85 – 115 MINS TO A29 (MAP 21)

75 – 105 MINS FROM A29 (MAP 21)

trailblazer

0   1/4 mile

0   APPROX SCALE   500m

20

ROUTE GUIDE AND MAPS

85 – 115 MINS FROM A285 (MAP 19) TO A29 (MAP 21)

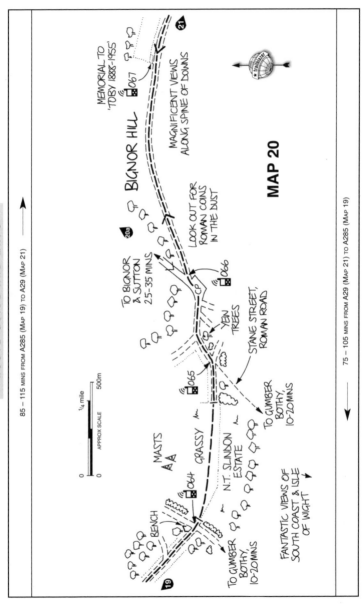

MEMORIAL TO
"TOBY 1885-1955"

067

BIGNOR HILL

MAGNIFICENT VIEWS
ALONG SPINE OF DOWNS

MAP 20

TO BIGNOR
& SUTTON
25-35 MINS

20a

LOOK OUT FOR
ROMAN COINS
IN THE DUST

066

CP

YEW TREES

STANE STREET,
ROMAN ROAD

TO GUMBER BOTHY,
10-20 MINS

065

¼ mile

500m

APPROX SCALE

0   0

MASTS

064

GRASSY

BENCH

N.T. SLINDON ESTATE

TO GUMBER BOTHY,
10-20 MINS

FANTASTIC VIEWS OF
SOUTH COAST & ISLE
OF WIGHT

19

75 – 105 MINS FROM A29 (MAP 21) TO A285 (MAP 19)

SUTTON & BIGNOR **MAP 20a**

The main reason for dropping off the hills to these twin villages is to see the fabulous mosaics at **Bignor Roman Villa** (see p114) but you can also stay comfortably here and eat well. There's a ***teashop*** at the villa.

The **church** at Sutton dates from the 11th century; publisher John Murray (1909-95) is buried in the churchyard.

Very close to the Roman Villa is an excellent B&B, ***Stane House*** (☎ 01798-869454, 💻 www.stanehouse.co.uk; 2D/1T, all en suite; ☕; WI-FI; Ⓛ), with rooms from £40pp (£65 sgl occ).

A mile further on is ***The White Horse Inn*** (☎ 01798-869221, 💻 www.white horse-sutton.co.uk; 5D all en suite; ☕; WI-FI; 🐕 in bar only; Ⓛ); food daily noon-2pm, Tue-Sat 6-9pm), a magnificent isolated country pub with B&B for £32.50-42.50pp (sgl occ from £65), though they often have special offers on their website so it is worth checking there. They also have a large restaurant and the food is exquisite: all home-cooked and sourced locally, with the bread, sausages and ice cream made on the premises. The pub is closed between 3pm and 6pm and on Sunday and Monday evenings.

Compass's No 99 and 99A **bus services** call at both Sutton and Bignor (see public transport map and table on pp44-6).

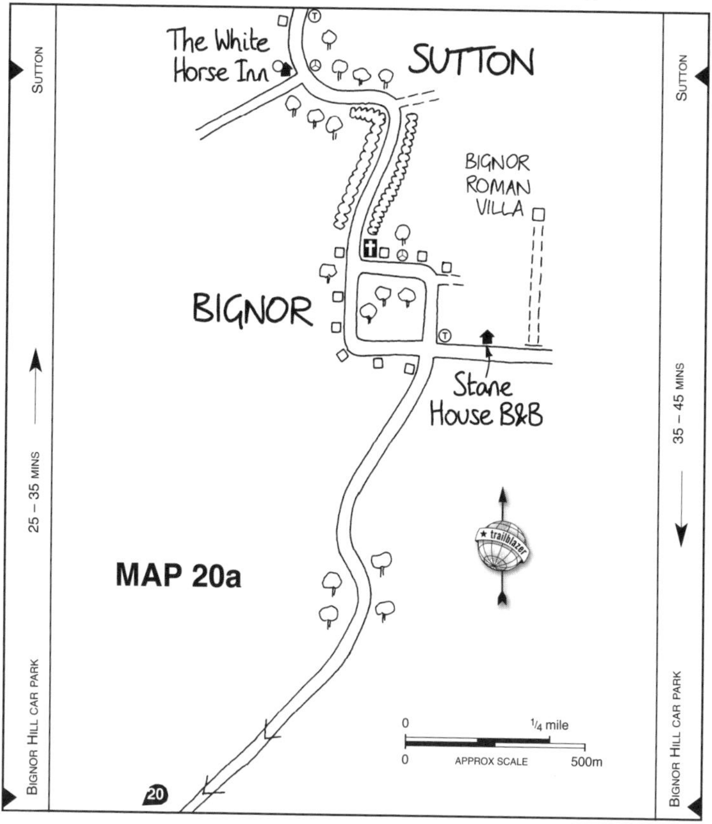

(cont'd from p109) Of far greater interest is **Stane St** (Map 20, p112), the Roman road built around 50AD to connect Noviomagus (Chichester) with Londinium (London).

Close to Bignor Hill, a mile south of the Way, is the excellent National Trust camping barn *Gumber Bothy* (see Map 20; ☎ 01243-814484; mid Mar to end Oct) which has simple accommodation for £10pp. They also allow **camping** here for the same price. Facilities include showers, toilets, a basic kitchen with a gas cooker, a barbecue and a pay phone. Booking in advance is recommended. Note that there is no vehicle access here.

The Way follows part of the old Roman road over **Bignor Hill**. Look out for the signpost in Latin in the car park (not actually of Roman origin!) and look out, too, for any Roman coins that may be buried among the flint and chalk. It's well worth going down to **Bignor** (see p113) from here to see the mosaics at **Bignor Roman Villa**.

❑ **Bignor Roman Villa**   **Map 20a, p113**

Just off the old Roman road of Stane Street are the remains of Bignor Roman Villa (☎ 01798-869259, 🖳 www.bignorroman villa.co.uk; daily Mar-Oct 10am-5pm, last entry 4pm; admission £6). It was discovered by a farmer, George Tupper, who was ploughing his field in 1811.

Believed to date from the 3rd century AD, Bignor Villa was one of the biggest in England and probably home to a wealthy farmer considering its enviable position on fertile land close to the main road between Chichester and London. Bignor is most famous for the superb floor mosaics, said to be some of the world's best-preserved examples. Many are in near perfect condition, including a 24-metre length of the 70-metre corridor. This is the longest mosaic on display in Britain.

There's a *teashop* (open 10.30am-4pm) but it serves only tea, coffee and cakes; no sandwiches or hot meals.

BURY   **MAP 21**

This unassuming village offers accommodation, food and a **post office** though it's open only on Tuesday (9.30am-5pm).

The Barn at Penfolds B&B (☎ 01798-831496, 🖳 www.thebarnatpenfolds.co.uk; 2D en suite; ☛; WI-FI; Ⓛ), on Houghton Lane, offers B&B from £35pp (sgl occ £55). They also have a cosy shepherd's hut (heated and insulated) with its own shower and a deck area outside. It's £85 per night for two in the double bed.

Harkaway (☎ 01798-831843, 🖳 www .harkaway.freeuk.com; 1D en suite, 1S/1T share a bathroom; ☛; WI-FI), on Houghton Lane, offers B&B from £30pp.

The Squire & Horse Inn (☎ 01798-831343, 🖳 www.squireandhorsebury.co.uk; food Mon-Sat noon-2pm & 6-9pm, Sun noon-8.30pm), by the main road, is a free-house with an award-winning chef and a busy restaurant. Main dishes include steak, Sussex ale and mushroom steamed pudding (£12.95), and rump of lamb (£16.50).

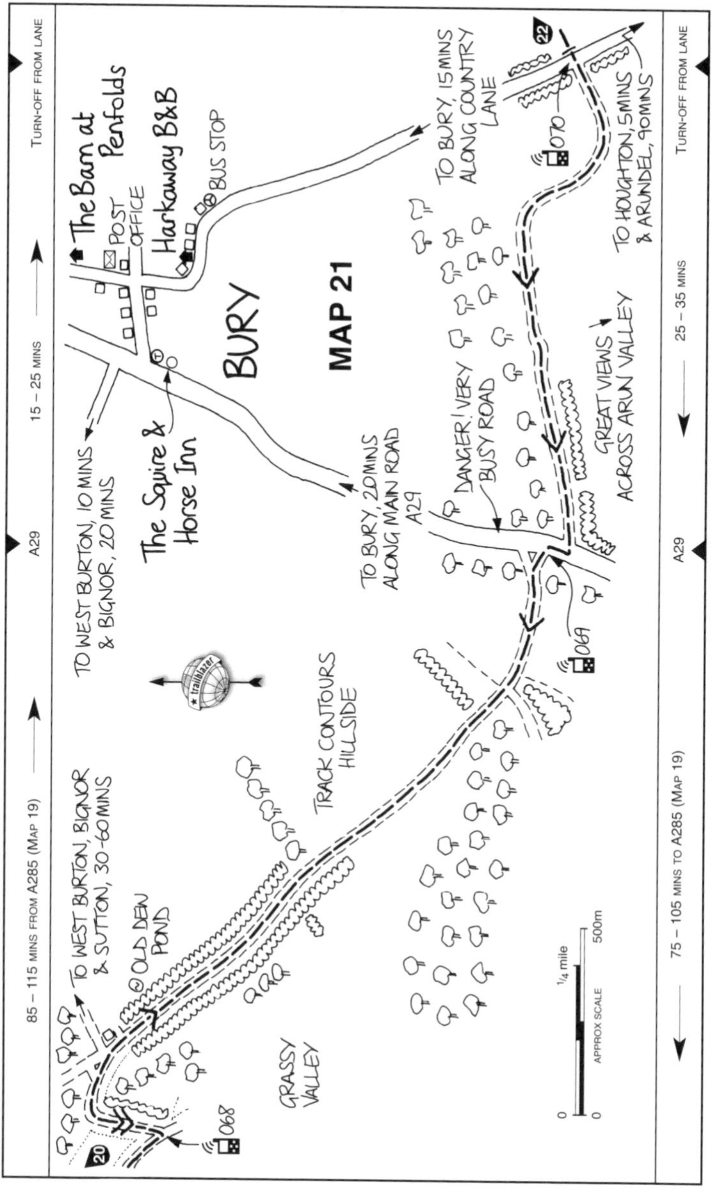

TURN-OFF FROM LANE

TURN-OFF FROM LANE

The Barn at Penfolds

POST OFFICE

Harkaway B&B

BUS STOP

22

TO BURY, 15 MINS ALONG COUNTRY LANE

070

TO HOUGHTON, 5 MINS & ARUNDEL, 90 MINS

BURY

MAP 21

DANGER! VERY BUSY ROAD

The Squire & Horse Inn

GREAT VIEWS ACROSS ARUN VALLEY

TO WEST BURTON, 10 MINS & BIGNOR, 20 MINS

TO BURY, 20 MINS ALONG MAIN ROAD

A29

15 – 25 MINS

A29

25 – 35 MINS

06A

trailblazer

TRACK CONTOURS HILLSIDE

85 – 115 MINS FROM A285 (MAP 19)

TO WEST BURTON, BIGNOR & SUTTON, 30 – 60 MINS

OLD DEN POND

GRASSY VALLEY

20

068

¼ mile

APPROX SCALE

500m

0

0

75 – 105 MINS TO A285 (MAP 19)

ROUTE GUIDE AND MAPS

Continuing along the Way, there are sensational views to the east along the length of the Downs.

Follow the route across the main road and down into the Arun valley for the villages of **Houghton Bridge** and **Amberley**. If you have time it is well worth visiting **Arundel** (see p119), about a mile further south along the River Arun. You can reach it by following the riverside footpath but the easier route is to jump on the train at Houghton Bridge.

HOUGHTON BRIDGE   MAP 22

The village of Houghton Bridge can easily be reached from the SDW as the trail almost passes through it. The **railway station** (called, a little confusingly, Amberley Station) has regular services to London Victoria and south to Arundel and beyond; see the public transport map and table, pp44-6. There are, however, no useful **bus** services other than those operated on school-day mornings by Sussex Bus (🖳 www.thesussexbus.com): their No 619 goes in the early morning to Amberley, Storrington, Thakeham and Steyning and in the mid afternoon by both Sussex Bus (No 719: from Steyning via Storrington, and Amberley to Houghton) and Compass (No 619: Storrington to Houghton/Amberley).

Right by the station you'll find the entrance to **Amberley Working Museum** (☎ 01798-831370, 🖳 www.amberleymuseum.co.uk; mid Feb to end Oct, Wed-Sun & Bank hols, plus every day during school holidays 10am-5pm, last entry 4.30pm; admission £10; call for details), situated in an old chalk pit. This extensive museum features a blacksmith's and foundry, as well as workshops producing traditional items such as brooms and walking sticks. The quarry tunnel at Amberley was actually used as a film location in the James Bond film *A View To A Kill* in 1984.

Foxleigh Barn has a **campsite**, or you could wild **camp** at High Titten.

For B&B, there's *Cherry Tree Cottage* (☎ 01798-831052, 🖳 www.cherry treecottage.org.uk; 1T private bathroom; ☞; WI-FI; Ⓛ), right by the railway bridge. A stay in this family home costs from £40pp (sgl occ from £50). They have dogs so can't accept visiting dogs.

Foxleigh Barn (☎ 01798-839113, 🖳 pete@foxleighbarn.co.uk; 1S/1T/1D all en suite; ☞; WI-FI; Ⓛ) is conveniently located right on the SDW, by the B2139. Open Easter to October they charge £45pp (£70 for sgl or sgl occ) for B&B. They also offer **camping** (£20) and facilities include toilets, shower and camp kitchen. A rent-a-tent and bedding option is available for £30, including a cook your own breakfast.

You can get breakfasts and light lunches at *Riverside* (☎ 01798-831066, 🖳 dinebytheriver.co.uk; Easter to Oct daily 9am-5pm, Oct to Easter Mon-Fri 10am-4pm, Sat & Sun 9am-4 or 5pm). This café, bar and restaurant is especially popular when the weather is good as they have a riverside garden where they serve all-day breakfasts, pizzas, and cakes amongst other items. In summer they are also open in the evening (Thur-Sat 6.30-8.30pm) and serve English and Spanish tapas as well as pizzas.

Just across the road is *The Bridge Inn* (☎ 01798-831619, 🖳 www.bridgeinnamberley.com; food Mon-Fri noon-2.30pm, Sat & Sun noon-4pm, Mon-Sat 6-9pm, Sun 5.30-8pm). It's relaxed but busy on summer evenings and serves very good food. The chef is from Corfu and there are often delicious Greek specialities on the menu, such as *afelia* (slow-cooked pork stew) for £13.

AMBERLEY   MAP 22

Perched on a sandstone ridge below the chalk Downs with the wild marshland of **Amberley Brooks** stretching to the north, Amberley claims to be the prettiest village on the Downs and it would be hard to argue otherwise. The quiet lane leading to the church and castle is lined with thatched cottages; hollyhocks and foxgloves bloom in the small front gardens in the summer months. Unlike other downland villages where local flint is prominent in the archi-

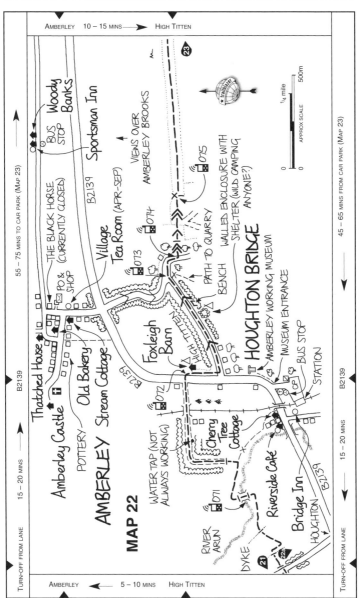

MAP 22

AMBERLEY Stream Cottage

tecture, many of Amberley's cottages were built using local sandstone, making the village distinctive. There are records referring to Amberley dating back to 680AD.

The pretty **church** was built by Bishop Luffa between 1091 and 1125. Next to the church is the **castle** (now a hotel, see Where to stay) which used to be the bishop's residence until it was recognised as a castle upon completion of the walls in 1377. More information on the history of the village and the local area can be found at Amberley Working Museum (see p116).

There is a very good community-run village **shop** (🖳 www.amberleyvillage stores.co.uk; Mon-Sat 7am-5pm, Sun & bank hols 8am-5pm or 4pm in winter) and **post office** (Mon, Thur & Fri 9am-1pm, Tue 9am-noon). They currently stock an excellent range of local artisan bread.

The nearest **railway station** is called Amberley Station but it is at Houghton Bridge. See p116 for details of the schoolday bus services that call here.

Where to stay and eat

The Thatched House (☎ 01798-831329, 🖳 www.thatchedhouseamberley.co.uk; 1D/1T with private bathroom; 🐾; WI-FI) isn't actually thatched but is nonetheless an excellent place to stay. Even though they have two rooms they only let one at a time unless people know each other. B&B costs from £45pp (£60 sgl occ), though rates are higher during Goodwood.

Away from the village, about a mile down the lane at Crossgates is *The Sportsman Inn* (☎ 01798-831787, 🖳 the sportsmanamberley.com; 1T/3D/1Tr, all en suite; 🐾; WI-FI in bar only; 🐾; ⓛ; food Mon-Sat noon-2.30pm & 6.30-9pm, Sun noon-4pm), a pleasant place which offers B&B for £45pp (sgl occ £55, £110 for three sharing). It's a popular pub serving real ales from local breweries. There's a wide choice

of pub food but you should book in advance at weekends. Next door is *Woody Banks* (☎ 01798-831295, 🖳 www.woodybanks.co .uk; 1T private shower room; ⓛ) with B&B for £35-39.50pp (sgl occ on request); the room also has its own sitting room.

Back in the village there are two places that may be worth trying although the first may have closed and the second only just be open. *Stream Cottage* (☎ 01798-831266, 🖳 www.streamcottage.co.uk; 1D private bathroom; 🐾; WI-FI) offers B&B for £50pp (sgl occ £80). They may, sadly, be closing later in 2015. *The Old Bakery* (🖳 www.amberleybedandbreakfast.co.uk) is currently being refurbished and will reopen in summer 2015. See website for details.

If you're celebrating getting this far and can afford it, there's every luxury at *Amberley Castle* (☎ 01798-831992, 🖳 www.amberleycastle.co.uk; 19D all en suite; 🐾; WI-FI). A double room with a whirlpool bathroom costs around £137.50pp (sgl occ full room rate), though it is always worth enquiring about special offers. There's a grand restaurant (with a dress code) serving a tasting menu for £85pp or a two-course meal for £65pp. Afternoon tea is £30pp. Booking is recommended.

Amberley Village Tea Room (☎ 01798-839196, 🖳 www.amberleyvillagetearoom .co.uk; 🐾; Apr-Sep, Thur-Tue 10am-5.30pm, also Sat-Sun in Mar & Oct) is on the main street just south of the PO & shop. Like the Amberley shop they pride themselves on sourcing locally produced food and their clotted cream teas (£5) are very popular. They also serve toasted teacakes, crumpets, tea breads and mouthwatering slices of homemade chocolate cake (£3).

Unfortunately the quirky and eccentric pub, *The Black Horse*, has still not reopened. There are plans for the villagers to run it as a community pub.

❏ Important note – walking times
Unless otherwise specified, **all times in this book refer only to the time spent walking**. You will need to add 20-30% to allow for rests, photography, checking the map, drinking water etc. When planning the day's hike count on 5-7 hours' actual walking.

ARUNDEL   MAP 22a, p121

The town of Arundel is about an hour and a half from the South Downs Way via the riverside path from Houghton Bridge or a five-minute train ride from Amberley station. Those who are walking the entire South Downs Way in one trip will find that a visit to this historic town makes an ideal rest day.

Arundel boasts a fine cathedral but it is the perfectly preserved castle with its grand turreted walls that really catches the eye. **Arundel Festival** (🖳 www.arundelfesti val.co.uk) is held in the castle in August.

What to see and do

This gothic-style **cathedral** (🖳 www.arun delcathedral.org) is somewhat upstaged by the immense castle down the road but is still a fine building in its own right. Founded by Henry, the 15th Duke of Norfolk, the cathedral is relatively new, dating back to 1873. A good time to visit is during the Corpus Christi festivities in early June when the main aisle of the cathedral is covered in a spectacular carpet of flowers.

The **castle** (☎ 01903-882173, 🖳 www.arundelcastle.org; Easter to early Nov Tue-Sun 10am-5pm, plus Mon during Aug and bank holidays) is the centrepiece of this historical town. Rising grandly from the trees it looms over the Arun Valley and is everything you imagine an English castle to be, complete with imposing walls, turrets and winding stone staircases. Of Norman origin it is now home to the dukes of Norfolk but is open to the public most of the year.

There are four levels of ticket ranging from Bronze (grounds and chapel only £9) to Gold Plus (castle rooms and bedrooms, castle keep, chapel and grounds £18).

The **Arundel Museum** (☎ 01903-885866, 🖳 www.arundelmuseum.org; daily 10am-4pm; £3) has reopened in a new building just off River Rd by the car park. The museum's exhibits focus on local history with an interesting display on the castle, the Catholic dukes of Norfolk and their association with the town. Also of particular interest is the 12th-century coffin with the finely decorated lid, the Roman sword

dating from the 4th-century and the old photographs portraying local life through the years.

The **Arundel Wildfowl and Wetlands Trust Centre** (☎ 01903-883355, 🖳 www.wwt.org.uk; daily summer 9.30am-5.30pm, rest of year 9.30am-4.30pm; admission £10.90, free for WWT members, save 10% if you book online) is a natural wetland site bordered by ancient woodland and is a perfect diversion for anyone interested in birds. The hides provide opportunities for viewing a variety of warblers and waders as well as the odd buzzard circling above the oak trees.

Services

There's a **tourist information point** (☎ 01903-737838, 🖳 www.sussexbythesea .com; daily 10am-4pm) just off River Rd in the museum. For public **internet** access, the **library** (Mon-Wed 1-5pm, Thur-Sat 9am-1pm) is at the western end of Tarrant St.

Food supplies can be found at the small **shop**, McColl's, near the bridge at the bottom of the High St, while across the bridge is a Co-op (daily 7am-10pm).

The **post office** (Mon-Fri 9am-5.30pm, Sat to 12.30pm) lies just across the road from McColl's.

Some pharmaceutical items are available in the Co-op but the nearest **pharmacy** is now inconveniently located in the local NHS health surgery on Canada Rd (beyond the roundabout at the western end of Maltravers St). There are several **banks** on the High St.

Chocoholics will be pleased to know that Arundel is home to **Castle Chocolates** (☎ 01903-884419; daily 10am-5.30pm), 11 Tarrant St, who claim to produce what is 'probably the finest confectionery, chocolate and fudge in the South of England'. For fudge they now have competition with **Roly's Fudge Pantry**, doing brisk trade at the bottom of the High St (No 25).

Public transport

[See the public transport map and table, pp44-6] Those coming to Arundel by **train** will find that the **railway station** is a ten-minute walk from the town centre; services are operated by Southern.

National Express's 315 **coach** service calls here. Stagecoach's No 700 (Coastliner) **bus** service operates from here to Brighton. Compass Travel's **bus** No 85/85A is the best choice for travel to Chichester; the bus stop is near the bridge.

For a **taxi** call (☎ 01903-884444).

Where to stay

Arundel is a popular tourist centre so you must book well in advance. During some weekends (eg during local events, see p16) there may be a two-night minimum stay for some places.

On the road leading from the town centre to the railway station is *Arundel Park Hotel* (☎ 01903-882588, 🖳 www.arundelparkhotel.co.uk; 1S/10D/3T/ 1Tr, all en suite; ☜; WI-FI; ⓛ); it has plenty of rooms and an unpretentious style. B&B costs £32.50-37.50pp (sgl/sgl occ from £55/65, three sharing from £95). Nearby is *Portreeves B&B* (☎ 01903-885392, 🖳 www.portreeves.co.uk; 2D, T or Tr, all en suite; ☜; WI-FI; 🐾). It's a well-run, friendly place offering B&B from £42.50pp (sgl occ £65) in their apartments.

In the centre of Arundel in a former fisherman's cottage at 14 River Rd is *Chain Locker B&B* (☎ 01903-882661, 🖳 www .chainlocker.org.uk; 1D, private bathroom; ☜; WI-FI; 🐾). It's a small place and they don't do breakfast but it's wonderful value at just £45 for the room (ie for two people).

Arundel House (☎ 01903-882136, 🖳 www.arundelhousewestsussex.com; 5D all en suite; WI-FI; ⓛ), near the post office at 11 High St, is an intimate little boutique restaurant with rooms. It's in a good location and a gorgeous place to stay. B&B costs £37.50-62.50pp (sgl occ £75 Sun-Thur; full room rate at weekends).

Nearby is the elegant *Swan Hotel* (☎ 01903-882314, 🖳 www.swanarundel.co .uk; 4T/7D/3Tr, all en suite; ☜; WI-FI; 🐾 £10; ⓛ) with B&B from £57.50pp but it can cost around £82.50pp (sgl occ from £75; three sharing £135).

The Town House (☎ 01903-883847, 🖳 www.thetownhouse.co.uk; 4D/2D or T, all en suite; ☜; WI-FI), opposite the castle at the top of the High St (No 65), is a very attractive place with immaculate and stylish rooms all with flat-screen TVs. Expect to pay £52.50-70pp (sgl occ from £75). It also has an excellent restaurant (see Where to eat and drink).

On Queen's Lane, a few minutes from the centre, is *Arden Guest House* (☎ 01903-884184, 🖳 www.ardenguesthouse.net; 7D or T; WI-FI) which is under new ownership. Some rooms are en suite (£35.50-46.50pp) but the others share facilities (£29.50-39.50pp); contact them for single occupancy rates and also rates during Goodwood.

Finally, *Byass House* (☎ 01903-882129, 🖳 www.byasshouse.com; 1D private bathroom/1D or T en suite; ☜; WI-FI; 🐾) is a beautiful red-brick Georgian townhouse at 59 Maltravers St; B&B is from £42.50pp (sgl occ from £60).

Where to eat and drink

Arundel is bursting with excellent pubs and restaurants. The best place to start looking is on the High St where you will find decent, filling, cheap snacks at the bottom of the hill in *The Moathouse Café and Restaurant* (☎ 01903-883297; Mon-Sat 8am-5pm, to 3pm on Thur in winter, Sun 9am-5pm) at 9 High St. Soup of the day is £2.50 and they do salad boxes from £3.

If you're looking for the ingredients of a good picnic, *Pallant of Arundel* (☎ 01903-882288; Mon-Sat 9am-6pm, to 5pm in Jan, Sun 10am-5pm) is the town's deli and specialist grocery store. They will even prepare a picnic hamper for you – from £45 for the 'very finest fare'.

Some of the best coffee in town is served at the little *Tarrant St Espresso* (☎ 01903-885350; Tue-Fri 7.30am-4pm, Sat & Sun 9am-4pm). They also do filled rolls and salads. Further along Tarrant St in Sparks Yard there's *The Loft* (Mon-Sat 9.30am-5.30pm, Sun 11am-5pm) offering beer, wine and meals.

Partners Café (☎ 01903-882018; Tue-Fri 8am-4pm, Sat & Sun 8am-4.30pm), 25a High St, is particularly recommended for its breakfasts but also does lunches and teas.

There are several traditional tearooms in Arundel. *Belinda's Tea Rooms* (☎ 01903-882977; daily 9am-5pm) has been

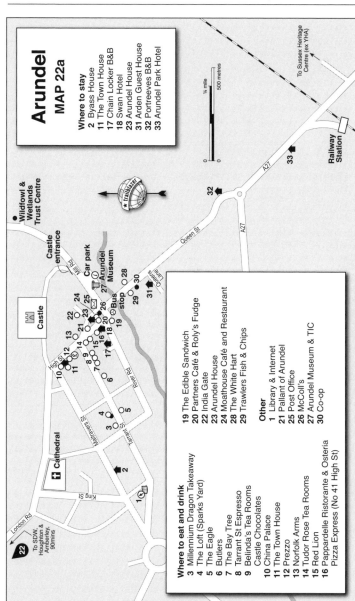

Arundel
MAP 22a

Where to stay
2 Byass House
11 The Town House
17 Chain Locker B&B
18 Swan Hotel
23 Arundel House
31 Arden Guest House
32 Portreeves B&B
33 Arundel Park Hotel

Where to eat and drink
3 Millennium Dragon Takeaway
4 The Loft (Sparks Yard)
5 The Eagle
6 Butlers
7 The Bay Tree
8 Tarrant St Espresso
9 Belinda's Tea Rooms
   Castle Chocolates
10 China Palace
11 The Town House
12 Prezzo
13 Norfolk Arms
14 Tudor Rose Tea Rooms
15 Red Lion
16 Pappardelle Ristorante & Osteria
   Pizza Express (No 41 High St)

19 The Edible Sandwich
20 Partners Café & Roly's Fudge
22 India Gate
23 Arundel House
24 Moathouse Café and Restaurant
28 The White Hart
29 Trawlers Fish & Chips

Other
1 Library & Internet
21 Pallant of Arundel
25 Post Office
26 McColl's
27 Arundel Museum & TIC
30 Co-op

serving teas and light lunches on Tarrant St for several decades now. You could also try *Tudor Rose Tea Rooms* on the High St.

Arundel House (see Where to stay; Tue-Sat noon-2pm & 6-9.30pm) is an excellent place to eat. There are lunches and dinners for £16.595/21.95 for two/three courses.

On the other side of the road there's a line of eateries starting with *The Red Lion* (☎ 01903-882214; food daily noon-9pm) at No 45, a large no-nonsense pub with rear garden serving cheap and filling dishes.

The *White Hart* (☎ 01903-884422; food daily Mon-Sat noon-9pm, Sun noon-4.30pm) serves Harveys beers and has an interesting menu including tapas as well as the usual pub grub.

A short stagger from The Red Lion is the Italian-run *Pappardelle Ristorante & Osteria* (☎ 01903-882025, 🖥 www.pappardelle.co.uk). The informal Osteria downstairs is open daily 9am-11pm and serves drinks and light meals with antipasto from £4.95 and open sandwiches (£7.95). The traditional Ristorante is open Mon 6.30-9.30pm, Tue-Sat noon-2pm and 6.30-9.30pm (to 10pm on Sat). The pizzas are excellent. If it's a pizza you're after there are also branches of *Pizza Express* and *Prezzo* on the High St.

India Gate (☎ 01903-884224; daily noon-2.30pm & 5.30-11.30pm), just off the High St at 3 Mill Lane, has all the usual curries: main dishes from £7.75.

Chinese food can be found at the other end of the High St at No 67: *China Palace* (☎ 01903-883702; daily noon-2.15pm & 6pm-midnight) is a smarter than average Chinese (Cantonese) restaurant.

For sandwiches and pastries for lunch there's the *Edible Sandwich* (☎ 01903-885969; Mon-Fri 5.30am-dark, Sat 7am-dark, Sun 8am-dark) by the river.

The Norfolk Arms (☎ 01903-882101; food daily noon-2pm & 7-9pm, shorter hours outside the tourist season), at 22 High St, has a traditional restaurant serving English dishes.

More top-notch food can be found at *The Town House* (see Where to stay; food Tue-Sat noon-2pm & 7-9.30pm) which has a smart restaurant where meals – two courses at lunchtime/in the evening will set you back £17.50/25.50 and three courses cost £21.50/29.50 – are taken under the fabulous 16th-century Florentine carved ceiling. The food gets rave reviews.

The Bay Tree (☎ 01903-883679, 🖥 www.thebaytreearundel.co.uk) daily 10.30am -4.30pm & 6.30-9.30pm) at 21 Tarrant St, serves contemporary British food and is consistently recommended. You may need to book for dinner. Nearby at No 25, *Butlers* (☎ 01903-882222; Mon-Sat noon-2.15pm & 7-9pm, Sun noon-2pm) offers two-course lunches for £12.95 Mon-Sat and two-course dinners for £14.95 Mon-Fri. Their Sunday roast lunches are popular.

One of the best pubs in town is *The Eagle* (☎ 01903-882304, 🖥 www.theeaglearundel.co.uk; daily 11am-11pm), on Tarrant St. They serve an excellent array of beers and sometimes have live music at weekends. It's a popular place: locals spill out onto the pavement on warm summer evenings. There's a Cellar Restaurant and they do bar snacks every day at lunchtime and a roast on Sunday. The wild boar sausages are recommended.

After supping the final pint most punters stumble over the road to *The Millennium Dragon Takeaway* (☎ 01903-883017; Mon, Wed, Thur 5-11.30pm, Fri & Sat 5pm-midnight, Sun 5.30-11pm), at 32 Tarrant St. The best chippy in town is *Trawlers Fish & Chips* (open Mon-Sat 11.45am-2pm & 5-9pm) on Queen St.

AMBERLEY TO STEYNING   MAPS 22-27a

The first half of this **10-mile (16km, 3½-5hrs)** stretch is an easy stroll along the high crest of the Downs with great views over the swamp-like **Amberley Wild Brooks** and the Low Weald. The quickest way to Storrington (Map 24) is along the path leading off the Way at GPS Waypoint 079. Alternatively take the road leading off from the Rackham Hill car park.

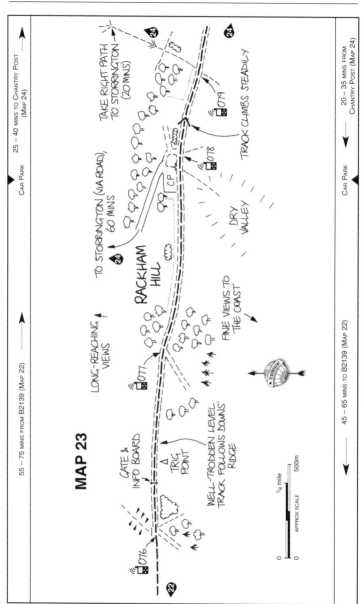

MAP 23

55 – 75 MINS FROM B2139 (MAP 22)

25 – 40 MINS TO CHANTRY POST (MAP 24)

CAR PARK

GATE & INFO BOARD

TRIG POINT

WELL-TRODDEN LEVEL TRACK FOLLOWS DOWNS' RIDGE

LONG-REACHING VIEWS

RACKHAM HILL

TO STORRINGTON (VIA ROAD), 60 MINS

TAKE RIGHT PATH TO STORRINGTON (20 MINS)

TRACK CLIMBS STEADILY

DRY VALLEY

FINE VIEWS TO THE COAST

CP

077

078

079

076

45 – 65 MINS TO B2139 (MAP 22)

CAR PARK

20 – 35 MINS FROM CHANTRY POST (MAP 24)

¼ mile

500m

APPROX SCALE

0

0

22

24

STORRINGTON   MAP 24

In comparison to many of the other towns and villages along the Downs the busy little town of Storrington is functional rather than attractive. It is a convenient place for topping up on supplies, getting a bite to eat or for finding a bed for the night but apart from that there is little reason to make the detour.

There's a small **museum** (🖥 www .storringtonmuseum.org; Wed & Sat 10am-4pm, Sun 10am-1pm; free) covering the local history of the area. Near the museum is a wonderfully ornate **Indian doorway**, set into the wall on Browns Lane.

Services

Storrington has everything you would expect in a prosperous town. The reception at the **library** (☎ 01903-839050; Mon-Fri 9.30am-5.30pm, Sat 10am-4pm) doubles up as the **tourist information point** and they also have **internet** access (£1/hour). Waitrose **supermarket** (Mon-Sat 8am-8pm, Sun 10am-4pm) is in a small shopping arcade just off the High St. At the other end of the High St is the **post office** (Mon-Fri 9am-5.30pm, Sat 9am-4pm) and just round the corner at 1 North St is Lloyds **pharmacy** and there's a branch of Boots on the High St. There are also three banks with **ATMs** on the High St.

Stagecoach's No 1 **bus** service calls here en route between Midhurst and Worthing. Compass's bus No 100 travels between Burgess Hill and Pulborough and their No 74/74A goes to Horsham; see the public transport map and table, pp44-6.

Where to stay

There is a much wider choice of places to stay in Arundel (see p120) and Steyning (see p130) but if you do find yourself looking for a bed in Storrington the most accessible B&B from the Way is *Ashton House* (☎ 01903-746661, 🖥 www.ashtonhouse .net; 2D/1T, all en suite; ♥; WI-FI; ℗) on the lane leading from the Downs into the town. All the rooms have fridges and one of the doubles is actually a self-contained studio with a 'snack-preparation area'. B&B is from £45pp (sgl occ £65).

In the town centre, the 400-year-old *White Horse Hotel* (☎ 01903-745760, 🖥 www.thewhitehorsestorrington.com; 10D/3D or T, all en suite; WI-FI; ℗) offers rooms from £42.50pp (sgl occ full room rate). The new owners are currently renovating part of the hotel.

Where to eat and drink

The short High St has several cafés and pubs including *Vintage Rose Café* (☎ 01903-744100, 🖥 www.vintagerosecafe.co.uk; Mon-Fri 9am-5pm, Sat 9.30am-4pm) which serves teas and coffees – on interestingly mismatched china – and light lunches.

For a cheap snack there's *Truffles Bakery* (☎ 01903-742459; Mon-Fri 8am-5.30pm, Sat 8am-5pm), near Waitrose.

Pubs include *The Anchor Inn* (☎ 01903-742665; food daily noon-9pm), at the eastern end and the marginally more attractive *The Moon* (☎ 01903-744773, 🖥 www.themoonpub.co.uk; food Mon-Fri noon-2.30pm & 6-9.30pm, Sat noon-3pm & 6-9.30pm, Sun carvery noon-2.30pm, burgers & pizzas 2.30-8.30pm). There's also the *White Horse Hotel* (see Where to stay; food Tue-Sat noon-1.45pm, Mon-Sat 6-8.45pm, Sun noon-2.45pm).

Storrington has a popular Indian restaurant: *Cottage Tandoori* (☎ 01903-743605; daily noon-2.30pm & 6-11pm).

The best restaurant in town is the 15th-century *Old Forge* (☎ 01903-743402, 🖥 www.oldforge.co.uk; Wed, Thur, Fri & Sun lunch from 12.30pm, last reservation 1.15pm, Thur, Fri & Sat dinner from 7.15pm, last reservation 8.45pm) where the quality of the food justifies the prices. A two-course lunch including a glass of wine costs £18.50 and a two-course evening meal costs £23.50. It is popular with locals and tourists alike; book in advance. They also have a **deli** (Mon-Sat 9.30am-4pm) which serves home-made soups, sandwiches and plenty more besides.

The main rival for fine dining in Storrington sits just across the road: *13 Church Street* (☎ 01903-746964, 🖥 www.thirteenchurchstreet.co.uk; Tue-Sat noon-3pm & 6-10.30pm) serves freshly prepared Thai specialities.

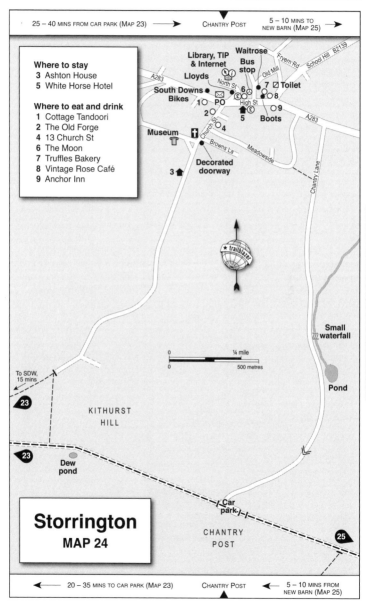

25 – 40 MINS FROM CAR PARK (MAP 23) ⟶   CHANTRY POST   5 – 10 MINS TO NEW BARN (MAP 25) ⟶

Where to stay
3 Ashton House
5 White Horse Hotel

Where to eat and drink
1 Cottage Tandoori
2 The Old Forge
4 13 Church St
6 The Moon
7 Truffles Bakery
8 Vintage Rose Café
9 Anchor Inn

Library, TIP & Internet
Lloyds
South Downs Bikes
PO
Waitrose
Bus stop
Toilet
Boots
Museum
Decorated doorway

North St
High St
Church St
Browns La
Meadowside
Fryern Rd
School Hill
Old Mill
A283
B2139
Chantry Lane

Small waterfall
Pond

To SDW, 15 mins

KITHURST HILL

Dew pond

0   ¼ mile
0   500 metres

Storrington
MAP 24

Car park

CHANTRY POST

23
25

⟵ 20 – 35 MINS TO CAR PARK (MAP 23)   CHANTRY POST   ⟵ 5 – 10 MINS FROM NEW BARN (MAP 25)

ROUTE GUIDE AND MAPS

WASHINGTON — MAP 25

Despite the proximity of the busy A24 dual carriageway this village is a peaceful place with most of the traffic noise being absorbed by the trees. There is an alternative South Downs Way path which leads the walker directly into the village.

There's B&B from £37pp at friendly *Holt House* (☎ 01903-893542; 1D en suite, 1D/1T shared bathroom; ☛; WI-FI; ☒; ⓛ) at the end of the road that runs off The Holt.

You'll find good food in the welcoming *Frankland Arms* (☎ 01903-892220, ☐ www.franklandarms.co.uk; ☒; food Mon-Fri noon-2.30pm & 6-9pm, Sat noon-3pm & 6-9.30pm, Sun noon-4pm). The pub is open all day (10am-11pm) and the restaurant serves a range of dishes from bangers & mash (£10.45) to steak & ale pie (£10.80). There's no food served on Sunday evenings.

North of the village on London Rd, *Washington Caravan & Camping Park* (☎ 01903-892869, ☐ www.washcamp.com; ☒; open all year) charges £6 per tent for backpackers plus £5pp; a shower costs 20p and they also have laundry facilities.

Stagecoach's **bus** No 1 stops here en route between Midhurst and Worthing. Compass's No 100 (Burgess Hill to Storrington) also calls here as does their No 23 (Crawley to Worthing) service. However, this is operated by Metrobus during the week. See public transport map and table, pp44-6.

The A24 dual carriageway (Map 25) is something of a blot on the landscape but it is soon forgotten once the steep climb up Chanctonbury Hill (Map 26) begins.

At the top there are the somewhat storm-ravaged remains of **Chanctonbury Ring**, a beautiful circle of beech trees that was shaken into a ragged mess during the famous storm of October 1987.

The descent for access to the beautiful small town of **Steyning** (Map 27a, p131) is a leisurely one with fine views over Steyning Bowl and down to the coastal towns of Worthing and Lancing.

❏ Chanctonbury Ring — Map 26, p128

This exposed hilltop is one of the great viewpoints of the South Downs but more significantly it is the site of an Iron Age hill-fort believed to date back to the sixth century BC. Today it is equally famous for the copse of beech trees that were planted on the site of the fort by Charles Goring in 1760 and which grew to become one of the most famous landmarks in Sussex. Sadly, the copse was badly damaged by the storm of October 1987 and despite a replanting programme the skyline has not yet recovered its distinctive crown of trees.

© HENRY STEDMAN

Chanctonbury Ring is also known for its folklore, tales of witchcraft, fairies and other mysterious goings-on. Perhaps the most famous story goes that while Satan was digging the nearby Devil's Dyke valley, spadefuls of earth landed here creating the hill you see today. The ring is also said to be haunted. It may be a beauty spot by day but it takes a brave person to spend the night there.

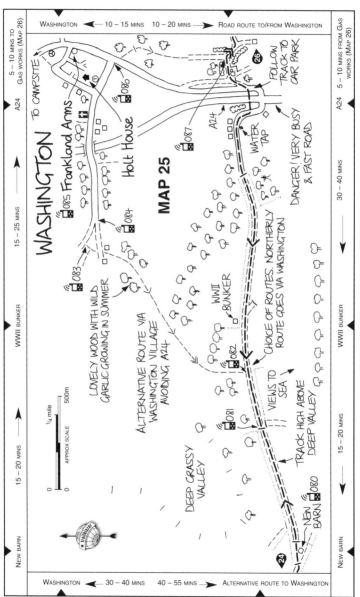

WASHINGTON ← 10 – 15 MINS   10 – 20 MINS → ROAD ROUTE TO/FROM WASHINGTON

A24

26

FOLLOW TRACK TO CAR PARK

⌂ 086

TO CAMPSITE

WASHINGTON

Holt House

Frankland Arms ⌂ 085

⌂ 087

A24

WATER TAP

DANGER / VERY BUSY & FAST ROAD

MAP 25

⌂ 084

A24

15 – 25 MINS

⌂ 083

LONELY WOOD WITH WILD GARLIC GROWING IN SUMMER

WWII BUNKER

WWII BUNKER

ALTERNATIVE ROUTE VIA WASHINGTON VILLAGE AVOIDING A24

CHOICE OF ROUTES: NORTHERLY ROUTE GOES VIA WASHINGTON

30 – 40 MINS

¼ mile   500m

⌂ 082

APPROX SCALE

0   0

VIEWS TO SEA

⌂ 081

TRACK HIGH ABOVE DEEP VALLEY

15 – 20 MINS

15 – 20 MINS

DEEP GRASSY VALLEY

Trailblazer

NEW BARN ⌂ 080

24

NEW BARN

NEW BARN

WASHINGTON ← 30 – 40 MINS   40 – 55 MINS → ALTERNATIVE ROUTE TO WASHINGTON

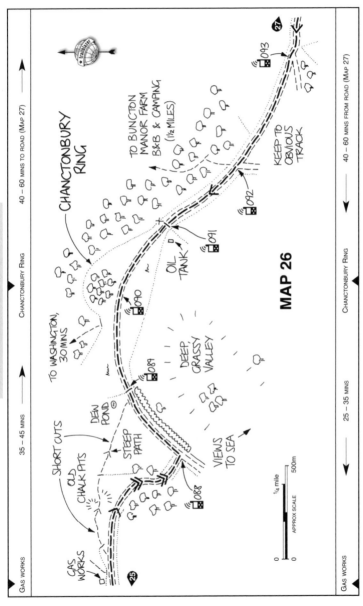

ROUTE GUIDE AND MAPS

GAS WORKS   35 – 45 MINS   CHANCTONBURY RING   40 – 60 MINS TO ROAD (MAP 27)

GAS WORKS   25 – 35 MINS   CHANCTONBURY RING   40 – 60 MINS FROM ROAD (MAP 27)

MAP 26

CHANCTONBURY RING

GAS WORKS

SHORT CUTS

OLD CHALK PITS

DEW POND

STEEP PATH

TO WASHINGTON, 30 MINS

VIEWS TO SEA

DEEP GRASSY VALLEY

OIL TANK

TO BUNCTON MANOR FARM B&B & CAMPING (½ MILES)

KEEP TO OBVIOUS TRACK

089
090
091
092
093
088

¼ mile
APPROX SCALE
500m
0
0

26
27

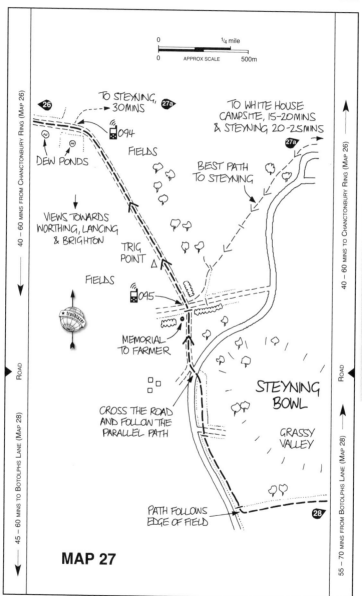

TO STEYNING, 30 MINS

26

27a

TO WHITE HOUSE CAMPSITE, 15-20 MINS & STEYNING 20-25 MINS

27a

📱094

DEW PONDS

FIELDS

BEST PATH TO STEYNING

VIEWS TOWARDS WORTHING, LANCING & BRIGHTON

TRIG POINT △

FIELDS

📱095

MEMORIAL TO FARMER

STEYNING BOWL

CROSS THE ROAD AND FOLLOW THE PARALLEL PATH

GRASSY VALLEY

PATH FOLLOWS EDGE OF FIELD

28

MAP 27

40 – 60 MINS FROM CHANCTONBURY RING (MAP 26)

Road

45 – 60 MINS TO BOTOLPHS LANE (MAP 28)

40 – 60 MINS TO CHANCTONBURY RING (MAP 26)

Road

55 – 70 MINS FROM BOTOLPHS LANE (MAP 28)

ROUTE GUIDE AND MAPS

0   ¼ mile
0   APPROX SCALE   500m

STEYNING — MAP 27a

Steyning, about one mile north of the path, is well worth the minor detour and not just to replenish supplies and energy. This small town has retained all the charm of a downland village and it is worth taking an afternoon off to wander around and maybe visit one or two of the sights. There are some beautiful old buildings, particularly along Church St where the **Grammar School (Brotherhood Hall)**, dating from 1614, really catches the eye with its black timber framing.

Next to the library is the small **Steyning Museum** (☎ 01903-813333, 🖳 www.steyningmuseum.org.uk; open Tue, Wed, Fri & Sat 10.30am-12.30pm & 2.30-4.30pm, Sun 2.30-4.30pm only, closes at 4pm Oct-Mar, open Bank Hol Mons) with displays on local history. Entrance is free.

Services

There is an **information point** in the **library** (☎ 01903-270330; Mon-Fri 10am-5pm, Sat 10am-2pm); there is also **internet** access there.

The High St has plenty of **banks** and **cash machines** and there's a **post office** (Mon-Fri 9am-5.30pm, Sat 9am-12.30pm) too. The main **supermarket**, Co-op (daily 6am-10pm, Sun 9am-6pm) is also on the High St. Further down is a **chemist** and, virtually opposite, there is also a good **bookshop** that sells maps.

Compass's **bus** No 100 calls here en route between Burgess Hill and Pulborough (where there is a railway station). Brighton & Hove Buses' service No 2 also stops here and at Upper Beeding en route to Brighton; see the public transport map and table, pp44-6.

Where to stay

There are two places to **camp** in the area. Just to the south-west of town off Newham Lane is ***White House Caravan and Campsite*** (☎ 01903-813737; 🐕; end Mar-Oct) and it's £10 for a tent pitch and up to two people. Note that there is no shower block and only one toilet here. The walk into town takes about eight minutes. The other place for camping is also a B&B, 2½ miles west of Steyning: ***Buncton Manor Farm*** (☎ 01903-812736, 🖳 www.bunctonmanor.supanet.com; 1D/1T shared private bathroom; ▾; WI-FI; Ⓛ) is on the A283, 1½ miles north of the SDW (see Map 26, WPT 092). There's B&B for £36.50pp. On their small **campsite** they charge £8 for a camper and tent, including the use of the hot shower and chemical toilet.

Walker-friendly ***Uppingham B&B*** (☎ 01903-812099, 🖳 www.uppingham-steyning.co.uk; 1D en suite, 1S/1T with shared bathroom; ▾; 🐕; WI-FI; Ⓛ) is in Kings Barn Villas, on the east side of Steyning. B&B is from £32.50pp.

Springwells Hotel (☎ 01903-812446, 🖳 www.springwells.co.uk; 1S/4D/2D or T en suite, 1S/1D share bathroom; ▾; WI-FI; 🐕; Ⓛ), 9 High St, offers B&B in an en suite room for £49.50-74.50pp (sgl/sgl occ £69-99); if the bathroom is shared the rate is £37-44.50pp (sgl/sgl occ £59-79). Two of the rooms have four-poster beds. One of the other delights of this lovely place is the heated swimming pool in the old walled garden.

Though the bar can sometimes be noisy, ***Chequer Inn*** (☎ 01903-814437, 🖳 www.chequerinnsteyning.co.uk; 1D/1T/1Qd, all en suite; WI-FI; Ⓛ), at 41 High St, offers comfortable B&B from £50pp (sgl occ £60, three/four sharing £130/150). Note that they cannot offer breakfast before 7.30am.

A cheaper option a little further from the centre is ***5 Coxham Lane*** (☎ 01903-812286; 1S/1T, shared bathroom; ▾; 🐕) charging from £25pp.

Where to eat and drink

The High St is the place for food. Cheap eats can be had at the bakery ***Truffles*** (☎ 01903-816140; Mon-Sat 7.30am-5.30pm, Sun 8am-5pm; the café open 30 mins later than the shop, and during the week closes an hour earlier).

A classier place is ***The Steyning Tea Rooms*** (☎ 01903-810064; daily 10am-6pm), which does very good breakfasts – including traditional bacon sandwiches or scrambled eggs with smoked salmon – as well as light lunches and cream teas.

For lunch packs there are takeaway

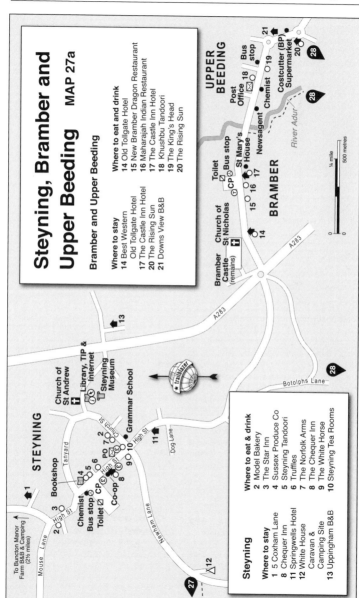

Steyning, Bramber and Upper Beeding MAP 27a

Bramber and Upper Beeding

Where to stay
14 Best Western
   Old Tollgate Hotel
17 The Castle Inn Hotel
20 The Rising Sun
21 Downs View B&B

Where to eat and drink
14 Old Tollgate Hotel
15 New Bramber Dragon Restaurant
16 Maharajah Indian Restaurant
17 The Castle Inn Hotel
18 Khushbu Tandoori
19 The King's Head
20 The Rising Sun

Steyning

Where to stay
1 5 Coxham Lane
8 Chequer Inn
11 Springwells Hotel
12 White House
   Caravan &
   Camping Site
13 Uppingham B&B

Where to eat & drink
2 Model Bakery
3 The Star Inn
4 Sussex Produce Co
5 Steyning Tandoori
6 Truffles
7 The Norfolk Arms
8 The Chequer Inn
9 The White Horse
10 Steyning Tea Rooms

UPPER BEEDING

BRAMBER

STEYNING

buns, cakes and savouries at the *Model Bakery* (☎ 01903-813785; Mon-Fri 8.30am-5pm, Sat 8.30am-3pm), on Church St, with a second branch (☎ 01903-813126; Mon-Fri 8am-5pm, Sat 8am-1pm) at the northern end of the High St.

Probably the best place to eat in Steyning is the *Sussex Produce Company* (☎ 01903-815045, 💻 www.thesussexproducecompany.co.uk; Mon-Sat 8am-8pm & Sun 9am-5pm). This award-winning deli and local produce shop has an excellent café serving steak from Sussex Longhorn cattle and fish from the local port of Newhaven among all the other locally sourced ingredients. There's Harveys beer, Fairtrade coffee and if all you want is ingredients for a picnic how about a shitake mushroom and asparagus pies (£3.95)? To eat in the restaurant (open Friday and Saturday evening) you must book several days in advance.

The White Horse (☎ 01903-814084, 💻 www.whitehorsesteyning.co.uk; food: Mon-Sat noon-9.30pm, noon-9pm Sun), is a gastro-pub at the crossroads on the High St. The pub can get quite lively in the evening; the restaurant section is quieter.

Chequer Inn (see Where to stay; 🐾; food Mon-Sat 10am-2pm & 6.30-9pm, Sun 10am-2.30pm) is a more traditional pub. On Saturday they often either have a karaoke night or live music. At the bottom end of the High St there is another traditional pub, *The Star Inn* (☎ 01903-813078; food daily noon-2pm & 6.30-9pm) serving dishes such as steak and ale pie.

There is also an Indian restaurant: *Steyning Tandoori* (☎ 01903-813533; Sun-Thur noon-2pm & 5.30-11pm, Fri & Sat noon-2pm & 5.30-11.30pm) serves all the usual Indian and Nepali dishes. There's also a *fish and chip shop* (near the post office), though it's open two days a week only (Wed & Fri noon-2pm & 5-9pm).

Finally, for a straightforward pint of real ale, head to *The Norfolk Arms* (☎ 01903-812215) at 18 Church St. This is a real old-style pub where you go for a drink or three.

BRAMBER & UPPER BEEDING
MAP 27a, p131

Acting almost as suburbs of Steyning, the twin villages of Bramber and Upper Beeding lie either side of the River Adur.

The main attraction is **Bramber Castle** (free, dawn to dusk). It was built by William de Broase in 1073 on a prominent knoll behind the village. In truth there is not much left of it, save for a few old ramparts and some collapsed sections of wall but the old moat, despite now having no water and having been taken over by trees, is still clearly visible. The only surviving part of the castle that's still in use is the **Church of St Nicholas** which was built around the same time.

St Mary's House (☎ 01903-816205, 💻 www.stmarysbramber.co.uk; open May-Sep Thur, Sun & bank holidays 2-6pm; admission £9, concessions £8.50) is a magnificent place which claims to be the finest example of a 15th-century timber-framed house in Sussex. The perfectly manicured front garden, with its topiary and fish ponds, only adds to the charm.

Despite the house being a private residence the owners do allow visitors in to admire the antiques, an Elizabethan *trompe l'oeil* painted room, four-poster beds, a 'mysterious, ivy-clad monks' walk' and octagonal dining-room. It is a popular location for TV dramas, most notably *Dr Who*.

Services

On the main street in Upper Beeding there is a **newsagent** (Mon-Fri 5.30am-5pm, Sat 5.30am-1pm, Sun 6am-noon) as well as a **chemist** (Mon-Fri 9am-1pm & 2-5.30pm, Sat 9am-12.30pm) and small **post office** (Mon-Fri 9am-5.30pm, Sat 9am-12.30pm). There's also a small Costcutter **shop** (daily 7am-10pm), part of the garage on the way out of town.

Brighton & Hove Buses' No 2 **bus** service passes through both Bramber and Upper Beeding on its way from Steyning to Rottingdean. Compass Bus No 100 also calls at both on its way between Pulborough and Burgess Hill; see the public transport map and table, pp44-6.

Where to stay

In **Upper Beeding** *Downs View B&B* (☎ 01903-816125, 🖳 www.upperbeeding .com; 6D or T/1Tr or Qd all en suite; 📶; WI-FI; Ⓛ) gets great reviews from visitors and is a friendly place to stay. B&B in their comfortable rooms is from £45pp (£40pp in the triple) and single occupancy is from £55. The breakfasts include homemade bread, muffins and jams.

The Rising Sun (☎ 01903-814424, 🖳 www.therisingsunupperbeeding.co.uk; 3S share bathroom 📶/2D or T en suite; WI-FI; Ⓛ), a basic inn with small, clean rooms with B&B from just £35pp.

In **Bramber**, *The Castle Inn Hotel* (☎ 01903-812102, 🖳 www.castleinnhotel .co.uk; 1D/5Tr/6D or T, one of the triples can sleep up to 5 people; all en suite; 📶; 🐾 £10; WI-FI; Ⓛ) has B&B from £20 to £40pp (sgl occ £40; three/four/five sharing room rate plus £25pp).

If you have cleaned the mud from your boots you could splash out on the *Best Western Old Tollgate Hotel* (☎ 01903-879494, 🖳 www.oldtollgatehotel .com; 28D, two with four posters/6D or T/ 4T, all en suite; 📶; WI-FI; Ⓛ) which incorporates a smart restaurant and lots of pristine rooms and charges around £40pp (sgl occ full room rate). However, their rates vary by the day and are generally better if you book in advance, also at times they have some special offers, so it is worth checking online.

Where to eat and drink

In **Bramber** there is a surprising number of food outlets for such a small village. One of the best places is *The Castle Inn Hotel* (see Where to stay; food Mon-Fri noon-2.30pm & 6-9pm, Sat & Sun noon-9pm but in winter Sun noon-4pm & 6-9pm).

Eating at *Old Tollgate Hotel* (see Where to stay; food Mon-Fri 7-9.30am, Sat & Sun 8-10am; Mon-Sat noon-2pm, Sun noon-9.30pm; Mon-Sat 6-9.30pm) is a classy experience with a three-course dinner (including dessert and a cheese) for £26.50.

For a cheaper night out head for *New Bramber Dragon Restaurant* (☎ 01903-812408, 🖳 newbramberdragon.com; Tue-Sun 5-11pm) where a typical Chinese dish such as sweet and sour pork will cost £6.30. They also serve Thai food.

The *Maharajah Indian Restaurant* (☎ 01903-814746; Mon-Fri noon-2pm & 5.30-11.30pm, Fri & Sat 5.30pm-midnight) claims to be the 'largest and most famous Indian restaurant in Sussex'.

Moving into **Upper Beeding** there is more food from the Indian subcontinent to take away at *Khushbu* (☎ 01903-816646; daily 5.30-11pm). *The King's Head* (☎ 01903-812196; food Mon-Fri noon-2.30pm & 6-9pm, Sat & Sun noon-3pm & 6-9pm) does some fine grub too.

There is also pub food at *The Rising Sun* (see Where to stay; 🐾; food Wed-Mon noon-2.30pm, Thur-Sat 6-9pm) at the far end of the village.

STEYNING TO PYECOMBE

MAPS 27a-32

The going is easy for most of this **10-mile (16 km, 4-5½hrs)** section with a good track leading the way along the level escarpment of the Downs. There are, once again, great views in all directions but particularly to the north across the Weald.

Despite the ugly pub and car park at the top of the hill the highlight of this stretch has to be **Devil's Dyke** (Map 31, p139), a spectacular dry valley said to have been carved out by Satan himself in order to let the sea flood over the lowland Weald and destroy all the churches. Geologists have blown this theory out of the water by proving that it is in fact a result of folding of the chalk strata due to pressure building between the African and Eurasian plates.

After leaving Devil's Dyke the Way drops down to a farm and then over the flanks of **Newtimber Hill**, a National Trust property and a veritable oasis of calm after the crowds that flock to Devil's Dyke.

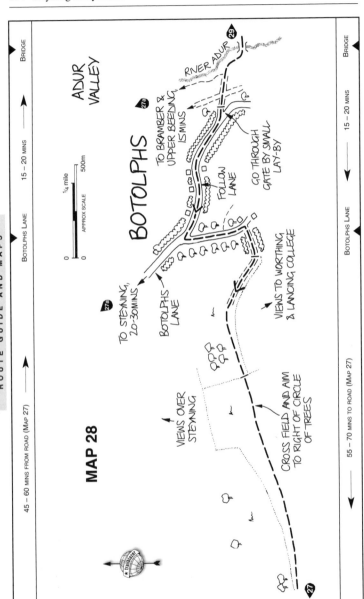

MAP 28

45 – 60 MINS FROM ROAD (MAP 27)

BOTOLPHS LANE

15 – 20 MINS

BRIDGE

55 – 70 MINS TO ROAD (MAP 27)

BOTOLPHS LANE

15 – 20 MINS

BRIDGE

ADUR VALLEY

BOTOLPHS

RIVER ADUR

TO BRAMBER & UPPER BEEDING, 15 MINS

GO THROUGH GATE BY SMALL LAY-BY

FOLLOW LANE

TO STEYNING, 20-30 MINS

BOTOLPHS LANE

VIEWS TO WORTHING & LANCING COLLEGE

VIEWS OVER STEYNING

CROSS FIELD AND AIM TO RIGHT OF CIRCLE OF TREES

¼ mile

500m

APPROX SCALE

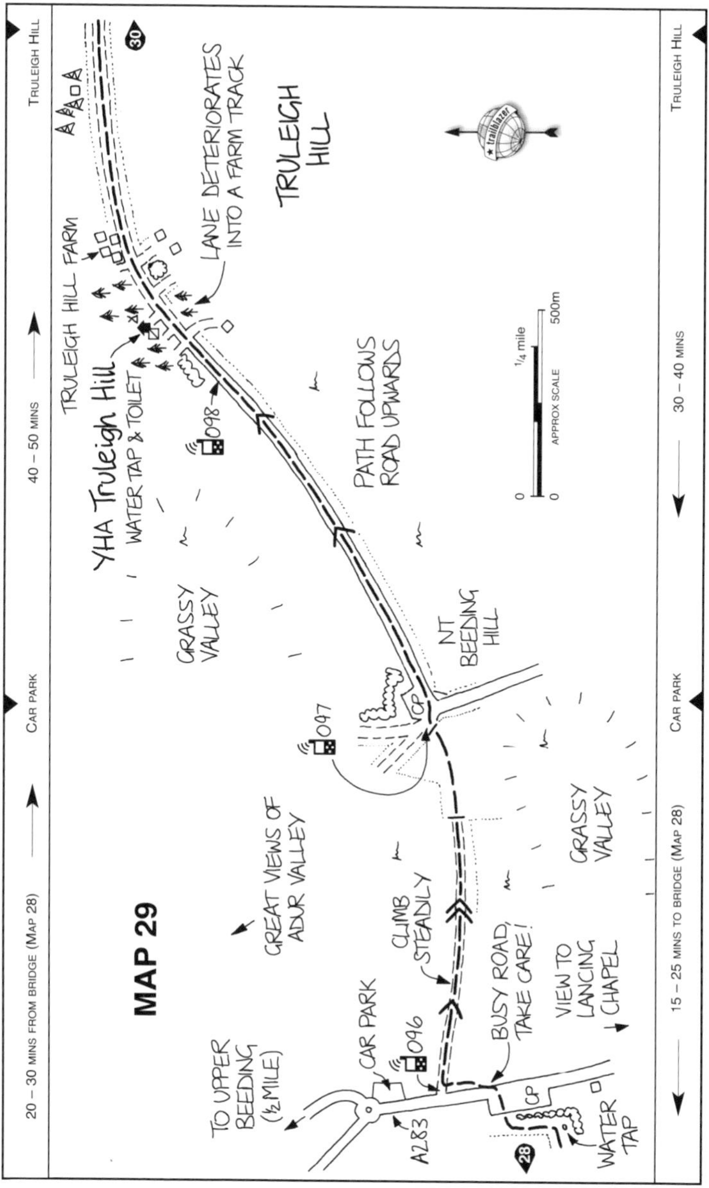

20 – 30 MINS FROM BRIDGE (MAP 28)
CAR PARK
40 – 50 MINS
TRULEIGH HILL
15 – 25 MINS TO BRIDGE (MAP 28)
CAR PARK
30 – 40 MINS
TRULEIGH HILL
MAP 29
TO UPPER BEEDING (½ MILE)
CAR PARK
096
A283
28
WATER TAP
CP
BUSY ROAD, TAKE CARE!
VIEW TO LANCING CHAPEL
CLIMB STEADILY
GREAT VIEWS OF ADUR VALLEY
GRASSY VALLEY
097
CP
NT BEEDING HILL
GRASSY VALLEY
PATH FOLLOWS ROAD UPWARDS
098
YHA Truleigh Hill
WATER TAP & TOILET
TRULEIGH HILL FARM
LANE DETERIORATES INTO A FARM TRACK
TRULEIGH HILL
30
trailblazer
APPROX SCALE
0
¼ mile
0
500m

TRULEIGH HILL **MAP 29, p135**
By the South Downs Way is *Truleigh Hill YHA Hostel* (☎ 0845-371 9047, 🖳 www.yha.org.uk/hostel/truleigh-hill; rooms have 2-6 beds: from £14pp; private rooms from £37; WI-FI; ⒧; Mar-Sep). The purpose-built hostel has all the usual facilities including a drying room and serves meals

but also has a shop and kitchen for those preferring to self-cater. There's a day room with toilet open all day as well as a drying room. **Camping** (Mar-Oct; £9.50pp) is also available and campers can use the toilet in the day room. There is also a water tap outside the front door.

FULKING **MAP 30**
Fulking is a tiny village with little of specific interest to the walker except for the delightful *Shepherd & Dog Inn* (☎ 01273-857382, 🖳 shepherdanddogpub.co.uk; food Mon-Fri noon-9pm, Sat noon-3pm & 5-9pm, Sun noon-6pm). It's everything that a proper country pub should be with plenty of real ales and good food and a beer garden with views of the Downs. The pub gets its name from Fulking's reputation for having

a rather large population of sheep: in the early 19th century the village was home to ten times as many sheep as people and the pub was the place where the shepherds would meet after a hard day's shearing to spend their earnings on the local brew.

Next to the pub car park is the locally famous **Victorian fountain**, placed there in memory of John Ruskin, the man responsible for installing the village's water supply.

POYNINGS **MAP 31, p139**
The hidden leafy village of Poynings sits at the foot of the escarpment away from the hustle and bustle high above at the beauty spot of Devil's Dyke. Poynings is a scenic two-mile walk from the Dyke.

Where to stay and eat
Saddlescombe Farm (☎ 01273-857712, 🖳 saddlescombefarmcampsite@national trust.org.uk; Apr-Sep; 🐾 on a lead) is a five-acre natural (ie basic – there are no showers just washbasins, a toilet and a water tap) **campsite** (£5pp) run by the National Trust. At the farm, there's the *Hikers Rest Teashop* (Wed-Sun & BH Mon 11am-3.30pm) serving cream teas, cakes, sandwiches and snacks. Nearby is one of the last examples of a **donkey wheel** used to pump water from the well.

A place that is both walker and cyclist friendly is *Dyke Lane Cottage* (☎

01273-857335, 🖳 amberric@hotmail.co .uk; 1T private bathroom/2D en suite; WI-FI; 🐾; ⒧); B&B here costs from £35pp (sgl occ £40). Note that the bathroom for the twin is downstairs.

Set in the heart of the village, *The Royal Oak* (☎ 01273-857389, 🖳 www .royaloakpoynings.pub; food daily noon-9.30pm) serves fabulous food, not least the Harveys beer-battered fish, triple-cooked chips and mushy peas for £13.

If descending to The Royal Oak does not appeal, the only other choice is the characterless and completely out-of-place *Devil's Dyke* pub (☎ 01273-857256, 🖳 www.vintageinn.co.uk/thedevilsdykebrigh ton; food Mon-Sat 11.30am-10pm, Sun noon-10pm) at the top of the hill, whose only redeeming feature is its proximity to the Way. Main courses cost £8-13. You can sit outside and watch the hang-gliders if the conditions are right and people are flying.

❏ **Important note – walking times**
Unless otherwise specified, **all times in this book refer only to the time spent walking**. You will need to add 20-30% to allow for rests, photography, checking the map, drinking water etc. When planning the day's hike count on 5-7 hours' actual walking.

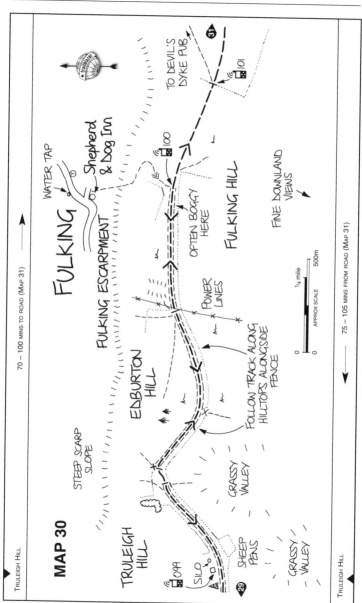

70 – 100 MINS TO ROAD (MAP 31)

MAP 30

TRULEIGH HILL

SILO

SHEEP PENS

GRASSY VALLEY

GRASSY VALLEY

STEEP SCARP SLOPE

FULKING

FULKING ESCARPMENT

EDBURTON HILL

WATER TAP

Shepherd & Dog Inn

TO DEVIL'S DYKE PUB

FULKING HILL

OFTEN BOGGY HERE

FINE DOWNLAND VIEWS

POWER LINES

FOLLOW TRACK ALONG HILLTOPS ALONGSIDE FENCE

GRASSY VALLEY

¼ mile

500m

0

0

APPROX SCALE

75 – 105 MINS FROM ROAD (MAP 31)

PYECOMBE　　　　　**MAP 32, p141**

Pyecombe, like many a downland village, has some very pretty ivy-clad flint houses but the peace and tranquillity that it evidently once had has been somewhat spoilt by the constant hum of traffic from the A23 which converges with the A273 just below the village. The trees hide the roads from view but struggle to do the same with the constant drone. Nevertheless, it's a convenient place to stay being right on the Way and with several B&Bs and a pub.

The Norman **church** (open 9am-6pm, 4pm in winter) is very welcoming, allowing you to make yourself a cup of coffee or tea in their kitchen, or use the **toilet**. The former **forge** in the house opposite was once the source of some of the best shepherds' crooks in southern England.

If you're looking for a picnic lunch, the BP petrol station just south of the village has an **M&S food outlet** stocked with treats.

Metrobus's No 270 (East Grinstead to Brighton) **bus** stops here as do their 271 (Crawley to Brighton via Hassocks) and 273 (Crawley to Brighton) services; see pp44-6.

Where to stay and eat

Right on the Way, *Hobbs Cottage* (☎ 01273-846150, 🖳 wendy.desborough@btinternet.com; 1T en suite/1T private bathroom; ☛; WI-FI) couldn't be better located. It's a well-run, friendly place charging £40pp in the en suite twin and £35pp for the other twin room (sgl occ £50/45). If you have a larger group they can accommodate up to seven people with folding beds.

Also right on the Way, *Dolphin Cottage* (☎ 01273-842468, 🖳 annspring@hotmail.co.uk; 1D/1T private bathroom; WI-FI) is another good B&B, opposite the church. They charge from £40pp (£50 sgl occ).

The White House (☎ 01273-846563, 🖳 louloua@onetel.net; 1S/2D or T shared bathroom ☛; 🐾; WI-FI) charges £40pp (sgl/sgl occ from £40/50). Both walker and dog friendly, this is a really great place to stay and they now also have a field for **campers** (contact them in advance to check it's open), with a toilet, shower and breakfast available. They offer a pick-up/drop off/luggage-transfer service; they also have a drying area and will do laundry.

The Plough (☎ 01273-842796, 🖳 www.theploughpyecombe.co.uk; food Mon-Fri 11.30am-10pm, Sat & Sun noon-10pm) commands unenviable views of the traffic hurtling down the A23 to and from Brighton. Despite this it is a good pub with tasty food; their bar menu is available till 5pm (Mon-Sat); the à la carte menu all the time. They also do takeaways.

CLAYTON　　　　　**off MAP 32, p141**

The main attraction of Clayton is not the small village at the foot of the hill but the two windmills (see below) just two minutes from the path.

There's no B&B in the village itself but out on the bend on the main road, about five minutes' walk away, is the *Jack & Jill Inn* (☎ 01273-843595, 🖳 www.thejackandjillinn.co.uk; 3T/1D all en suite; WI-FI in bar only; Ⓛ; food Mon-Fri noon-2pm & 6-9pm, Sat & Sun noon-9pm) with B&B for £37.50-42.50pp (sgl occ £55-60); room only £5pp less. The bar is open all day, every day and serves a selection of real ales.

❏ **Jack and Jill Windmills**

The twin windmills above Clayton, known as Jack and Jill (Map 32), are famous local landmarks that can be seen for miles around. There is evidence that suggests the first windmill was erected way back in 1765. The names of the windmills are said to originate from the 1920s when tourists first came to visit. The post mill Jill, the white windmill, has been fully restored and occasionally grinds out some wholemeal flour. It is the only one of the two that is open to the public (🖳 www.jillwindmill.org.uk; May-Sep, most Sun & bank hols 2-5pm). Admission is free and there is a *tea shop*.

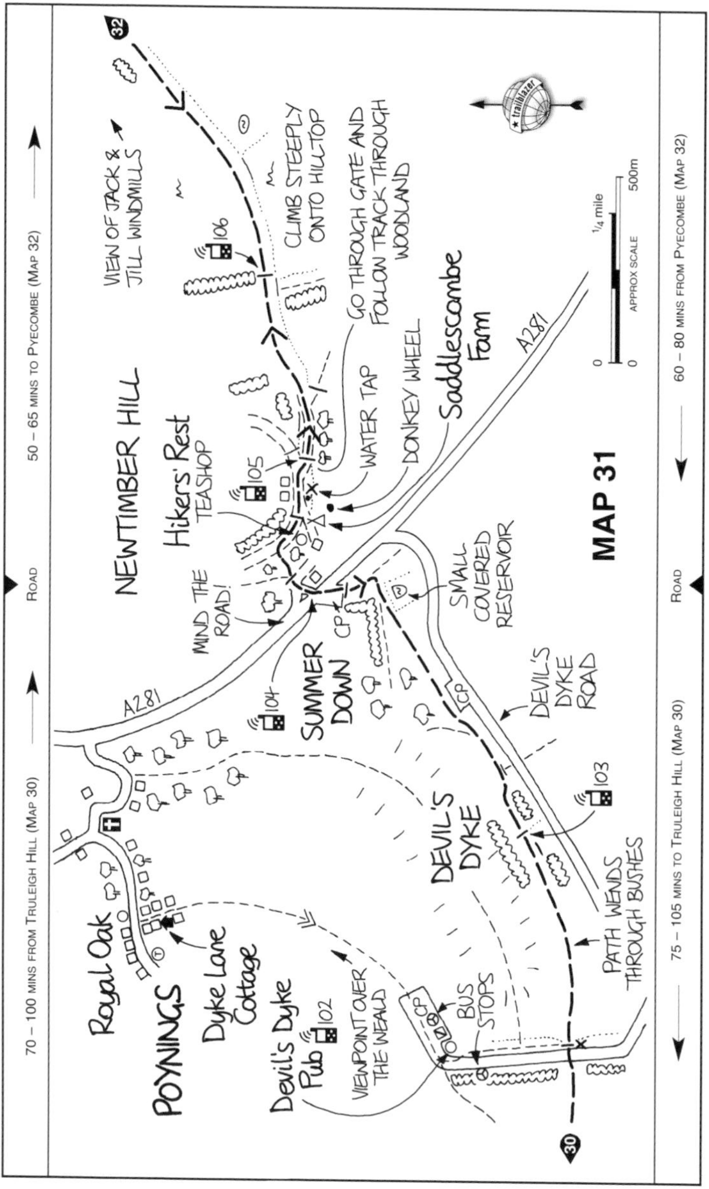

50 – 65 MINS TO PYECOMBE (MAP 32)
ROAD
70 – 100 MINS FROM TRULEIGH HILL (MAP 30)
75 – 105 MINS TO TRULEIGH HILL (MAP 30)
ROAD
60 – 80 MINS FROM PYECOMBE (MAP 32)
32
VIEW OF JACK & JILL WINDMILLS
CLIMB STEEPLY ONTO HILLTOP
106
GO THROUGH GATE AND FOLLOW TRACK THROUGH WOODLAND
NEWTIMBER HILL
Hikers' Rest
TEASHOP
105
WATER TAP
DONKEY WHEEL
Saddlescombe Farm
A281
MIND THE ROAD!
CP
SUMMER DOWN
104
SMALL COVERED RESERVOIR
MAP 31
0
1/4 mile
0
500m
APPROX SCALE
trailblazer
A281
CP
DEVIL'S DYKE ROAD
DEVIL'S DYKE
103
PATH WENDS THROUGH BUSHES
Royal Oak
POYNINGS
Dyke Lane Cottage
Devil's Dyke Pub
102
VIEWPOINT OVER THE WEALD
CP
BUS STOPS
30

ROUTE GUIDE AND MAPS

PYECOMBE TO SOUTHEASE   MAPS 32-38

This reasonably long stretch, **14½ miles (23.5km, 5-7hrs)** provides sweeping views north. The high ground in the distance is the High Weald, a large area of sandstone incorporating Ashdown Forest, the home of Winnie the Pooh, while to the south is Brighton and the English Channel.

The high point of this section is **Ditchling Beacon** (Map 33, p143). The name refers to the pyres that were burnt here and at other sites along the Downs such as Beacon Hill (see p85) in Hampshire. The beacons were lit to warn of impending attack, most notably during the time of the Spanish Armada. More recently they were used for celebrating Millennium Eve and the Queen's Diamond Jubilee in 2012.

Ditchling Beacon is another National Nature Reserve but is also a popular tourist spot. Access is made particularly easy by the road that winds in hairpins up the escarpment from Ditchling village; Brighton & Hove Buses No 79 **bus** service runs between the car park at Ditchling Beacon and Brighton Railway station; see public transport map and table, pp44-6.

After leaving the hustle and bustle of the Beacon the route continues towards **Black Cap** (Map 34, p144) where the track takes a sharp right-hand turn. Those wishing to visit **Lewes** (see p145) should head straight on at this point: however, it is important to note that it is at least an hour's walk from here.

For those continuing on the Way, once over the A27 dual carriageway the path returns to the ridge of the Downs before crossing the Greenwich Meridian to reach the villages of **Rodmell** and **Southease** (Map 38, p155) where the smell of the sea will probably be prevalent and the chalk cliffs of Seaford Head can be seen in the distance.

DITCHLING   MAP 33a, p142

It is about a mile from the Downs to this village but if you are trying to decide on a place to spend the night this is a good choice and worth the short detour. Ditchling is among the prettiest of the pretty, perhaps bettered only by Alfriston and Amberley. There is a multitude of historic buildings centred around the crossroads but the oldest of all is the fine 13th-century Norman **St Margaret's Church**.

Opposite the church you can see the house, **Wings Place**, bought by Henry VIII for his fourth wife, Anne of Cleves (see Plumpton p142 and Lewes p145) as part of a 'pay off' at the end of their marriage.

Not far from the church, in the old Victorian village school, is the recently refurbished **Ditchling Museum** (☎ 01273-844744, 🖳 www.ditchlingmuseumartcraft .org.uk; open mid-Jan to mid-Dec, Tue-Sat

11am-5pm, Sun noon-5pm; £6.50). It's well worth visiting with impressive collections by famous local artists and craftspeople such as the sculptor and engraver Eric Gill, the printer Hilary Pepler, the weaver Ethel Mairet and the painters David Jones and Sir Frank Brangwyn.

Services

There are two small **village shops** with limited provisions. One is a short way up the High St next to Church Lane while the other, incorporating the **post office** (☎ 01273-842736; post office Mon-Fri 9am-5.30pm & Sat 9am-12.30pm, shop Mon-Fri 8am-1pm & 2.15pm-6pm, Sat 8am-1pm, Sun 8am-2pm), is at the crossroads in the centre of the village.

Close by is **Ditchling Pharmacy** (Mon-Thur 9am-1pm & 2-5.30pm, Fri 9am-1pm & 2-6.30pm).

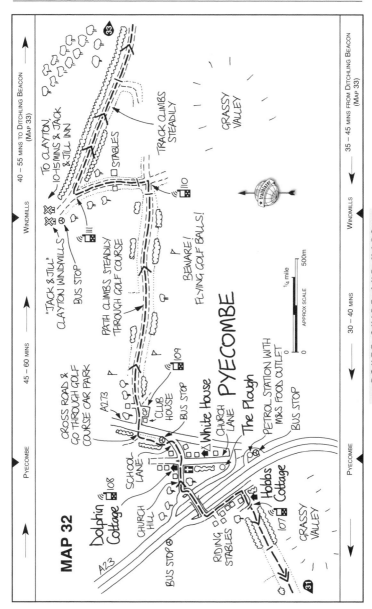

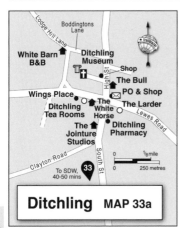

Ditchling **MAP 33a**

Where to stay and eat

The Bull (☎ 01273-843147, 🖳 www.the
bullditchling.com; 4D en suite; food Mon-
Fri noon-2.30pm & 6-9.30pm, Sat noon-
9.30pm, Sun noon-9pm; WI-FI), is a wonderful old pub on the High St. There's very
comfortable B&B from £50pp rising to
£80pp (sgl occ full room rate) at weekends
when they also have a minimum two-night
stay. It's a good place to eat though you
may have to book a table at weekends.
Confit pork belly with butterbeans is £15;
fillet of bream with clams is £18.

There's also *The White Horse* (☎
01273-842006; 🖳 www.whitehorseditch
ling.com; 2D/1D or T en suite, 2D/2D or T
private bathroom; ☛; WI-FI; (L)). which
charges from £35pp to £55pp (sgl occ from
£60); note that the rooms with private bathroom are small. Food (Mon-Fri noon-3pm
& 6-9.30pm, Sat noon-9.30pm, Sun noon-
4pm & 6-9pm) is available in the pub or in

their restaurant; main dishes include beef &
ale pie (£12.50) and aubergine bake
(£9.95).

If staying in a pub does not appeal
there are more peaceful options away from
the busy main road that runs through the
village. The *White Barn* (☎ 01273-842920,
🖳 www.thewhitebarnbandb.co.uk; 1D private bathroom; ☛; WI-FI; (L)), on Lodge Hill
Lane, with B&B for £37.50pp (sgl occ from
£50). The big double bed is extremely comfortable! The breakfast they offer is continental; they don't do a full English now.

There's very comfortable B&B in the
attractive studios once used by the artist Sir
Frank Brangwyn: *The Jointure Studios* (☎
01273-841244, 🖳 jointurestudios.word
press.com; 1D or T with bathroom, kitchen
and living room; ☛; WI-FI) at 11 South St.
B&B is £60pp sharing.

The most luxurious accommodation in
the area is also closest to the Way, at *Tovey
Lodge* (Map 33; ☎ 01273-256156, 🖳 www
.toveylodge.co.uk; 1D/4D or T, all en suite;
☛; 🐕 £5; WI-FI; (L)) on Underhill Lane.
There's an indoor swimming-pool, spa hot
tub and sauna. They charge according to
season and demand, with room rates ranging from £50pp to £100pp (sgl occ £90-
185).

For breakfast and lunch try *Ditchling
Tea Rooms* (☎ 01273-842708, 🖳 www
.ditchlingtearooms.com; Apr-Oct daily
8am-5pm, Oct-Mar Mon-Fri 8am-4pm, Sat
& Sun 8am-5pm), where you can have a
cooked breakfast (from £6.50), a range of
sandwiches/baguettes (from £4.75), or
afternoon tea (scone, cream and jam £4.95).

To make up a picnic visit *The Larder*
(☎ 01273-845333, open Mon-Sat 9am-
6pm), a deli stocking local produce. You
can also get hot drinks to take away.

PLUMPTON   MAP 34, p144
Famous for its agricultural college,
Plumpton is also the location for the private-
ly owned **Plumpton Place**, a 16th-century
mansion complete with moat, once owned
by Anne of Cleves after it was given to her
by Henry VIII. The best view of the mansion
is from the Way on the top of the hill.

Plumpton railway station is actually in
Plumpton Green, 2½ miles due north of
Plumpton. It's a stop on the London to
Eastbourne/Ore line; **train** services are
operated by Southern. Compass's **bus** No
166 will take you to Lewes or Haywards
Heath. See the public transport map and
table, pp44-6.

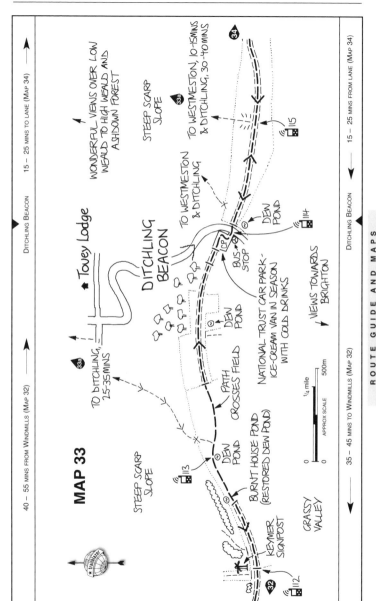

MAP 33

40 – 55 MINS FROM WINDMILLS (MAP 32)

15 – 25 MINS TO LANE (MAP 34)

DITCHLING BEACON

WONDERFUL VIEWS OVER LOW WEALD TO HIGH WEALD AND ASHDOWN FOREST

STEEP SCARP SLOPE

↑ Tovey Lodge

DITCHLING BEACON

TO WESTMESTON 10–15MINS & DITCHLING, 30–40MINS

TO WESTMESTON & DITCHLING

TO DITCHLING, 25-35MINS

DEW POND

DEW POND

BUS STOP

DEW POND

PATH CROSSES FIELD

NATIONAL TRUST CAR PARK-ICE-CREAM VAN IN SEASON WITH COLD DRINKS

VIEWS TOWARDS BRIGHTON

STEEP SCARP SLOPE

DEW POND

BURNT HOUSE POND (RESTORED DEW POND)

KEYMER SIGNPOST

GRASSY VALLEY

APPROX SCALE

0   ¼ mile

0   500m

DITCHLING BEACON

15 – 25 MINS FROM LANE (MAP 34)

35 – 45 MINS TO WINDMILLS (MAP 32)

ROUTE GUIDE AND MAPS

ROUTE GUIDE AND MAPS

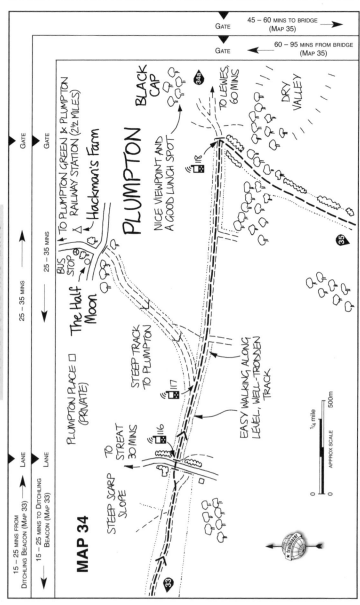

MAP 34

45 – 60 MINS TO BRIDGE
(MAP 35)

60 – 95 MINS FROM BRIDGE
(MAP 35)

GATE

GATE

GATE

GATE

15 – 25 MINS FROM
DITCHLING BEACON (MAP 33)

15 – 25 MINS TO DITCHLING
BEACON (MAP 33)

LANE

LANE

25 – 35 MINS

25 – 35 MINS

BLACK CAP

TO LEWES, 60 MINS

DRY VALLEY

TO PLUMPTON GREEN & PLUMPTON RAILWAY STATION (2½ MILES)

Hackman's Farm

PLUMPTON

NICE VIEWPOINT AND A GOOD LUNCH SPOT

118

BUS STOP

The Half Moon

PLUMPTON PLACE ☐ (PRIVATE)

STEEP TRACK TO PLUMPTON

117

EASY WALKING ALONG LEVEL, WELL-TRODDEN TRACK

TO STREAT 30 MINS

116

STEEP SCARP SLOPE

¼ mile

APPROX SCALE

500m

33

Campers will find pitches at two local sites. *Hackman's Farm* (☎ 01273-890348; Feb-Oct; 🐾 if on a lead) charges £6.50pp. Campers can use the toilet at the back of the cottage and there's also a water tap there. Further along the Way – and right on it – (Map 35, p151) there's *Housedean Farm* (see p148).

The Half Moon (☎ 01273-890253, 🖥 www.halfmoonplumpton.com; bar Mon-Sat noon-11pm, Sun noon-6pm; food Mon-Sat noon-3pm & 6-9pm, Sun noon-4pm) is an excellent local pub with a wide selection of interesting dishes including marinated frogs' legs (£4) but also steaks (from £18). During the week at lunch-time they serve a 2-/3-course meal for £12/15. All their meat and fish is sourced locally with food miles travelled noted. There are also real ales on tap, locally brewed and changed on a regular basis. The main kitchen is closed 3-6pm year-round but in the summer during the week they serve snacks such as filled ciabatta at that time.

LEWES   MAP 34a, p147

'Lewes ... lying like a box of toys under a great amphitheatre of chalky hills ... on the whole it is set down better than any town I have seen in England'   **William Morris**

Lewes, the county town of East Sussex, is still an attractive place to visit and one of the most desirable places to live in the South East. Like Totnes in Devon, it's a Transition Town (🖥 www.transitiontown lewes.org), populated by a vibrant community of people some of whom are dedicated to following this movement based on permaculture and sustainability. They've even issued their own currency (see box p148).

For the visitor it's interesting to see somewhere that's paying more than lip service to being green. It also means there's a profusion of places to buy and eat good healthy food; it's well worth spending the night here.

Lewes lies in a strategic position by the River Ouse with Mount Caburn rising steeply to the west. This did not go unnoticed by William the Conqueror who had William de Warrene fortify the town soon after the Battle of Hastings in 1066.

The town's focal point is **Lewes Castle** (see box below), which sits proudly at the very highest point on a grassy bluff.

Down the hill from the castle, **Anne of Cleves House** (☎ 01273-474610, 🖥 www .sussexpast.co.uk; Feb-Oct Tue-Sat 10am-5pm, Sun & Mon 11am-5pm; admission £5.40, or £11.40 with combined Lewes Castle ticket) is open to the public – unlike Plumpton Place (see p142) and Wing's Place (see p140) which were also given as a gift from Henry VIII to his fourth wife Anne of Cleves. This house is well worth visiting for its beautiful interior with timber beams and oak furnishings. There is a *café* here and a Tudor tea garden.

Lewes still has some excellent bookshops, the oldest of which, the **Fifteenth Century Bookshop**, can be found at the top of the High St near the castle entrance. The timber-framed building that houses the shop is worth a visit in itself.

At the same end of the High St is **Bull House** where Thomas Paine, the founder of American Independence, lived between 1768 and 1774. During his time in Lewes he acted as the local tobacconist and

---

❏ Lewes Castle & Barbican House Museum

This Norman **castle** (☎ 01273-486290, 🖥 www.sussexpast.co.uk; open daily year-round except Mon in Jan, 10am-5.30pm Mar-Oct, 10am-3.45pm Nov-Feb; admission £7.20 or combined ticket for Anne of Cleves House £11.40) was built by Lieutenant William de Warenne shortly after the Battle of Hastings in 1066. The well-preserved castle gate and walls can be explored and the ticket also gives access to the **Barbican House Museum** opposite, which contains artefacts from the castle and an interactive display covering the history of the town and castle.

exciseman. A commemorative plaque can be seen on the outside wall.

Priory Park and the ruins of the 11th century **Priory of St Pancras** are worth visiting and the ruins are well labelled with interesting panels. There's also a little herb garden of medicinal herbs once grown by the monks. The park and the ruins are always open and there's no entry charge.

Real-ale drinkers cannot go to Lewes without visiting **Harveys Brewery** (☎ 01273-480209, 🖳 www.harveys.org.uk) though with a waiting list of more than a year for guided tours most fans will get no further than the shop. Harveys is the oldest brewery in Sussex and has been producing real ales for well over 200 years using hops from Sussex and Kent and water from their own spring. The company is still run by the same family that founded it seven generations ago. The **shop** (☎ 01273-480217; Mon-Sat 9.30am-5.30pm) sells a vast array of Harveys' related paraphernalia.

Services
The **tourist information centre** (☎ 01273-483448, 🖳 lewes.tic@lewes.gov.uk; Apr-Sep Mon-Sat 9am-4.30pm, Sun & bank hols 10am-2pm; Oct-Mar Mon-Fri 9.30am-4.30pm, Sat 10am-2pm, closed Sun) is on the corner of Fisher St and the High St at No 187. They can help find local accommodation and also sell maps, books and guides.

The **post office** (Mon-Fri 9am-5.30pm, Sat 9am-12.30pm) is on the High St where there is also a **chemist** and there are plenty of **banks** with **cash machines**. Waitrose **supermarket** is on Eastgate St and walking equipment can be found at **The Outdoor Shop** (☎ 01273-487840; Mon-Sat 9am-5.30pm) at the lower end of the High St near the river. In the same area there's a **Waterstones bookshop** and *café* (Mon-Sat 9am-6pm, Sun 9am-4.30pm).

Public transport
[See the public transport map and table, pp44-6]. Convenient and regular **trains** from Lewes run south to Seaford & Eastbourne and north to Gatwick Airport & London Victoria; services from Ashford International station to Brighton as well as

Ore/Eastbourne/Seaford to Brighton also call here.

There are also several useful **bus** services (the bus station is on Eastgate St): Brighton and Hove Buses' No 28 runs to Brighton and their No 29 service stops here en route between Brighton and Tunbridge Wells. Compass provides several useful services: for Rodmell, Southease and Newhaven take their No 123; the 124/126 service operates between Barcombe and Alfriston and the 143 service goes to Eastbourne; for Plumpton or Haywards Heath take their No 166.

For a **taxi** try Lewes Taxis (☎ 01273-483232) or GM Taxis (☎ 01273-473737).

Where to stay
There is no shortage of rooms in Lewes but as with any other popular tourist town booking in advance is advised.

1 Garden Cottages (☎ 01273-473343, 🖳 www.lewesroom.co.uk; 1D/1T en suite; ➤; WI-FI; Ⓛ), 59 South St, is an attractive B&B on the eastern edge of the town. You'll get a good continental breakfast and eggs (a full English an additional £5pp) and the friendly owner is a mine of information about the area. She charges £40pp (£50 sgl occ) and there is a two-night minimum stay in summer for advance bookings. The double room has its own entrance.

The hospitable owner of *One Harveys Way* (☎ 01273-480865, 🖳 andrewkr37@gmail.com; 1S/1T shared bathroom; ➤; WI-FI) charges £35pp with a healthy breakfast of cereal and toast. A cooked breakfast costs £5 extra.

Castle Banks Cottage (☎ 01273-476291, 🖳 www.castlebankscottage.co.uk; 1S/1T, shared bathroom but basins in each bedroom; ➤; WI-FI), 4 Castle Banks, is in a quiet street behind the castle. They charge £40pp (sgl £40, sgl occ £55) with a full cooked breakfast (vegetarian options available) which you can have in the garden on sunny days.

The Prospect B&B (☎ 01273-472883, 🖳 www.theprospectbandb.co.uk; 1D or T en suite; WI-FI) is on St Martin's Lane in the centre of town. They charge from £45pp (sgl occ £60); the breakfasts are excellent and include home-baked bread. They do have an additional room for people travelling in a group of four and willing to share the bathroom.

Montys (☎ 01273-476750, 🖥 www .montysaccommodation.co.uk; 3D, all en suite; 🛏; WI-FI; Ⓛ), Broughton House, 16 High St, charges £50-70pp (sgl occ full room rate); two of the rooms are self con-

tained and have a kitchenette, one also has a four-poster bed and free-standing bath. The rate includes a continental breakfast with home-made muesli or granola.

Felix House (☎ 01273-473250, 🖥 www.lewesbedandbreakfast.co.uk; 1S/2D en suite; 🛏; WI-FI), 22 Gundreda Rd, is ideally placed for walkers being halfway between the Way and Lewes town centre. If

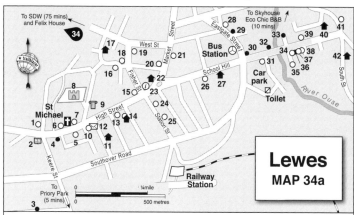

Where to eat and drink
1 Baltica Café
5 Shanaz Indian Restaurant
6 Castle Sandwich Bar
7 Panda Garden
10 Beckworths
13 Charcoal Grill
14 Pelham House
15 Ask
16 Lewes Arms
18 The Friar Fish and Chip Shop
19 Carnival Chinese Takeaway
20 Café at the Needlemakers
21 Famiglia Lazzati
24 The Royal Oak
25 Limetree Kitchen
26 Robson's of Lewes
28 Chaula's Café Restaurant
31 Forfars Bakery
34 Gardener's Arms
35 John Harvey Tavern
37 Le Magasin
38 Bill's Produce Store
39 The Real Eating Company
41 Buttercup Café

Where to stay
11 The Prospect B&B
14 Pelham House
17 Castle Banks Cottage
22 The Crown Inn
27 Montys
40 One Harveys Way
42 1 Garden Cottages

Other
2 15th Century Bookshop
3 Anne of Cleves House
4 Bull House
8 Lewes Castle
9 Barbican House Museum
12 Post Office
23 TIC
29 Waitrose supermarket
30 Chemist
32 Waterstones Bookshop
33 Harveys Brewery and shop
36 The Outdoor Shop

ROUTE GUIDE AND MAPS

you're walking in on Hill Rd, turn right onto King Henry's Rd, right again onto De Warenne Rd and Gundreda Rd is on the right. They charge £42.50pp (sgl/sgl occ £45/65) for B&B including a full cooked breakfast. There is a two-night minimum stay in summer for advance bookings

There's also accommodation at *The Crown Inn* (☎ 01273-480670, 🖳 www .crowninnlewes.co.uk; 2D/1T/2Qd, all en suite; 🖤; WI-FI in bar area only; 🐾; Ⓛ). They charge from £40pp (sgl occ £60-80, £100-160 for three/four sharing).

A classy place is *Pelham House* (☎ 01273-488600, 🖳 www.pelhamhouse.com; 2S/29D, all en suite; 🖤; WI-FI) with B&B for £40-80pp (sgl/sgl occ from £79). However, if they're not booked up they may offer B&B from £30pp (two sharing £60).

For something completely different *Skyhouse Eco Chic B&B* (☎ 07468-691 860, 🖳 www.skyhousesussex.com; 3D en suite; 🖤; WI-FI) is a luxury eco B&B in a new zero-carbon house a 10-minute walk from the town centre. It's £75pp but there's a 10% discount if you arrive on foot.

Between Lewes and Kingston-nr-Lewes
Housedean Farm Campsite (Map 35; ☎ 07919-668816, 🖳 www.housedean.co.uk; 🐾; Mar-Oct) is right on the SDW. In addition to its 25 pitches (£11pp) they have bell tents (sleep six people on double beds; unfurnished/furnished £65/80), a camping pod (sleeps two; bedding not provided; £40) and a shepherd's hut (£160). There are toilets, showers and a fire pit at each pitch. There's a minimum 2-night stay policy in June to August unless there is late availability. Booking can be done online. The stop for buses to Lewes and Brighton is nearby.

Half a mile up the A27 from here and also convenient for the SDW (though being right by the road it's hardly the most beautiful location) the *Newmarket Inn* (Map 35; ☎ 01273-470021, 🖳 www.relaxinnz.co .uk; 10D en suite; 🖤; WI-FI) has B&B from £34.50pp (sgl occ £44). The cheap pub grub served here is good.

Where to eat and drink
Most of Lewes's cafés, pubs and restaurants are on or just off the upper High St.

❏ The Lewes Pound
In 2008, Lewes town took the unusual step of issuing its own currency, to be used alongside sterling. The idea behind the 'Lewes Pound' (🖳 www.thelewespound.org) is to encourage demand for local goods and services, and the logic behind it is simple: money spent in shops in the town that are merely another branch of a national chain does not stay in the local economy; but money spent in shops owned by locals or on local services does. So while the Lewes Pound would not be accepted in, for example, the local outlet of a nationwide superstore, of which there are several in Lewes, it would be accepted by a local trader – who would then spend it locally with another local trader, and so on and so on. Thus, by ensuring that money is spent locally and so stays within the community, the wealth of the locals is safeguarded.

People buy Lewes Pounds (with sterling) at one of the issuing points (including Lewes Town Hall, Mays General Store on Cliffe High St, and Richards & Son, Butchers, on Western Rd) – or off the website 🖳 www.thelewespound.org – then spend them with participating traders.

Whilst the establishing of a new currency may seem like a highly bizarre step to take, it isn't without precedent; indeed, Lewes itself had its own currency for over a century between 1789 and 1895. The issuers of the latest Lewes Pound, however, admit that their currency is not actually legal tender, in that there is no obligation on the part of retailers to accept the pound.

Some residents, however, see the Lewes Pound as an unnecessary complication. They argue, rightly, that they can support local traders by buying from them using good old-fashioned sterling. And it's true that the Lewes Pound doesn't seem to be quite as much in evidence as it was in the past.

On the eastern side of town, **Buttercup Café** (☎ 01273-477664, 🖳 thebuttercup cafe.wordpress.com; open Mon-Fri 9.30am-4pm, Sat 9am-4pm, may also open Sun in summer) is a quirky little café serving breakfasts, lunches and teas. Set amongst an antique shop and a studio it's right at home here in Lewes. The menu's interesting and the food is delicious and very good value. It's worth checking the website as they sometimes do themed supper evenings and host exhibitions in the studio.

Right at the western end of town near the castle, at 145 High St, is a similarly-popular restaurant, **Baltica Café** (☎ 01273-483449, 🖳 www.baltictrader.co.uk; open Tue-Sat 10am-5pm, Sun 11am-4pm). Part of a Polish ceramics shop the menu includes some excellent Polish dishes such as pierogi filled with pork and vegetables (£9.95) and goulash (£8.95). A two-course lunch is £9.95. There are also delicious pastries and they serve Zywiec beer.

Another recommended place is the **Café at the Needlemakers** (☎ 01273-486258, 🖳 www.needlemakers.co.uk; open Mon-Sat 9.30am-5.30pm, also open Sun in summer). The coffee is excellent and there's a mouthwatering range of homemade cakes, scones and muffins. They also do salads and open sandwiches. There are lots of interesting shops to look round at the Needlemakers.

Bill's Produce Store (☎ 01273-476918, 🖳 www.bills-website.co.uk; Mon-Thur 8am-10.30pm, Fri & Sat 8am-11pm, Sun 9am-10.30pm) is a great place with tables outside on the cobbled street. The store incorporates a very colourful fruit and veg shop as well as a restaurant and is always busy with locals and tourists alike.

Limetree Kitchen (☎ 01273-478636, 🖳 www.limetreekitchen.co.uk; Wed-Sat noon-2.30pm & 6.30-9.30pm, Sun noon-2.30pm), 14 Station St, is an excellent restaurant (one of the best places to eat in Lewes) and a café. Main dishes for dinner might include salt marsh lamb with parma ham (£18), or sea bass with orzo and clams (£18). There are two-/three-course set lunch menus for £13.50/£19.

The Real Eating Company (☎ 01273-402650, 🖳 www.real-eating.co.uk; food Mon-Sat 8.30am-10pm, Sun 10am-9pm), 18 Cliffe St, is a café-restaurant serving drinks and light meals and grills. Burgers are from £11.95, an 8oz flat-iron steak is £14.95 and a lobster roll is £16.95.

Almost opposite is **Le Magasin** (☎ 01273-474720) and it does just as it claims: serving restaurant food for bistro prices in a café atmosphere. It's highly recommended and you can get breakfast here 8am-noon daily (from 9am Sun), lunch daily noon-3pm and dinner Thur-Sat 6-9pm.

There's a good restaurant at **Pelham House** (see Where to stay; daily noon-2.30pm & 6.30-9.30pm). For two/three courses it's £21.50/27.50.

For Italian food you could try **Ask** (☎ 01273-479330; Mon-Sat 11.30am-11pm, Sun 11.30am-10pm) where all the usual pizza and pasta dishes are served. There's also **Famiglia Lazzati** (☎ 01273-479539; Mon-Fri 5-10pm, Sat & Sun noon-10pm) on Market St; it's small and cheerful and the pizzas are good value.

There are several Indian restaurants. **Chaula's Café Restaurant** (☎ 01273-476 707; Sun-Thur 11am-3pm & 5-10.30pm, Fri & Sat 11am-11pm), at 6 Eastgate St near the bus station, is a cheap place to get a filling meal. Back on the High St there's **Shanaz Indian Restaurant** (☎ 01273-488028; daily noon-2pm & 6-11pm).

There are numerous small cafés and takeaways. The **Charcoal Grill** (☎ 01273-471126; Sun-Thur noon-midnight, Fri & Sat noon-1am) has takeaway pizzas, kebabs and burgers. For cheap homemade pizzas, sandwiches or cakes try **Beckworths** (☎ 01273-474502; Mon-Sat 9am-5pm) which is set in a tiny timber-framed house at 67 High St: it is also a deli which serves a variety of cold meats. Further up the High St, **Castle Sandwich Bar** (☎ 01273-478080; Mon-Fri 9.30am-3pm, Sat 11am-2pm) has very reasonably priced sandwiches.

The Friar Fish and Chip Shop (☎ 01273-472016; Tue-Sat noon-1.45pm & 5-9.30pm) is on the aptly named Fisher St. On the same street there's the **Carnival Chinese Takeaway** (☎ 01273-474221; Wed-Mon 5-11pm). **Panda Garden** (☎ 01273-473235; Tue-Fri noon-2pm & daily 6-10.30pm) is on the High St near the castle. Another place to find something quick to eat is on the lower High St by the river where *Forfars Bakery* (☎ 01273-474827; Mon-Sat 7am-5pm) has sandwiches and jacket potatoes from £3. There's also *Robson's of Lewes* (☎ 01273-480654; Mon-Sat 9am-5pm, Sun 10am-5pm) on the High St, a coffee shop and takeaway. They serve breakfasts, light lunches and teas.

With a brewery in town it's not surprising that there's a wide choice of pubs. The *John Harvey Tavern* (☎ 01273-479880; food Mon-Sat noon-2pm & 6-9.30pm, Sun noon-4.30pm), part of the famous brewery, is just off the High St. The menu is full of tasty-looking dishes and there is also, of course, plenty of Harveys

Ale to wash it all down. Another good spot for a pint of the local brew and many others since it's a real ale pub is *The Gardener's Arms* (☎ 01273-474808) which is conveniently situated a short way down the High St; it is a popular place with locals wanting a quiet drink.

The Lewes Arms (☎ 01273-473152; food Mon-Fri noon-8.30pm, Sat noon-9pm, Sun noon-8pm) is a lovely traditional pub with snugs and quiet corners where you can enjoy a beer; they offer good pub fare.

On Station St there's a selection of real ales and more pub grub at *The Royal Oak* (☎ 01273-474803; food Mon-Sat noon-2.30pm & 6-9pm, Sun noon-5pm). There's live music on Thursday nights (often folk music).

❏ **Paragliding**
At certain points on the Downs, particularly around the Lewes area (Ditchling Beacon and Mount Caburn), colourful canopies can be seen floating effortlessly, high above the hilltops. These paragliders are attracted to the scarp slope of the Downs by thermal updrafts which develop through the course of warm summer days. Anyone can try paragliding with the following companies offering expert tuition to help fledgling fliers take their first flight. The sensation of running along a hilltop only for your feet to leave the ground and find yourself floating like a weightless feather in a cool breeze is certainly a unique way to appreciate the countryside.
● **Airsports Paragliding** (☎ 01903-879241, 🖳 www.airsportsparagliding.co.uk) Offers five-day beginners' courses at their site near Steyning from £495 per person.
● **Airworks Paragliding Centre** (☎ 01273-434002, 🖳 www.airworks.co.uk) One-, five- and ten-day courses for £130, £590 and £990 respectively, operated from their base at Glynde. They can also give tuition in hang-gliding.
● **Freeflight Paragliding** (☎ 01273-628793, 🖳 www.freeflightbrighton.co.uk) Offers tasters from £100 and four-day courses from £500 near Steyning.

KINGSTON-NEAR-LEWES
MAP 36, p152
Kingston-near-Lewes is one of the larger downland villages. From the top of the hill the rather out-of-place housing estate is all too obvious but once you're down in the village it is well hidden. The main street, lined with pretty cottages, comes as a pleasant surprise.

There's a **campsite** half a mile from here on the way to Lewes: *Spring Barn Farm* (☎ 01273-488450, 🖳 www.spring barnfarm.com; £10pp) with showers and toilets. There's a farm shop and the restaurant serves hot food daily until 4pm.

On The Avenue *Nightingales* (☎ 01273-475673, 🖳 nightingalesbandb.co.uk; 1D/1T, both en suite; ☞; WI-FI) offers B&B for £42.50-45pp (sgl occ £60). If the owner's hens haven't been eaten by the fox, you may have some for breakfast.

The Juggs (☎ 01273-472523; 🐾; bar daily 11am-11pm; food daily noon-9pm) is an excellent pub with a pretty front garden. The unusual name refers to the baskets once used for carrying fish from Brighton to the market in Lewes.

The only **bus** service to call here is the No 123 (Newhaven to Malling) operated by Compass Travel; see pp44-6.

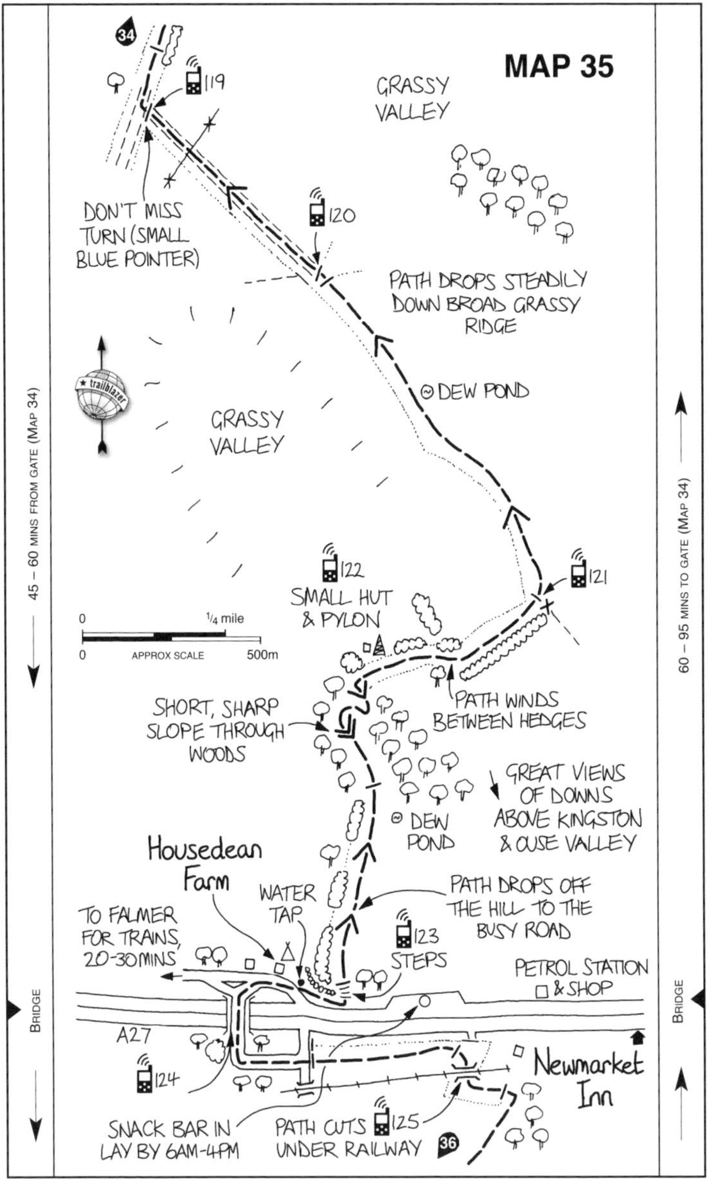

MAP 35

34

📱119

GRASSY
VALLEY

DON'T MISS
TURN (SMALL
BLUE POINTER)

📱120

PATH DROPS STEADILY
DOWN BROAD GRASSY
RIDGE

⊙ DEW POND

45 – 60 MINS FROM GATE (MAP 34)

GRASSY
VALLEY

0   ¼ mile
0   APPROX SCALE   500m

📱122
SMALL HUT
& PYLON

📱121

60 – 95 MINS TO GATE (MAP 34)

PATH WINDS
BETWEEN HEDGES

SHORT, SHARP
SLOPE THROUGH
WOODS

GREAT VIEWS
OF DOWNS
ABOVE KINGSTON
& OUSE VALLEY

⊙ DEW
POND

Housedean
Farm

WATER
TAP

PATH DROPS OFF
THE HILL TO THE
BUSY ROAD

TO FALMER
FOR TRAINS,
20-30MINS

📱123
STEPS

PETROL STATION
☐ & SHOP

BRIDGE

A27

📱124

BRIDGE

Newmarket
Inn

SNACK BAR IN
LAY BY 6AM-4PM

PATH CUTS
UNDER RAILWAY

📱125

36

ROUTE GUIDE AND MAPS

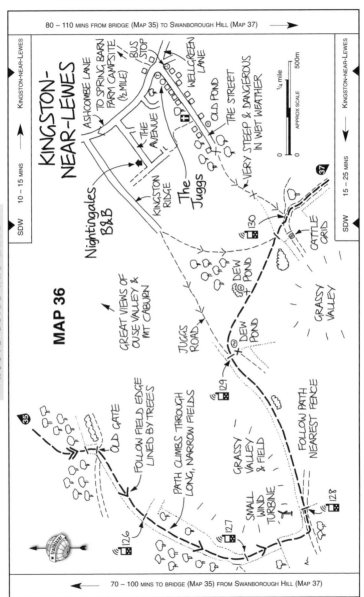

80 – 110 MINS FROM BRIDGE (MAP 35) TO SWANBOROUGH HILL (MAP 37)

KINGSTON-NEAR-LEWES

SDW 10 – 15 MINS

KINGSTON-NEAR-LEWES

KINGSTON-NEAR-LEWES

KINGSTON-NEAR-LEWES

SDW 15 – 25 MINS

KINGSTON-NEAR-LEWES

ASHCOMBE LANE
TO SPRING BARN / FARM CAMPSITE (½ MILE)

BUS STOP

WELLGREEN LANE

OLD POND

THE STREET

THE AVENUE

VERY STEEP & DANGEROUS IN WET WEATHER

KINGSTON RIDGE

The Juggs

Nightingales B&B

MAP 36

GREAT VIEWS OF OUSE VALLEY & MT CABURN

¼ mile

500m

APPROX SCALE

0

0

37

130

CATTLE GRID

DEW POND

GRASSY VALLEY

JUGGS ROAD

DEW POND

35

OLD GATE

FOLLOW FIELD EDGE LINED BY TREES

PATH CLIMBS THROUGH LONG, NARROW FIELDS

129

GRASSY VALLEY & FIELD

FOLLOW PATH NEAREST FENCE

SMALL WIND TURBINE

128

127

126

70 – 100 MINS TO BRIDGE (MAP 35) FROM SWANBOROUGH HILL (MAP 37)

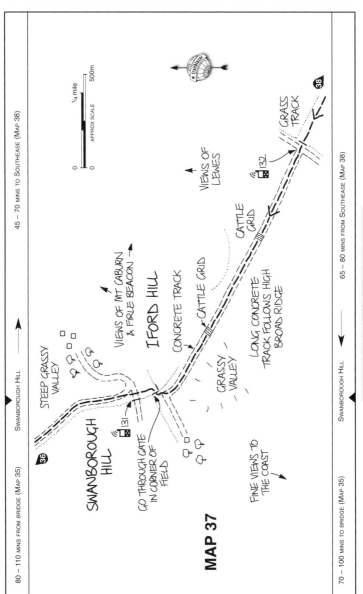

TELSCOMBE   **off MAP 38**
Telscombe YHA Hostel (☎ 0845-371 9663,
🖥 www.yha.org.uk/hostel/telscombe; 5 x
4-bed rooms, 1 x 2-bed; from £13, private
rooms from £29) is best reached by leaving
the South Downs Way at the farm buildings

at the bottom of the steep path down Mill
Hill. Note that the hostel is often taken by
groups for sole occupancy so it is essential
to book in advance. The hostel is self catering only but there is a shop selling basic
provisions. There is also a drying room.

RODMELL   **MAP 38**
Rodmell is famous for having been home
to Virginia Woolf (see box below) and her
husband Leonard. **Monk's House** (☎
01273-474760, Apr-Oct Wed-Sun 1-5pm,
£5.80 or free to NT members), where they
once lived, is now open to the public.
    The only **bus** service is Compass's No
123 (Lewes–Newhaven); see pp44-6.

Where to stay, eat and drink
Opposite the pub is the friendly *Sunnyside
Cottage B&B* (☎ 01273-476876; 1T, or Tr,
en suite; 🐾; Ⓛ) with B&B at £36pp (sgl
occ also £36) including a good cooked
breakfast. The accommodation is like a separate flat though the entrance is through the
main house. The sitting room has a single
sofa bed so three can sleep here but access
to the shower and toilet is through the main
bedroom. Nearby, *Rodmell House* (☎
01273-479620; 🖥 www.rodmell.net/index
.php?page=1228; 1S/1D, en suite; 🐾; Ⓛ)
offers B&B from £37.50pp. The single
room isn't available on Fri or Sat.

Deep Thatch Cottage (☎ 01273-
477086; 🖥 deepthatchcottage.co.uk; 1T/
2D en suite; WI-FI; 🐾 £5 per dog; Ⓛ),
offers accommodation in three apartments
each with bedroom, bathroom and kitchen.
Everything for breakfast is supplied for you
to prepare yourself though, if arranged in
advance, a cooked breakfast is available for
£5pp (not in the Annexe apartment). They
charge £42.50-47.50pp.
    Ash Tree Cottage (☎ 01273-477982,
🖥 www.ashtreerodmellbandb.co.uk; 1D en
suite; WI-FI; Ⓛ) is also self-contained and
has its own entrance, patio and garden; a
continental breakfast is provided. They
charge from £37.50pp (from £60 sgl occ).
    The Abergavenny Arms (☎ 01273-
472416, 🖥 www.abergavennyarms.com;
bar daily noon-11pm; food Apr-Oct Mon-
Sat noon-3pm & 6-9pm, Oct-Mar same but
till 2.30pm Mon-Sat) is a great place to take
a break and sit by the log fire if it's cold. The
filled rustic rolls (£6) make a perfect light
lunch. The well inside the pub was once the
main source of water for the entire village.

❏ **Virginia Woolf and the Bloomsbury Group**
Born in 1882 in London, Virginia Woolf was a highly accomplished novelist, writing
such titles as *The Voyage Out*, *Night and Day*, and *Jacob's Room*. In 1912 she married Leonard Woolf. Their links with Sussex began in 1919 when they moved to the
18th-century **Monk's House** in Rodmell. Their friends included a number of famous
artists and writers of the time, not least Virginia's sister the artist Vanessa Bell. Along
with the poet TS Eliot and the artists Duncan Grant, Roger Fry and Clive Bell they
were known collectively as the Bloomsbury Group.
    Many of the paintings from the Bloomsbury Group can be seen in the gallery at
the former home of Vanessa Bell and Duncan Grant, **Charleston Manor** (see p156),
and also in the small church of St Michael and All Angels at **Berwick** (see p160).
    Woolf's life was beset by frequent and sometimes enduring spells of mental
breakdown. She tried to kill herself through defenestration (ie throwing herself from a
window) before finally, on 18 March 1941, filling her pockets with stones and drown-
ing herself in the nearby River Ouse. Her husband was left with a suicide note in which
she spelt out the depths of her love for him: 'If anybody could have saved me it would
have been you. Everything has gone from me but the certainty of your goodness'.

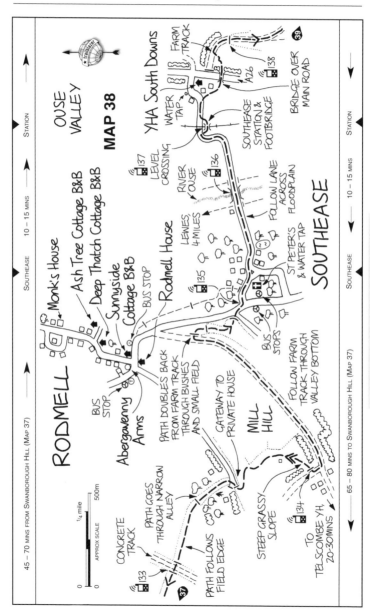

45 – 70 MINS FROM SWANBOROUGH HILL (MAP 37)

STATION

SOUTHEASE   10 – 15 MINS

OUSE VALLEY

MAP 38

YHA South Downs

Monk's House

Ash Tree Cottage B&B

Deep Thatch Cottage B&B

Sunnyside Cottage B&B

Rodmell House

BUS STOP

RODMELL

BUS STOP

Abergavenny Arms

PATH DOUBLES BACK FROM FARM TRACK THROUGH BUSHES AND SMALL FIELD

GATEWAY TO PRIVATE HOUSE

PATH GOES THROUGH NARROW ALLEY

CONCRETE TRACK

PATH FOLLOWS FIELD EDGE

¹⁄₄ mile
500m
APPROX SCALE

37

133

134

TO TELSCOMBE YH, 20-30MINS

STEEP GRASSY SLOPE

MILL HILL

FOLLOW FARM TRACK THROUGH VALLEY BOTTOM

65 – 80 MINS TO SWANBOROUGH HILL (MAP 37)

SOUTHEASE   10 – 15 MINS

STATION

SOUTHEASE

ST PETER'S & WATER TAP

BUS STOPS

LEWES, 4 MILES

135

136

FOLLOW LANE ACROSS FLOODPLAIN

RIVER OUSE

137

LEVEL CROSSING

SOUTHEASE STATION & FOOTBRIDGE

WATER TAP

138

A26

FARM TRACK

39

BRIDGE OVER MAIN ROAD

ROUTE GUIDE AND MAPS

SOUTHEASE MAP 38, p155

Pretty little Southease is tucked away from any main roads, with a tiny Saxon church, **St Peter's**, incorporating an unusual Norman round tower. This round tower is one of three in Sussex, all in the Ouse Valley and all built in the first half of the 12th century. Inside the church are the remains of some 13th-century wall paintings which once covered the whole church; they were revealed again in the 1930s.

YHA South Downs (☎ 0845-371 9574, 💻 www.yha.org.uk/hostel/south-downs; rooms with 2-8 beds; some are en suite and some have double beds; from £20pp, private rooms from £35), opened in 2013 near Southease railway station. It has a restaurant (which is licensed), a drying room and laundry facilities. Other options are **camping** (£11pp) and heated **camping pods** (2 x 3-/4-bed, from £30.50/40.50); bedding is not provided in the pods so you need to have a sleeping bag.

Because Southease is on the **railway** line between Brighton and Seaford it's an ideal place to start or end a day walk; services operate approximately once an hour. Compass Travel's **bus** No 123, between Lewes and Newhaven, stops here; see the public transport map and table, pp44-6.

SOUTHEASE TO ALFRISTON MAPS 38-42

Continuing along the crest of the escarpment, with the high point at Firle Beacon (Map 40), this stretch affords easy walking for **7¾ miles (12.5km, 2½-3½hrs)** with fine views to the coast and across the lowlands to **Mount Caburn**, probably the most grandiose name for any hill of 150 metres altitude. Once past **Bostal Hill** (Map 41) the path drops steadily down to pretty wee Alfriston.

WEST FIRLE off MAP 40, p158

This small village among the trees lies at the foot of the Downs escarpment. **Firle Stores & Post Office** (☎ 01273-858219; Mon-Fri 9am-1pm & 2-5.30pm, Sat 9am-1pm and also May-Sep until 3pm on Sat and 10.30am-4pm on Sun), offers plenty of choice for your lunchbox.

The Ram Inn (☎ 01273-858222; 💻 www.raminn.co.uk; 2D/2T en suite; ♥; 🐕 £20; WI-FI; Ⓛ) charges £47.50-72.50pp (sgl occ £80-145) for B&B. Food (main dishes £10-19) is served in what was formerly the Court Room where judges once passed sentence on misbehaving villagers. The real ales are worth the detour and the bar is open 11.30am-11.30pm every day with the kitchen open daily 9am-9.30pm.

About a mile from the village is **Charleston Manor** (☎ 01323-811626, 💻 www.charleston.org.uk; late Mar-Oct Wed-Sun daily 1-6pm (-5.30pm Sun), July & Aug from noon, admission £12.50 by timed ticket) which houses a gallery of work by the Bloomsbury group of artists (see box p154), and hosts a festival each May (see p16). Charleston is a stop on Compass Travel's No 126 (as well as their No 124 school-day Alfriston to Ringmer) **bus** service; when it is open it is also a stop on Cuckmere Community Bus's infrequent No 40 service. See pp44-6.

ALCISTON off MAP 41, p159

Alciston is yet another beautiful but tiny downland village with little to draw the walker here apart from ***The Rose Cottage Inn*** (☎ 01323-870377, 💻 www.therosecottageinn.com; 1S with kitchenette/2D in self-contained flats; ♥; WI-FI in bar area only; food Mon-Sat noon-2pm & 6.30-9.30pm, Sun noon-3pm), a genuine country pub that has been around for over 350 years. Timber framing and open fires add to the charm and there is also a good choice of locally brewed ales. There is a mouthwatering menu based on locally sourced produce: the restaurant menu contains a wide selection of fish dishes as well as standard pub fare. The self-contained flats (with kitchen/lounge diner, toilet & shower room) cost £35-37.50pp (sgl occ full room rate); the single room costs £40. Note that there is a **two-night** minimum stay.

Alciston is a stop on Cuckmere Community Buses' infrequent Nos 42 and 44 **bus** services. See pp44-6.

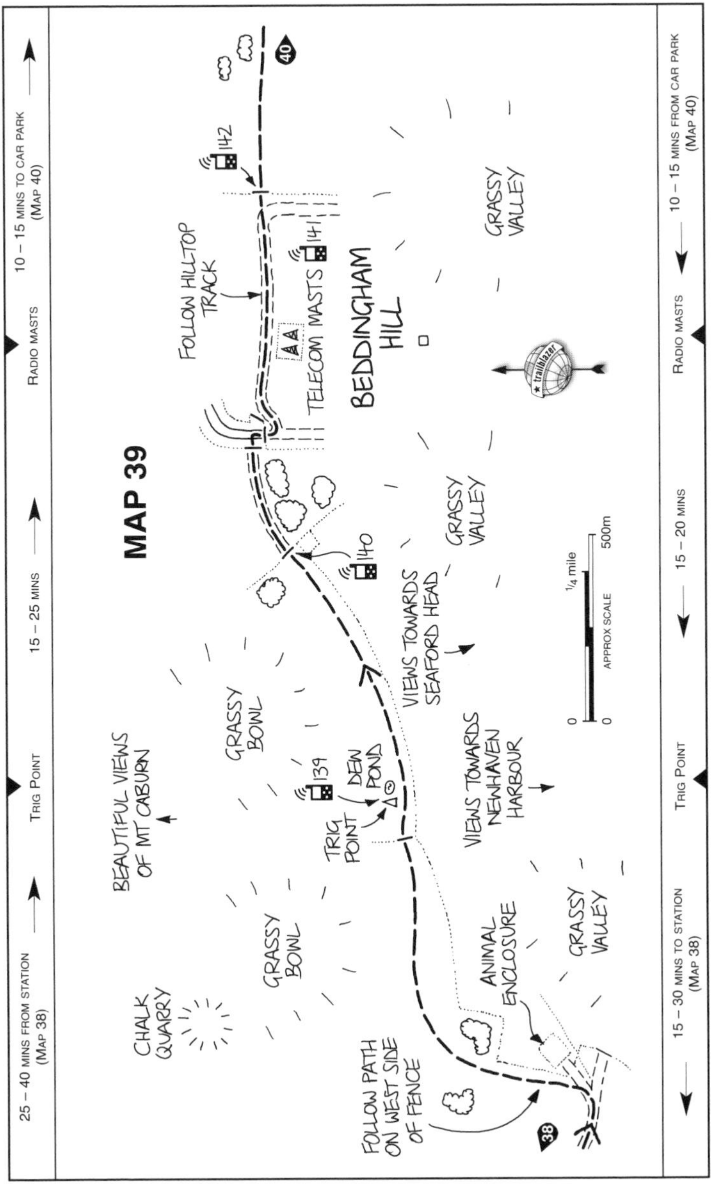

MAP 39

25 – 40 MINS FROM STATION (MAP 38) ← | TRIG POINT ← | 15 – 25 MINS → | RADIO MASTS ▶ | 10 – 15 MINS TO CAR PARK (MAP 40) →

CHALK QUARRY

GRASSY BOWL

BEAUTIFUL VIEWS OF MT CABURN ↑

GRASSY BOWL

FOLLOW PATH ON WEST SIDE OF FENCE

38

ANIMAL ENCLOSURE

GRASSY VALLEY

TRIG POINT

DEW POND

139

VIEWS TOWARDS NEWHAVEN HARBOUR

VIEWS TOWARDS SEAFORD HEAD

140

GRASSY VALLEY

FOLLOW HILLTOP TRACK

142

141

TELECOM MASTS

BEDDINGHAM HILL

GRASSY VALLEY

GRASSY VALLEY

40

¼ mile
APPROX SCALE
0   500m

15 – 30 MINS TO STATION (MAP 38) ← | TRIG POINT | ← 15 – 20 MINS → | RADIO MASTS | 10 – 15 MINS FROM CAR PARK (MAP 40) →

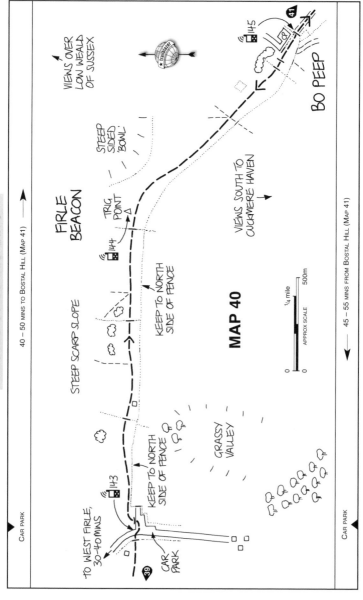

CAR PARK

40 – 50 MINS TO BOSTAL HILL (MAP 41) →

VIEWS OVER
LOW WEALD
OF SUSSEX

★ trailblazer

FIRLE
BEACON

STEEP
SIDED
'BOWL'

STEEP SCARP SLOPE

TRIG
POINT △

🏠 144

KEEP TO NORTH
SIDE OF FENCE

MAP 40

VIEWS SOUTH TO
CUCKMERE HAVEN

🏠 145

BO PEEP

41

¼ mile

0   500m
0   APPROX SCALE

🏠 143

KEEP TO NORTH
SIDE OF FENCE

GRASSY
VALLEY

TO WEST FIRLE,
30–40MINS →

CAR
PARK

39

CAR PARK

← 45 – 55 MINS FROM BOSTAL HILL (MAP 41)

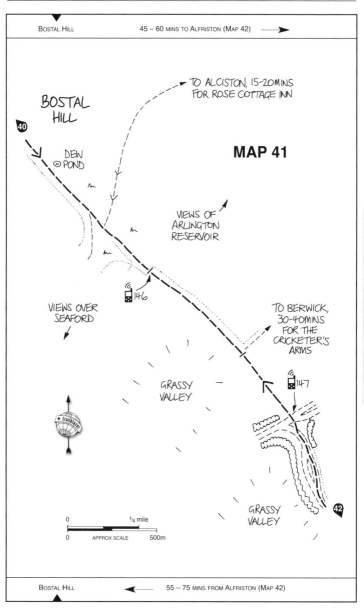

BOSTAL HILL   45 – 60 MINS TO ALFRISTON (MAP 42) ⟶

BOSTAL
HILL

40

DEW
POND

TO ALCISTON, 15-20MINS
FOR ROSE COTTAGE INN

MAP 41

VIEWS OF
ARLINGTON
RESERVOIR

146

VIEWS OVER
SEAFORD

TO BERWICK,
30-40MINS
FOR THE
CRICKETER'S
ARMS

147

GRASSY
VALLEY

0   ¼ mile
0   APPROX SCALE   500m

GRASSY
VALLEY

42

ROUTE GUIDE AND MAPS

BOSTAL HILL   ⟵   55 – 75 MINS FROM ALFRISTON (MAP 42)

BERWICK   off MAP 41, p159

Berwick is famous for the Bloomsbury Group of Victorian artists which included Vanessa Bell, Roger Fry and Duncan Grant. Some of Vanessa Bell's work can be seen in the small **church** on the edge of the village.

For food head to *The Cricketer's Arms* (☎ 01323-870469, 🖳 www.cricketers berwick.co.uk; food Apr-Sep daily noon-8.30pm, mid Sep-Apr Mon-Fri noon-2.15pm & 6-8.30pm, Sat noon-8.30pm, Sun noon-8pm). Their menu generally includes sharing platters and pub favourites such as ham, eggs & chips (£11) and in the summer a range of salads.

Berwick is a stop on the Ore/Eastbourne to Brighton **railway** line as well as on the Ashford International to Brighton line on Sundays. Compass Travel's No 125 (Eastbourne to Lewes) **bus** service calls here as does its No 126 (Eastbourne to Berwick) service during the week. Cuckmere Community **Bus** (CCB) operates the 126 on Sundays and bank hol Mons. Their No 47 (Cuckmere Valley Rambler) service runs in summer. CCB also has some routes which operate on different days of the week. Many bus services connect with train arrivals here, making it a good place to start or end a day walk. See pp44-6.

ALFRISTON   MAP 42

Alfriston is another candidate for 'prettiest village on the South Downs Way'. However, this small collection of Tudor wood-beamed buildings slung higgledy-piggledy along a narrow main street is far from a well-kept secret. In high season coachloads of tourists come to 'ooh' and 'ahh' at the sights and have cream teas. Nevertheless, it is worth planning on spending a few hours to take it all in at a leisurely pace.

Whilst here make sure you take a look around the **church** and the **Clergy House** (see box below) by the church and the village green.

Services

The **post office** (Mon-Fri 9am-5.30pm, Sat 9am-12.30pm) on The Square doubles as the village **shop/deli** (Mon-Sat 8am-7pm, Sun 10am-5pm). It is worth a visit just to take in its almost authentic 'Olde Worlde' atmosphere. The now-forgotten 'Lamson' system of moving cash to a single cashier

whereby cannisters containing the money were shot along wires and tubes is still in place, though no longer used. The deli here is a great place to pick up the ingredients for a top-class picnic.

There's an excellent independent bookshop, **Much Ado Books** (☎ 01323-871222, 🖳 www.muchadobooks.com; Mon-Sat 10am-5pm, Sun 11am-5pm) with an interesting stock of old and new books, maps and guides. Another good place to browse is **Music Memorabilia**, a record and CD shop.

For those with a sweet tooth, **Munchlicious** (daily 10am-5pm) sells a bewildering array of chocolate; anything from Columbian to organic. They sell ice creams in the summer months and also have traditional sweets.

Compass's No 125 **bus** service (Lewes to Eastbourne) calls here as does its No 124 school-day service to/from Ringmer and its No 126 (Eastbourne to Berwick) service, though on Sundays this is operated by

---

❏ Alfriston Church and Clergy House

The 14th-century flint church by the river sits in the middle of a well-groomed lawn and is worth a look, as is the Clergy House (☎ 01323-871961, 🖳 www.nation altrust.org.uk; daily except Thur & Fri late Feb-mid Mar & Nov-mid Dec 11am-4pm, mid Mar-end Oct 10.30am-5pm; £5.50) nearby. This beautiful 14th-century, timber-framed thatched house was the first property the National Trust bought thanks to the local vicar who in 1896 suggested the building be safeguarded for the nation. Apart from anything else it's a good spot for lunch.

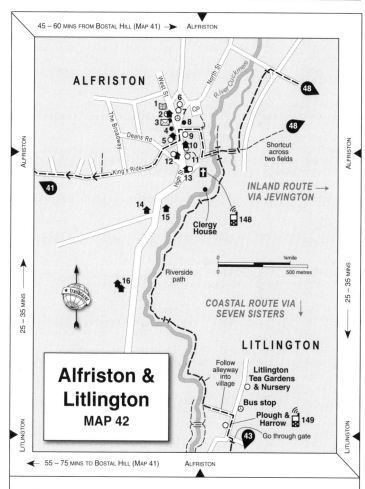

45 – 60 MINS FROM BOSTAL HILL (MAP 41) ⟶ ALFRISTON

ALFRISTON

ALFRISTON

ALFRISTON

West St

North St

River Cuckmere

The Broadway

Deans Rd

King's Ride

High St

CP

1
6
2
7
3
8
4
9
5
10
12
11
13

48

48

Shortcut across two fields

INLAND ROUTE ⟶ VIA JEVINGTON

148

Clergy House

Riverside path

COASTAL ROUTE VIA SEVEN SISTERS ↓

25 – 35 MINS

25 – 35 MINS

14
15

16

★ trailblazer

Alfriston & Litlington MAP 42

LITLINGTON

LITLINGTON

Follow alleyway into village

Litlington Tea Gardens & Nursery

Bus stop

Plough & Harrow 149

43 Go through gate

0 ¼mile
0 500 metres

⟵ 55 – 75 MINS TO BOSTAL HILL (MAP 41) ALFRISTON

ROUTE GUIDE AND MAPS

Where to stay
2 Ye Olde Smugglers Inne (Market Inn)
5 The Star Inn
10 The George Inn
12 Chestnuts B&B
13 Wingrove House
14 Dacres
15 Deans Place Hotel
16 Riverdale House & Highcroft B&B

Where to eat and drink
2 Ye Olde Smugglers Inne (Market Inn)
3 Deli (in Village Shop)
5 The Star Inn
6 Badgers Tea House
7 The Singing Kettle
9 The Apiary
10 The George Inn

11 Moonrakers
12 Chestnuts
13 Wingrove House

Other
1 Much Ado Books
3 Village Shop/Deli & PO
4 Music Memorabilia
8 Munchlicious

Cuckmere Community Bus (CCB); in the summer months CCB runs the No 47 at weekends; its Nos 40, 42 and 44 services operate some days of the week. See public transport map and table, pp44-6.

Where to stay

For the latest information on accommodation it's worth checking the village website: ☐ www.alfriston-village.co.uk

In the village itself there are few cheap options though B&B at *Chestnuts* (☎ 01323-870959, ☐ chestnutsalfriston.co.uk; 1D or T/1D/1T shared bathroom; ✒; 🐾; WI-FI; Ⓛ) costs £35-40pp (sgl occ £50-60). They also have a *tearoom* (Tue-Sat 10.30am-5pm, Sun 10.30am-4.30pm).

Dacres (☎ 01323-870447, ☐ pat syembry@gmail.com; 1Tr en suite; WI-FI; Ⓛ) charges from £45pp (sgl occ £55) for B&B or less £5 without breakfast. The room is open plan and more of a studio apartment; the excellent organic cooked breakfasts are served here and the hospitable owner will provide a vegetarian or vegan breakfast if preferred. There's also a lovely garden to relax in.

Riverdale House (☎ 01323-871038, ☐ www.riverdalehouse.co.uk; 3D/1D or T/1Tr; all en suite; ✒; WI-FI) is peacefully located on the edge of the village, off Seaford Rd. It's a very comfortable B&B and two aerobeds can be put in one of the doubles allowing four to sleep in the room. Rates range from £45 to £72.50pp (sgl occ rates on request; three/four sharing £110/150). Luggage transfer is available by prior arrangement: to/from Lewes and Eastbourne (£20 per trip). Sharing the same driveway as Riverdale next door, *Highcroft B&B* (☎ 01323-870553, ☐ www.highcroftalfriston.co.uk; 2D en suite, 1T private bathroom; ✒; WI-FI) charges £42.50-47.50pp (sgl occ £70-95); an additional bed can be put in one of the doubles (three sharing: room rate plus £25).

Wingrove House (☎ 01323-870276, ☐ www.wingrovehousealfriston.com; 7D, all en suite; ✒; WI-FI) is a restaurant with rooms in the 19th-century colonial style building. The rooms are luxurious and the food good. B&B costs £50-100pp.

The Star Inn (☎ 01323-870495, ☐ www.thestaralfriston.co.uk; 2S/21D/14T, all en suite; ✒; 🐾 £10; WI-FI; Ⓛ) is one of the oldest inns in England, said to date back to 1345. Prices for B&B vary considerably depending on season but expect to pay £45-70pp (sgl/sgl occ £70-140).

The George Inn (☎ 01323-870319, ☐ www.thegeorge-alfriston.com; 5D, all en suite; ✒; 🐾; WI-FI; Ⓛ) is a magnificent old building with oak beams. B&B costs £50-70pp (sgl occ £75-110) but they also have dinner, bed and breakfast rates. There is a minimum two-night booking policy at the weekend in the summer.

Ye Olde Smugglers Inne (aka The Market Inn; ☎ 01323-870241; ☐ www .yeoldesmugglersinne.co.uk; 1T/1D shared bathroom, 1D or T private bathroom, 1D en suite shower; ✒; 🐾 £5; WI-FI; Ⓛ) charges from £35pp plus £5 for breakfast. The name is derived from a famous gang of smugglers (see box p164) who once used the pub to plan smuggling ventures at Cuckmere Haven.

At the southern end of the village is the large *Deans Place Hotel* (☎ 01323-870248, ☐ www.deansplacehotel.co.uk; 3S/29D or T/4Tr, all en suite; ✒; 🐾 £5; WI-FI) a smart 14th-century country house hotel set in a big garden with manicured lawns and a swimming-pool (summer only). B&B costs £50-80pp (sgl £57.50-87.50; three sharing around £137.50); contact them also to enquire if they have any special deals.

Where to eat and drink

For such a small village Alfriston does well for pubs and cafés, many of which have long histories.

Badgers Tea House (☎ 01323-871336, ☐ www.badgersteahouse.com; Mon-Fri 9.30am-4pm, Sat & Sun 10am-4.30pm; note that they stop serving food at 3.30pm every day) is a traditional English teashop with a little walled garden to sit in. Housed in a building dating back to 1510, they serve breakfasts (from £8.95), a selection of home-made cakes, soups served with chunky bread (£5.95), light lunches (dressed crab £8.95) and cream teas (£6.50).

Of a similar ilk is *The Singing Kettle* (☎ 01323-870723; daily 10am-5pm) which does tasty snacks such as buck rarebit (cheese on toast with a poached egg on top), and *Chestnuts Tearoom* (see Where to stay; Tue-Sat 10.30am-5pm, Sun 10.30am-4.30pm).

Ye Olde Smugglers Inne (aka The Market Inn; see Where to stay; food daily noon-9pm) has friendly staff and an attractive conservatory at the back. They serve good-value pub grub with specials from £5 mid-week evenings.

One of the best pubs is undoubtedly *The George Inn* (see Where to stay; daily noon-9pm); the menu changes seasonally and mains cost from £13.

The Apiary (☎ 01323-870730, daily 10am-5pm) is a coffee shop one side and a dress shop the other. There's a nice garden and they also serve soups, paninis and cream teas (£6).

The Star Inn (see Where to stay; food daily noon-2.30pm & 6-9pm, all day in holiday periods) has bar meals and a restaurant which is usually candlelit and in winter there is a roaring fire. The two/three-course roast Sunday lunch menu is £13.95/£16.95, they have cheaper bar meals and they do a decent cream tea for £5.50.

Moonrakers Restaurant (☎ 01323-871199, 🖳 www.moonrakersrestaurant.co .uk; Mar-Oct Tue-Sun 10am-5pm, Oct-Mar weekends only; Fri & Sat from 7pm) is a tea room (serving afternoon tea) though they also offer breakfast, light lunches and also have a set three-course menu for £25.

Wingrove House (see Where to stay; Mon-Fri 6-9.30pm, Sat noon-2.30pm & 6-9.30pm, Sun noon-2.30pm & 6-7.30pm) is a restaurant with rooms. An excellent three-course dinner is £29 and might include 'oven roasted rack of Sussex marsh lamb, slow roasted shoulder and broad bean fricassee, fresh mint pesto'. The provenance of many of the locally sourced ingredients is given on the menu.

ALFRISTON TO EASTBOURNE (COASTAL ROUTE VIA CUCKMERE)
MAPS 42-47

These **10½ miles (17km, 4¼-5¾hrs** – plus another 1½ miles to Eastbourne; see town map p179) are arguably the highlight of the whole walk, including a stretch through the beautiful **Cuckmere Valley** (Map 43, p165) which culminates in wide meanders leading to what is one of the few undeveloped river mouths in the South-East.

The final assault on Eastbourne is a spectacular roller-coaster ride over the **Seven Sisters** (or should that be eight; see Map 44, p167 & Map 45, p168), a line of chalk cliffs that are less famous than their Dover counterparts but far more spectacular.

If that was not enough the path continues to reach the final high point of the whole walk: **Beachy Head**, a spectacular chalk cliff jutting into the English Channel with 360° views (Map 47, p170). Even the sprawling mess of Eastbourne is well worth admiring from here.

The path finishes at the foot of the hill where it meets abruptly with Eastbourne's suburbs. There is accommodation and refreshments in the neighbourhood of **Meads Village** (see p171) but if you want to go into Eastbourne there is a bus (see p178) or a rather tedious half-hour walk to the town centre. Alternatively, after walking one hundred miles there is no shame in calling a **taxi** to the town centre and Eastbourne Taxis (☎ 01323-720720) have a reliable fleet.

LITLINGTON
MAP 42, p161

Sitting on the eastern bank of the Cuckmere River, Litlington is yet another oh-so-charming little downland village complete with flint cottages. On the other side of the valley is a chalk-horse figure carved into the hillside by a certain James Pagden.

The local pub is *The Plough and Harrow* (☎ 01323-870632, 🖥 www.plough andharrowlitlington.co.uk; food Mon-Fri noon-3pm & 6-9pm, Sat noon-9pm, Sun noon-8.30pm) which serves a variety of bar meals ranging from a ploughman's lunch (£8.50) to pan-roasted guinea fowl (£13.50). The bar is open all day. This village is also home to *Litlington Tea Gardens & Nursery* (☎ 01323-870222; Apr-Nov Tue-Sun & bank hols 11am-5pm). If it's not too busy you could stop for a cup of tea and a scone in the lovely garden.

Litlington is a stop on Cuckmere Community Bus's No 47 **bus** service which operates at weekends in the summer months; also their No 40 service though this only runs on Tuesday and Friday. See the public transport map and table on pp44-6.

❏ **Smuggling**

Smuggling of wool, brandy and gin was rife along the Sussex coast with Cuckmere Haven and Birling Gap being favourite places for gangs of smugglers to load and unload their contraband in the late 18th and early 19th centuries. One of the most infamous groups was the Alfriston Gang who would smuggle goods to and from Cuckmere Haven along the Cuckmere River.

The leader of the Alfriston Gang was Stanton Collins who owned the now aptly named Ye Olde Smugglers Inne from where the group plotted their exploits. These included a raid on a Dutch ship wrecked at Cuckmere Haven. The figurehead of the ship, a red lion's head, still stands next to the Star Inn in the village. Stanton Collins was eventually arrested in 1831 for sheep rustling and was shipped off to Australia.

WESTDEAN & EXCEAT
MAP 43

On the north side of the small wooded ridge of chalk is the wonderfully secluded and secret **Westdean**, a tiny collection of beautiful cottages complete with duck pond, nestled in a wooded fold. On the other side of the ridge is **Exceat**, more a collection of tourist facilities than a village but with a very good information centre. This is the gateway to the **Seven Sisters Country Park** (see box p166) and the spectacular Cuckmere Valley and beach.

If Exceat is an overnight stop on your walk, try to arrive here early in the day to give yourself time to enjoy the area around the beach.

Services

The excellent **information centre** (now staffed by volunteers and open irregular hours) next to the path, has information on wildlife and conservation efforts in the Seven Sisters Country Park. **Bikes** can be hired (from £30 a day) next door at Seven Sisters Cycle Co (☎ 01323-870310, 🖥 www.cuckmere-cycle.co.uk; Apr-Oct daily 10am-6pm, Oct-Mar Tue-Sun 10am-5pm). There's a **water fountain** behind the toilet block.

Brighton & Hove Buses' Nos 12/12X, 12A and 13X **bus** services pass through Exceat and provide regular links between Brighton and Eastbourne. Cuckmere Community Bus's No 47 service stops at Seven Sisters Country Park at weekends in the summer months and their No 40 service calls at both Westdean and Exceat but only on Tuesday and Friday; see the public transport map and table, pp44-6.

Where to stay and eat

Saltmarsh Farmhouse (☎ 01323-870218), formerly known as Exceat Farmhouse, is currently being restored and will have five en suite B&B rooms available from summer 2015. However, the *restaurant* (10am-5pm), offering lunches, drinks and delicious home-made cakes, is open now.

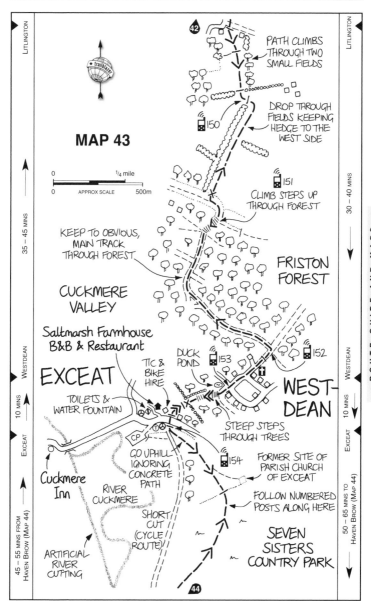

LITLINGTON

MAP 43

0   ¼ mile
0   APPROX SCALE   500m

42

PATH CLIMBS THROUGH TWO SMALL FIELDS

DROP THROUGH FIELDS KEEPING HEDGE TO THE WEST SIDE

150

151

CLIMB STEPS UP THROUGH FOREST

KEEP TO OBVIOUS, MAIN TRACK THROUGH FOREST

FRISTON FOREST

CUCKMERE VALLEY

Saltmarsh Farmhouse B&B & Restaurant

DUCK POND

153

152

EXCEAT

TIC & BIKE HIRE

WEST-DEAN

TOILETS & WATER FOUNTAIN

STEEP STEPS THROUGH TREES

CP

GO UPHILL IGNORING CONCRETE PATH

154

FORMER SITE OF PARISH CHURCH OF EXCEAT

Cuckmere Inn

RIVER CUCKMERE

FOLLOW NUMBERED POSTS ALONG HERE

SHORT CUT (CYCLE ROUTE)

SEVEN SISTERS COUNTRY PARK

ARTIFICIAL RIVER CUTTING

44

LITLINGTON

30 – 40 MINS

WESTDEAN

10 MINS

50 – 65 MINS TO HAVEN BROW (MAP 44)

35 – 45 MINS

WESTDEAN

10 MINS

EXCEAT

45 – 55 MINS FROM HAVEN BROW (MAP 44)

By the bridge, the large ***Cuckmere Inn*** (☎ 01323-892247, 🖳 www.vintageinn.co.uk/thecuckmereinnseaford; food Mon-Sat noon-10pm, Sun noon-9.30pm; WI-FI) has a big garden overlooking the River Cuckmere. Their menu includes standard pub fare; fish & chips from £8.50. It gets very busy during the summer due to its great location. If staying at Saltmarsh and visiting the pub in the evening, take a torch as the road between the two is unlit.

(Note that **Foxhole Campsite** is open only to educational groups. For information call ☎ 0345-608 0193).

❏ Seven Sisters Country Park

This extensive country park (🖳 www.sevensisters.org.uk) of rolling coastal downland includes the spectacular Seven Sisters chalk cliffs over which the South Downs Way passes. There is an excellent visitor centre at Exceat where you can glean all sorts of information from the displays and exhibitions.

Apart from the obvious attraction of the chalk cliffs and downland the park also includes Cuckmere Haven and estuary, one of the only river mouths in the south-east of England that has not been spoilt by development. That is not to say that the estuary is untouched. The natural meanders of the river, seen so spectacularly from the ridge above Exceat, have been left to sit as idle ponds thanks to the man-made channel that diverts the flow of the river more swiftly to the sea. Plans were underway to restore the Cuckmere Estuary to its natural state by filling in the man-made channel and allowing the blockade to gradually deteriorate. This would have restored the flow of the river through the meanders and encouraged the natural restoration of the salt-marsh and mudflats. However, by 2006 this plan had been suspended after a 'modelling miscalculation' by the project's environmental consultant was found.

The country park covers an area steeped in history. Some of the most fascinating stories involve the numerous shipwrecks that litter the seabed below the Seven Sisters' cliffs. The most significant of these is that of the Spanish ship *Nympha Americana* which, in 1747, ran aground halfway along the line of chalk cliffs, resulting in the deaths of thirty crewmen.

BIRLING GAP   MAP 45, p168

All that's in this gap is a small line of terraced houses that are falling into the sea, a B&B and a café/bar. Considering the beautiful position of the hamlet on a low saddle along the line of chalk cliffs, it's a shame that some of the buildings are so ugly and out of place. However, now that the hotel has been closed and been taken over by the National Trust as a café perhaps they can do something to make the place more in keeping with the surroundings. The attractive fish design fence is a good start.

Birling Gap is a stop on both the 12A and 13X bus services operated by Brighton and Hove Buses; see pp44-6.

The Boathouse B&B (☎ 01323-423073; 2D, both en suite) is perfectly located and the friendly owner offers B&B for £30pp (sgl occ £35).

National Trust Birling Gap Café (☎ 01323-423197, 🖳 www.nationaltrust.org.uk; food daily 10am-4pm, up to 6/7pm in the summer months) has seating both inside and outside; the menu includes a great range of cakes, salads and sandwiches; during the week hot meals (noon-2.30pm) are also available. A bacon roll and a pot of tea/coffee is £4.65, served 10-11.30am.

A 15- to 20-minute walk from Birling Gap, ***Belle Tout Lighthouse*** (Map 46; ☎ 01323-423185, 🖳 www.belletout.co.uk; 6D, all en suite; ❤; WI-FI) is now a luxury B&B with incredible coastal views. They charge £72.50-107.50pp (sgl occ £110-215). There's usually a two-night minimum stay policy but it's worth contacting them at short notice for a single-night stay. Outside the lighthouse there's a ***snack shop*** (mid-Feb to Oct) serving drinks and ice-creams.

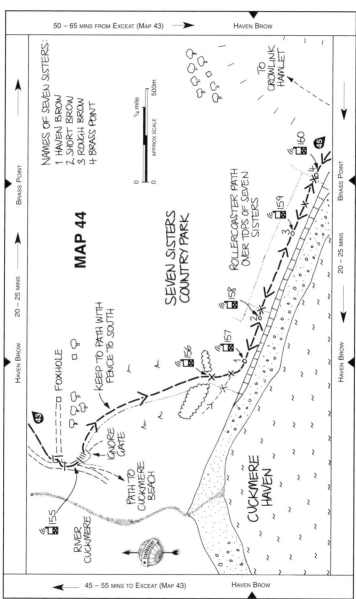

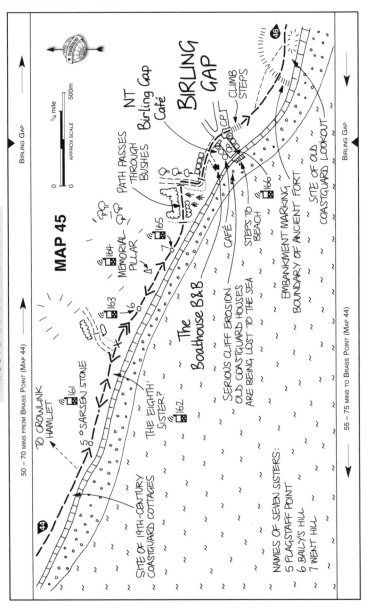

ROUTE GUIDE AND MAPS

50 – 70 MINS FROM BRASS POINT (MAP 44)

MAP 45

BIRLING GAP

trailblazer

¼ mile

500m

0   APPROX SCALE   0

BIRLING GAP

BIRLING GAP

NT
Birling Gap
Café

CLIMB
STEPS

CP

CP

PATH PASSES
THROUGH
BUSHES

165

MEMORIAL
PILLAR

164

166

163

The Boathouse B&B

TO CROWLINK
HAMLET

161

5 SARSEN STONE

THE 'EIGHTH'
SISTER?

162

SITE OF 19TH-CENTURY
COASTGUARD COTTAGES

CAFÉ

STEPS TO
BEACH

SERIOUS CLIFF EROSION.
OLD COASTGUARD HOUSES
ARE BEING LOST TO THE SEA

EMBANKMENT MARKING
BOUNDARY OF ANCIENT FORT

SITE OF OLD
COASTGUARD LOOKOUT

NAMES OF SEVEN SISTERS:
5 FLAGSTAFF POINT
6 BAILY'S HILL
7 WENT HILL

55 – 75 MINS TO BRASS POINT (MAP 44)

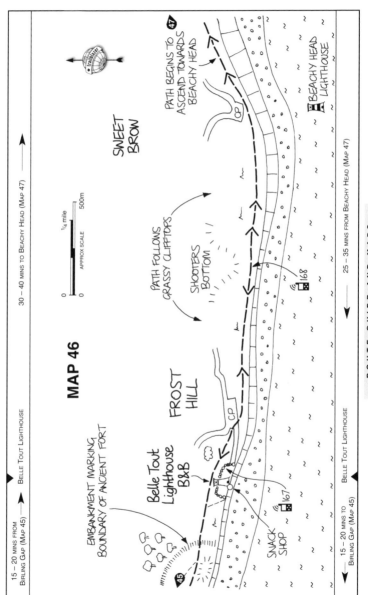

MAP 46

EMBANKMENT MARKING
BOUNDARY OF ANCIENT FORT

Belle Tout
Lighthouse B&B

PATH FOLLOWS
GRASSY CLIFFTOPS

SHOOTERS
BOTTOM

SWEET
BROW

FROST
HILL

47

PATH BEGINS TO
ASCEND TOWARDS
BEACHY HEAD

CP

CP

BEACHY HEAD
LIGHTHOUSE

168

167

SNACK
SHOP

45

¼ mile

0   500m

0

APPROX SCALE

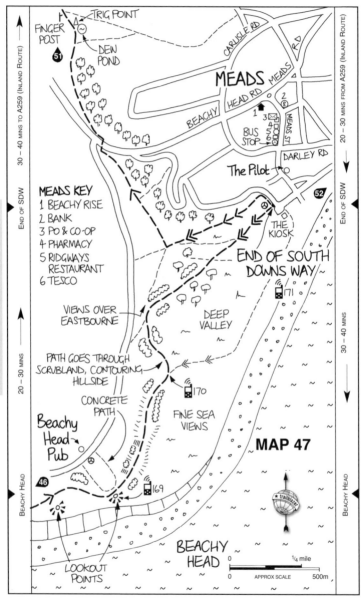

TRIG POINT

FINGER POST

51

DEW POND

CARLISLE RD

MEADS RD

MEADS

BEACHY HEAD RD

MEADS ST

1
BUS STOP
3
4
5
6
2

DARLEY RD

The Pilot

52

THE KIOSK

END OF SOUTH DOWNS WAY

171

MEADS KEY
1 BEACHY RISE
2 BANK
3 PO & CO-OP
4 PHARMACY
5 RIDGWAYS RESTAURANT
6 TESCO

VIEWS OVER EASTBOURNE

DEEP VALLEY

PATH GOES THROUGH SCRUBLAND, CONTOURING HILLSIDE

170

CONCRETE PATH

FINE SEA VIEWS

Beachy Head Pub

46

169

MAP 47

LOOKOUT POINTS

BEACHY HEAD

¼ mile

APPROX SCALE

500m

30 – 40 MINS TO A259 (INLAND ROUTE)

END OF SDW

20 – 30 MINS

BEACHY HEAD

20 – 30 MINS FROM A259 (INLAND ROUTE)

END OF SDW

30 – 40 MINS

BEACHY HEAD

ROUTE GUIDE AND MAPS

BEACHY HEAD   MAP 47

Beachy Head is, thankfully, relatively unspoilt with just one large chain pub near the top: *The Beachy Head* (☎ 01323-728060, 🖳 www.vintageinn.co.uk/the beachyheadeastbourne; food summer Mon-Sat noon-10pm, Sun noon-9.30pm, winter daily noon-9pm; WI-FI). It's not the best place to celebrate the walk's end but could be useful if you need to shelter from the weather. The food is good value.

Brighton & Hove's Nos 12A and 13X **bus** services as well as Stagecoaches' No 3/3A service call here; see public transport map and table, pp44-6.

MEADS VILLAGE   MAP 47

Meads Village is actually the most westerly suburb of Eastbourne. It is a quiet, well-to-do part of town with a genuine village feel. More importantly for South Downs Way walkers, it is positioned right at the official end of the walk, making a stop here a more appealing prospect than the half-hour walk into the hectic centre of Eastbourne.

To reach Meads Village head straight on where the South Downs Way reaches the ice-cream kiosk at the bottom of the hill and turn left at Holywell Rd.

Services

Everything one might need here is centred along one short stretch of Meads St. There is a **Co-op** (Mon-Sat 7.30am-9pm, Sun 8am-9pm) on the corner of Matlock Rd which also incorporates the **post office** (Mon-Fri 9am-5.30pm, Sat 9am-12.30pm), a **Tesco Express** (daily 6am-11pm) and a **bank** with an **ATM**.

For those requiring attention to blistered feet there's **Meads Pharmacy** (Mon-Fri 9am-1pm & 2-5.30pm, Sat 9am-1pm).

Stagecoach's No 3/3A bus service is the one to catch into central Eastbourne; see public transport map and table, pp44-6. This bus leaves from the foot of the hill at the end of the South Downs Way and also from Meads Village.

Where to stay and eat

The closest accommodation to the end of the walk – indeed the only option here – is *Beachy Rise* (☎ 01323-639171, 🖳 www .beachyrise.com; 2D/1T/1Tr, all en suite; ☛; WI-FI; Ⓛ), on Meads Rd, with B&B from £32.50pp (sgl occ £55; three sharing £90).

The Pilot (☎ 01323-723440; food summer Mon-Fri noon-2.30pm & 6-9pm, Sat noon-9pm, Sun noon-7pm; winter Mon-Sat to 8.30pm, Sun to 6pm), on a bend on Meads St, is the first pub reached after leaving the end of the South Downs Way. The bar is open all day which makes it convenient for a celebration drink. This place gets consistently good reviews.

If, after 100 miles, you feel the need to treat yourself and push the boat out book a table at the exclusive *Ridgways Restaurant* (☎ 01323-726805, 🖳 www.ridgwaysrestau rant.co.uk; Tue-Sun noon-1.45pm, Tue-Thur 6.30-8.30pm, Fri & Sat 7-8.45pm; booking strongly advised). They specialise in traditional English dishes; all main courses at lunch are £9.25; in the evening they have an à la carte menu and during the week there is a supper menu (£16.75/18.95 for 2/3 courses). The 'smart/casual wear only' notice means that the hiking boots will have to be left behind.

EASTBOURNE
For the guide to Eastbourne turn to p178.

> ❏ **Important note – walking times**
> Unless otherwise specified, **all times in this book refer only to the time spent walking**. You will need to add 20-30% to allow for rests, photography, checking the map, drinking water etc.

ALFRISTON TO EASTBOURNE (INLAND ROUTE VIA JEVINGTON)
MAP 42 p161 & MAPS 48-51

This inland **alternative route** is geared towards horse-riders and cyclists but walkers are welcome to use the bridleway too.

Although these **7½ miles (12km, 2¾-3½hrs** – plus another 1½ miles to Eastbourne centre) are not as spectacular as the coastal route there are still plenty of fine downland views to enjoy high up on **Windover Hill** (Map 48, opposite) while a detour to see the famous **Long Man of Wilmington** (see box below) is strongly recommended.

It is a good idea to keep an extra day spare for this section even if you have already walked the coastal route.

MILTON STREET   MAP 48

Milton Street is nothing more than a small collection of scattered houses. There is, however, a good pub here, *The Sussex Ox* (☎ 01323-870840, 🖳 www.thesussexox .co.uk; food served Mon-Sat noon-2.30pm & 6-9pm, Sun noon-3pm & 6-9pm). Note the pub is closed between 3pm and 6pm during the week from October to Easter but is open all day in the summer months. The menu is varied and changes daily but it usually features ox beef burger (£11.25), Sussex sausages (£11.95) and fish & chips (£10.95); as much as possible the meat they use comes from their own farm.

WILMINGTON   off MAP 48

Wilmington is best known for the Long Man, a huge chalk figure adorning Windover Hill above the village.

A little way from the South Downs Way on the main road north of the village is *Crossways Hotel* (☎ 01323-482455, 🖳 www.crosswayshotel.co.uk; 1S/4D/2T, all en suite; 🛏; WI-FI; Ⓛ) which is actually a restaurant with rooms. They offer B&B for £72.50-85pp (sgl £85) but also have two self-contained cottages (one with 1D, the other with 1D/1D or T) which can be booked for a minimum of two nights on a B&B basis, or for self-catering. From Tuesday to Saturday (7.30-8.30pm) they serve a four-course set meal including coffee and petit fours for £41; booking is recommended.

Wilmington is a stop on Compass's No 126 **bus** service; this is operated by Cuckmere Community Bus (CCB) on Sundays and bank holidays. CCB's No 47 summer service also calls here as does its No 40 (Tuesday and Friday only); see public transport map and table, pp44-6.

❏ **The Long Man of Wilmington**
No-one is quite sure when or why this large chalk figure appeared on the side of Windover Hill above Wilmington (Map 48, opposite).

Best viewed from the lane leading out of the village, he stands 70m tall and holds a vertical rod in each hand. Although it was only in 1969 that the white blocks were placed along the lines of the figure, suggestions as to when the original was made range from the prehistoric era or the Roman age to just a few hundred years ago.

As for the question of why, well that is even harder to answer. Some say he is a fertility symbol robbed of his genitalia; others claim he was carved out for fun by monks from the nearby Wilmington Priory. Or could it be that a real giant collapsed and died on that very spot?

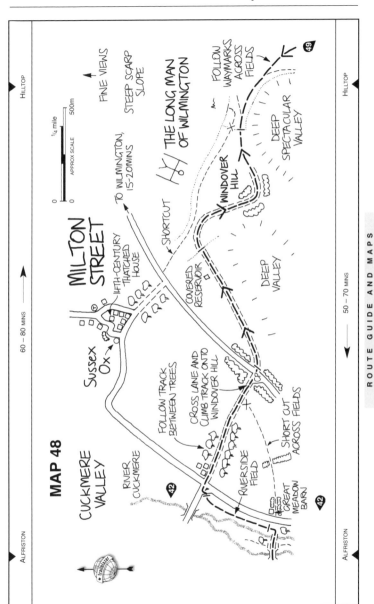

MAP 48

CUCKMERE VALLEY

RIVER CUCKMERE

ALFRISTON

60 – 80 MINS

HILLTOP

Sussex Ox

MILTON STREET

14TH-CENTURY THATCHED HOUSE

FINE VIEWS

STEEP SCARP SLOPE

APPROX SCALE

0   ¼ mile

0   500m

TO WILMINGTON, 15-20 MINS

THE LONG MAN OF WILMINGTON

FOLLOW WAYMARKS ACROSS FIELDS

49

SHORTCUT

WINDOVER HILL

DEEP SPECTACULAR VALLEY

HILLTOP

FOLLOW TRACK BETWEEN TREES

CROSS LANE AND CLIMB TRACK ONTO WINDOVER HILL

COVERED RESERVOIR

DEEP VALLEY

RIVERSIDE FIELD

SHORT CUT ACROSS FIELDS

GREAT MEADOW BARN

42

42

ALFRISTON

50 – 70 MINS

HILLTOP

JEVINGTON   MAP 49

Jevington, sitting comfortably in the Cuckmere valley, is another beautiful village that provides a good alternative stop to the somewhat exploited streets of Alfriston.

Jevington is a stop on Cuckmere Community Buses' No 41 service which operates on Tuesday and Thursday only; see public transport map and table, pp44-6.

Where to stay and eat

For accommodation in the village there is *The Paddocks* (☎ 01323-482499, 💻 www.thepaddockstables.co.uk; 1D/1T, both en suite; 🐾; 🐱 £5 per stay; WI-FI; ⓛ), a comfortable B&B charging from £35pp (sgl occ £45). They welcome dogs and there is also stabling to keep your horse, should you require it.

Jevington Tea Gardens (☎ 01323-489692) is currently closed but should reopen soon – phone for details. Their usual opening times were: Mar (Mother's Day) to Oct, Wed-Sun, 10.30am-5pm, also open bank hols). They served cream teas and coffees indoors or in the garden, light lunches such as toasties and soups; everything made on the premises. It was always worth stopping by here so we hope they reopen soon.

The village pub, the *Eight Bells* (☎ 01323-484442, 💻 www.theeightbellsjevington.co.uk; food Mon-Sat noon-3pm & 6-9pm, Sun summer noon-9pm, winter to 6pm), is a five-minute walk up the lane (the blind bend on the road is very dangerous as there is no pavement for pedestrians – it is safer to use the path by the church. The bar is open all day, every day and they have a wide range of pub meals as well as a pleasant garden, with views over the Downs, in which to eat them.

In the centre of the village, the Hungry Monk Restaurant (💻 www.hungrymonk.co.uk), which claimed to be the birthplace in 1972 of banoffi pie, has closed. You can still find the recipe on their website, though.

❏ Lullington Heath

This hidden National Nature Reserve near Jevington (see Map 49) is a short detour from the South Downs Way and is a good place to escape the crowds who tend to congregate around the tourist traps of Alfriston, Jevington and Wilmington.

The rough chalk grassland is a good place to see a variety of species of butterfly including the Chalkhill blue. In summer the shallow valley is often ablaze with the yellow flowers of gorse and broom. To the south of Lullington Heath is the expansive cover of **Friston Forest**, another good place to get lost and explore countless forest tracks.

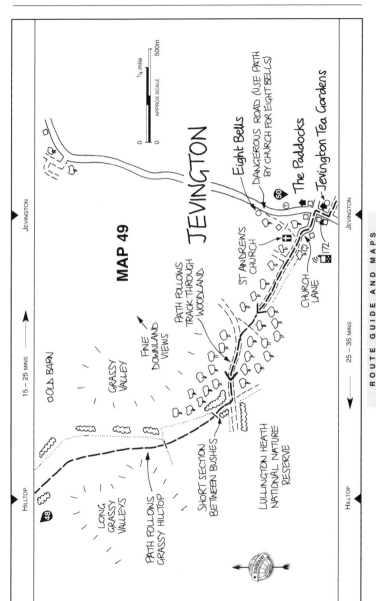

MAP 49

JEVINGTON

HILLTOP

15 – 25 MINS

JEVINGTON

OLD BARN

GRASSY VALLEY

FINE DOWNLAND VIEWS

PATH FOLLOWS TRACK THROUGH WOODLAND

ST ANDREW'S CHURCH

Eight Bells

DANGEROUS ROAD (USE PATH BY CHURCH FOR EIGHT BELLS)

The Paddocks

Jevington Tea Gardens

50

172

CHURCH LANE

LONG GRASSY VALLEYS

PATH FOLLOWS GRASSY HILLTOP

SHORT SECTION BETWEEN BUSHES

LULLINGTON HEATH NATIONAL NATURE RESERVE

48

HILLTOP

25 – 35 MINS

JEVINGTON

¼ mile

500m

APPROX SCALE

0

0

TRAILBLAZER

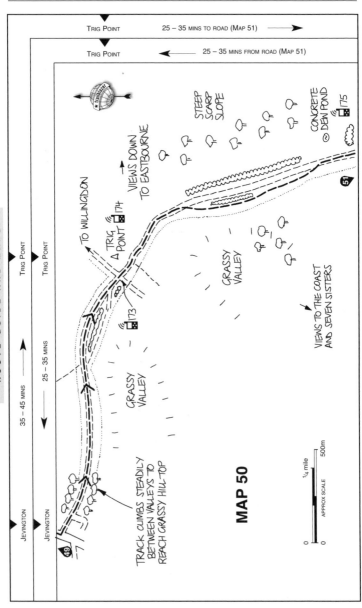

TRIG POINT   25 – 35 MINS TO ROAD (MAP 51) →

TRIG POINT   ← 25 – 35 MINS FROM ROAD (MAP 51)

STEEP SCARP SLOPE

CONCRETE @ DEW POND

175

VIEWS DOWN TO EASTBOURNE

TO WILLINGDON

△ TRIG POINT   174

173

51

TRIG POINT

TRIG POINT

GRASSY VALLEY

GRASSY VALLEY

GRASSY VALLEY

VIEWS TO THE COAST AND SEVEN SISTERS

35 – 45 MINS

25 – 35 MINS

JEVINGTON

JEVINGTON

49

TRACK CLIMBS STEADILY BETWEEN VALLEYS TO REACH GRASSY HILL-TOP

MAP 50

¼ mile   500m

APPROX SCALE

0   0

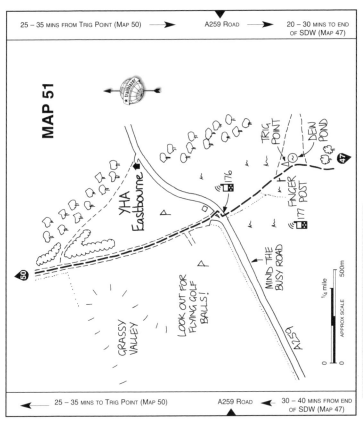

25 – 35 MINS FROM TRIG POINT (MAP 50) → A259 ROAD → 20 – 30 MINS TO END OF SDW (MAP 47)

MAP 51

YHA Eastbourne

TRIG POINT

DEW POND

FINGER POST

177 POST

176

MIND THE BUSY ROAD

A259

LOOK OUT FOR FLYING GOLF BALLS!

GRASSY VALLEY

¼ mile

0

APPROX SCALE

500m

0

50

47

25 – 35 MINS TO TRIG POINT (MAP 50) ← A259 ROAD ← 30 – 40 MINS FROM END OF SDW (MAP 47)

EASTBOURNE   MAP 52

Eastbourne is a typical English seaside resort, complete with a grand Victorian pier (despite the fire in 2014), though it does have something of a reputation as a retirement town.

Having received a lot of unfair criticism over the years as being one of the least adventurous resorts, particularly when compared to its upbeat neighbour Brighton, Eastbourne has recently undergone something of a revival. The signs on the edge of town shout out 'Welcome to the Sunshine Coast' and certainly this is one of the sunnier corners of the UK. However, whether this really is England's Costa del Sol is open to question.

Love it or hate it, Eastbourne, sprawled out below the hill and stretching along the coast, is a safe and friendly town. It may not have the history and charm of Winchester at the other end of the South Downs Way but Beachy Head, at least, makes for a fitting end to a long walk.

You can promenade along the 300m **pier** which was built from 1866-72 on stilts sitting in cups on the sea-bed allowing it to shift a little in stormy weather. In July 2014 the central domed building was destroyed by fire. Renovations are in progress and the pier is open again. It's a great place from which to watch the annual airshow, **Airbourne**, which takes place over several days in the middle of August.

Towner (☎ 01323-434670, 🖳 www .townereastbourne.org.uk; Tue-Sun, 10am-6pm; no entry charge) is an interesting contemporary art gallery on College Rd.

The **Wish Tower** is a Martello Tower, one of a number built along the coast to counter an invasion threat from Napoleon.

Services

The commercial centre is around Terminus Rd and the Arndale Shopping Centre, about 30 minutes' walk from the foot of the South Downs and the end of the Way.

The **tourist information centre** (TIC; ☎ 0871-663 0031, 🖳 www.visiteast bourne.com; July-Sept Mon-Fri 9.15am-5.30pm, Sat 9.15am-5pm, Sun 10am-1pm; Mar-June & Oct Mon-Fri 9.15am-5.30pm,

Sat 9.15am-4pm; Nov-Feb Mon-Fri 9.15am-4.30pm, Sat 9.15am-1pm) is off the northern end of Terminus Rd on Cornfield Rd. There is plenty of free information here, not only for Eastbourne but also the rest of South-East England and London too.

The **post office** (Mon-Sat 9am-5.30pm) is not far away on the corner of Langney Rd and along the pedestrianised section of Terminus Rd there are also **chemists** (Boots, Mon-Sat 8.30am-6pm & Sun 10.30am-4.30pm) and several **banks**.

Outdoor shops, **Millets** and **Blacks**, are on Terminus Rd (both open Mon-Sat 9am-5.30pm, Sun 10.30am-4.30pm). Also here is **Waterstones** bookshop (Mon-Sat 9am-5.30pm, Sun 10.30am-4.30pm), department stores **Debenhams** and **M&S**, and a **Curzon cinema**.

There is a big **Sainsbury's supermarket** in Arndale Shopping Centre, a **Premier** and **Tesco Express** on Seaside Rd, **Co-op** on Cornfield Rd and **Spar** on Terminus Rd. Most are open daily 7am-11pm.

Public transport

[See the public transport map and table, pp44-6] Eastbourne is connected by **train** to places along the south coast as well as to Gatwick Airport and London Victoria. National Express's **coach** 024 also goes to Gatwick and London Victoria. Their 315 service runs west along the coast to Helston in Cornwall.

Stagecoach's **bus** No 3/3A runs to Meads Village at the end of the South Downs Way. Brighton & Hove Buses go to Brighton (12/12X, 12A, 13X), all via Seaford and Newhaven, but their No 13X is an open-top bus that also calls at Birling Gap and Beachy Head. Compass Travel's No 143 service goes to Lewes and No 126 to Lewes via Alfriston; it is operated by Cuckmere Community Buses (CCB) on Sundays. CCB also run services (41 & 44) which call here on certain days of the week.

Try Eastbourne Taxis (☎ 01323-720720) if you need a **taxi**.

Where to stay

As a major seaside resort Eastbourne is overflowing with hotels and guesthouses.

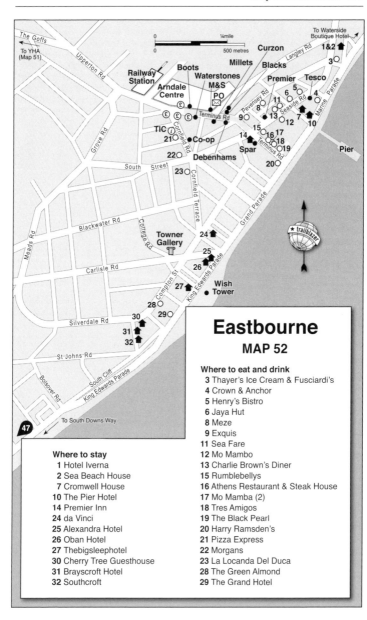

Eastbourne

MAP 52

Where to eat and drink
3 Thayer's Ice Cream & Fusciardi's
4 Crown & Anchor
5 Henry's Bistro
6 Jaya Hut
8 Meze
9 Exquis
11 Sea Fare
12 Mo Mambo
13 Charlie Brown's Diner
15 Rumblebellys
16 Athens Restaurant & Steak House
17 Mo Mamba (2)
18 Tres Amigos
19 The Black Pearl
20 Harry Ramsden's
21 Pizza Express
22 Morgans
23 La Locanda Del Duca
28 The Green Almond
29 The Grand Hotel

Where to stay
1 Hotel Iverna
2 Sea Beach House
7 Cromwell House
10 The Pier Hotel
14 Premier Inn
24 da Vinci
25 Alexandra Hotel
26 Oban Hotel
27 Thebigsleephotel
30 Cherry Tree Guesthouse
31 Brayscroft Hotel
32 Southcroft

YHA Eastbourne (☎ 0845-371 9316, 🖥 www.yha.org.uk/hostel/eastbourne; 30 beds in rooms with 2-7 beds; beds from £13, private room from £36) is self-catering only and one room is en suite. It's housed in a modern building by the A259 near the golf course on the western edge of Eastbourne. See Map 51, p177.

As you head into town from the end point of the SDW you'll find three good B&Bs in the same area. *Cherry Tree Guesthouse* (☎ 01323-722406, 🖥 www .cherrytree-eastbourne.co.uk; 3S/2T/3D/1 Tr, all en suite; ☛; WI-FI; Ⓛ) is at 15 Silverdale Rd; it's an Edwardian townhouse with B&B from £35-40pp (sgl occ £55, three sharing £120.

Just around the corner is *Brayscroft Hotel* (☎ 01323-647005, 🖥 www.brays crofthotel.co.uk; 1S/2T/3D, all en suite; ☛; WI-FI; Ⓛ), at 13 South Cliff Ave, another Edwardian house with lots of antique furniture and beds for £40-45pp (sgl/sgl occ £40-65); dinner from £15 (book in advance).

Next door at No 15 is *Southcroft* (☎ 01323-729071, 🖥 www.southcrofthotel.co .uk; 1S/3D or T/2D, all en suite; ☛; WI-FI; Ⓛ), a guesthouse which charges £20-47.50pp (sgl occ £35-80) for B&B.

Along the seafront and King Edward's Parade there's *Alexandra Hotel* (☎ 01323-720131, 🖥 alexandrahoteleastbourne .uk; 11S/10D/17T, all en suite; ☛; WI-FI) where B&B costs 36-52pp (sgl £38-47, sgl occ £56-82). There's also *Oban Hotel* (☎ 01323-731581, 🖥 www.oban-hotel.co.uk; 7S/9D/ 1D or T/13T, all en suite; ☛; WI-FI; Ⓛ), a large establishment with B&B from £42.50-47.50pp (sgl from £50).

da Vinci (☎ 01323-727173, 🖥 www.davinci.uk.com; 4S/8D/5D or T/2Tr or Qd, all en suite; ☛; WI-FI), on Howard Sq, has an art gallery downstairs and 'art-themed' rooms. It's a friendly, comfortable place and B&B costs from around £35pp. Phone them for the lowest prices

The chain *Premier Inn* (☎ 0871-5279448, 🖥 www.premierinn.com; 65D, all en suite; ☛; WI-FI), has opened a new hotel on Terminus Rd. Book online rather than calling the high-rate phone number and prices can be as low as £39 for the room (two people; a sofabed is available if

you need separate beds) or more than twice that if booked last minute. The rooms have very comfortable beds and 40-inch flat-screen TVs. There's a restaurant: a light/cooked breakfast costs £6.25/£8.75.

Right opposite the pier is the appropriately named *The Pier Hotel* (☎ 01323-649544, 🖥 pierhotel.relaxinnz.co.uk; 11S/ 11D/8T/1Tr, all en suite; ☛; WI-FI; 🐾), a place that's not without its charms and is in a great location. Rooms are fair value at around £39-44 for a single, £55-79 for a double. Also on the seafront are *Hotel Iverna* (☎ 01323-730768, 🖥 www.hotel-iverna.co.uk; 1S/2D/2T/1Qd, en suite or private facilities; ☛; 🐾), 32 Marine Parade, with B&B for £27.50-38pp (sgl occ rates on request but full room rate in summer; four sharing £145; and *Cromwell House* (☎ 01323-725288, 🖥 www.crom well-house.co.uk; 2S/2T/1D/3D or T, all en suite; WI-FI; Ⓛ), at 23 Cavendish Place, a Victorian townhouse with B&B from £30-40pp (sgl £30-40, sgl occ £50-60).

Sea Beach House (☎ 01323-410458, 🖥 www.seabeachhouse.com; 1S/5D/4T, all en suite; ☛; WI-FI; 🐾; Ⓛ), is at 40 Marine Parade. Some of the rooms have sea views and cost £36-42pp (sgl £38, sgl occ £38-53). Princess (later to become Queen) Victoria is said to have stayed here.

Thebigsleephotel (☎ 01323-722676, 🖥 www.thebigsleephotel.com; 10S/14D/ 12T/1Tr/1Qd and one room up to six; ☛; 🐾 £10; WI-FI) is a stylish, modern place on the seafront. Curiously pitched somewhere between a hostel and a boutique hotel, it's packed with facilities including pool and table tennis tables, 12-channel TVs in the rooms and even a bar serving takeaway food. Prices are reasonable: £22.50-47.50pp (sgl/sgl occ £29-75; three/four/six sharing £79-125) including continental breakfast (cooked breakfast additional £3.50pp).

If it's luxury and pampering you require after your walk, try *Waterside Boutique Hotel* (off Map 52; ☎ 01323-646566, 🖥 www.watersidehoteleastbourne .co.uk; 2D or T/16D, all en suite; ☛; WI-FI; Ⓛ), 11-12 Royal Parade; B&B costs £40-47.50pp. Some rooms have Jacuzzis; the spa treatments are extra.

Where to eat and drink

You'll find a surprisingly eclectic mix of restaurants and cafés, many of which are on or around **Seaside Rd** and **Terminus Rd**.

On Compton St, at 12 Grand Hotel Buildings, *The Green Almond* (☎ 01323-734470; Tue-Thur 10am-4pm, Fri & Sat noon-4pm & 7-11pm) is a vegetarian bistro that gets rave reviews. It's a small place so you usually need to book for the buffet lunches (noon-3pm, small/large plate for £6.50/£8.50). Dinner is £20.

At the western end of Seaside Rd are a number of cheap places open long hours: *Rumblebellys* (☎ 01323-728247) at No 7 and *Charlie Brown's Diner* (☎ 01323-726588) at No 54 for burgers, and *Mo Mambo's* (☎ 01323-732832) at No 71 for pasta and pizzas (with another branch on Terminus Rd). At No 74 Seaside Rd, *Jaya Hut* (☎ 01323-642775) is a budget Malaysian & Chinese restaurant/takeaway.

At 124 Seaside Rd there's what is probably the best place to have dinner in Eastbourne, the excellent *Henry's Bistro* (☎ 01323-371653, 🖳 henrysbistro.com; Mon-Thu 6-9pm, bookings only on Mon, Fri 6-10pm, Sat 6-10.30pm). Dinner might include Mongolian shredded lamb yum buns (£6.50) followed by garlic & ginger pork belly (£12.50) and then kaffir lime posset with raspberry sorbet (£5.50). During the week they often have two/three course set menus for £15.95/£19.95.

There are numerous places on the seaside end of Terminus Rd. *Athens Restaurant & Steak House* (☎ 01323-733278; daily 11.30am-2.30pm & 5.30-10.30pm), at No 195, gets excellent reviews. It's efficiently run by three generations of a hospitable Greek-Cypriot family and their moussaka (£12.50) is particularly good.

At 207 Terminus Rd is the cheerful *Tres Amigos* (☎ 01323-739944; Mon-Fri 5-10pm, Fri, Sat & Sun noon-10pm) with a range of tapas dishes, burritos and some special meal deals.

Also on Terminus Rd, nearer the seafront is *The Black Pearl* (☎ 01323-724435; 🖳 www.theblackpearleastbourne .co.ukfood, daily 10am-10pm) a seafood bar offering everything from fish and chips to lobsters and champagne.

Morgans (☎ 01323-644609; daily noon-10pm), at 119 South St, is a reliable restaurant and bistro where you can get anything from a cup of coffee to a full meal. Nearby on Cornfield Rd is a branch of *Pizza Express*.

At 1 Pevensey Rd, *Exquis* (☎ 01323-430885; Tue-Sat 6-11pm, also from noon Fri), is shabby outside but actually a delightful French bistro with a simple menu that's good value. *Meze* (☎ 01323-731893; daily noon-midnight), at 15 Pevensey Rd, is a good Turkish restaurant open long hours.

La Locana Del Duca (☎ 01323-737177; daily noon-2.30pm & 5.30-11pm, to 10.30pm on Sun), 26 Cornfield Terrace, is an authentic Italian place offering set menus for £18.95/20.95 for two/three courses and traditional favourites à la carte.

There are numerous pubs, some rather rougher than others. The *Crown & Anchor* (☎ 01323-642500; food daily noon-3pm & 5.30-9pm), on the seafront at 15 Marine Parade, often has live music at weekends.

As a seaside town Eastbourne would not be complete without lots of fish and chip shops. *Sea Fare* (☎ 01323-641893; daily 11.30-3.30pm & 4.30-9pm), at 66 Seaside Rd, is a good traditional chippie. There's also a branch of the *Harry Ramsden's* chain (☎ 01323-417454), on the seafront at the end of Terminus Rd.

Another seaside tradition is ice cream. Between Marine Parade and Seaside Rd are two competing outlets, both very good. The cheaper of the two, *Thayer's Ice Cream*, is a small family-run business with 32 different flavours. Bigger, brasher *Fusciardi's*, on the seafront, also has a sit-down café.

If your walk ends at about tea time and you wish to celebrate in style there can be no better place for a top-of-the-range cream tea than *The Grand Hotel* (☎ 01323-412345, 🖳 www.grandeastbourne.com). You should phone ahead to book. It's served daily from 2.45pm to 6pm when for £25.50 you get a full spread including sandwiches, scones, pudding and cakes. You can push the boat out even further with the Grand Champagne Tea (£33.50). The hotel is easy to find: you walk right past it on the way into Eastbourne from the end of the South Downs Way. Splash out – you deserve it!

APPENDIX A – GPS WAYPOINTS

Each GPS waypoint was taken on the route at the reference number marked on the map as below.

MAP	REF	GPS WAYPOINT		DESCRIPTION
Map 2	001	N51° 03.228'	W01° 16.749'	Join road
Map 2	002	N51° 02.862'	W01° 16.146'	Turn left onto track
Map 2	003	N51° 03.006'	W01° 15.865'	Leave track
Map 3	004	N51° 02.813'	W01° 14.842'	Road crossing
Map 3	005	N51° 02.997'	W01° 14.437'	Through gate on track
Map 3	006	N51° 03.433'	W01° 14.089'	Track junction at farmyard
Map 3	007	N51° 02.955'	W01° 12.769'	Crossroads
Map 4	008	N51° 02.727'	W01° 12.399'	Gate into field
Map 4	009	N51° 02.346'	W01° 12.081'	Cross A272 road
Map 4	010	N51° 01.586'	W01° 11.793'	Join lane leading uphill
Map 5	011	N51° 01.041'	W01° 11.358'	The Milbury's
Map 5	012	N51° 00.821'	W01° 10.521'	Gate to Wind Farm
Map 5	013	N51° 00.580'	W01° 09.631'	Track past houses
Map 6	014	N51° 00.059'	W01° 08.913'	Beacon Hill car park
Map 6	015	N50° 59.555'	W01° 08.413'	Stile to cross fields
Map 6	016	N50° 59.342'	W01° 08.227'	Stile to cross track
Map 7	017	N50° 59.040'	W01° 07.728'	The Shoe Inn, Exton
Map 7	018	N50° 59.252'	W01° 07.208'	Bridge over stream
Map 7	019	N50° 59.196'	W01° 06.725'	Cross disused railway
Map 7	020	N50° 58.854'	W01° 05.328'	Hill fort, Old Winchester Hill
Map 8	021	N50° 59.009'	W01° 04.712'	Turn off track
Map 8	022	N50° 59.279'	W01° 04.827'	Car park
Map 8	023	N50° 59.443'	W01° 04.934'	Gate at fork in road
Map 8	024	N50° 59.238'	W01° 04.546'	Join track
Map 8	025	N50° 59.296'	W01° 04.200'	Left turn at farmyard
Map 8	026	N50° 59.446'	W01° 03.153'	Turn onto tree-lined avenue
Map 8	027	N50° 59.066'	W01° 03.085'	Crossroads
Map 9	028	N50° 58.079'	W01° 02.373'	Wetherdown Hostel
Map 9	029	N50° 57.939'	W01° 01.698'	Road junction
Map 10	030	N50° 58.051'	W01° 00.110'	Homelands Farm
Map 10	031	N50° 58.026'	W00° 59.794'	Junction with Hogs Lodge Lane
Map 10	032	N50° 58.465'	W00° 59.274'	Butser Hill car park
Map 10	033	N50° 57.891'	W00° 58.866'	Gate before A3 road crossing
Map 11	034	N50° 57.450'	W00° 58.658'	Turn off track into woods
Map 11	035	N50° 58.095'	W00° 57.775'	Join other track
Map 12	036	N50° 58.372'	W00° 57.375'	Car park and road crossing
Map 12	037	N50° 58.206'	W00° 56.456'	Track junction
Map 12	038	N50° 58.153'	W00° 55.787'	Road junction
Map 13	039	N50° 57.980'	W00° 54.137'	Road crossing
Map 13	040	N50° 57.611'	W00° 53.213'	Car park, B2146 road crossing
Map 13	041	N50° 57.435'	W00° 52.672'	Car park, B2141 road crossing
Map 14	042	N50° 57.659'	W00° 51.469'	Turn-off to East Harting
Map 14	043	N50° 57.547'	W00° 51.119'	Trig point, Beacon Hill
Map 14	044	N50° 57.535'	W00° 50.447'	Path, not farm track!
Map 14	045	N50° 57.267'	W00° 49.981'	Track junction

MAP	REF	GPS WAYPOINT		DESCRIPTION
Map 15	046	N50° 56.760'	W00° 49.665'	Track crossroads
Map 15	047	N50° 56.999'	W00° 48.587'	Track crossroads
Map 15	048	N50° 56.873'	W00° 47.494'	Path junction, Cocking Down
Map 16	049	N50° 56.759'	W00° 47.002'	Track crossroads
Map 16	050	N50° 56.660'	W00° 46.360'	Junction near ball of chalk
Map 16	051	N50° 56.571'	W00° 45.338'	Car park at A268 crossing
Map 16	052	N50° 56.544'	W00° 45.002'	Water tap
Map 17	053	N50° 56.440'	W00° 44.226'	Fork in track
Map 17	054	N50° 56.463'	W00° 43.706'	Path junction
Map 17	055	N50° 56.466'	W00° 43.258'	Turn-off to Heyshott
Map 18	056	N50° 56.457'	W00° 42.857'	Path junction
Map 18	057	N50° 56.378'	W00° 42.375'	Track junction
Map 18	058	N50° 56.353'	W00° 42.128'	Track junction
Map 18	059	N50° 56.239'	W00° 40.938'	Signpost with memorials
Map 18	060	N50° 56.016'	W00° 39.082'	Track junction
Map 19	061	N50° 55.902'	W00° 39.598'	Track crossroads
Map 19	062	N50° 55.307'	W00° 38.925'	Cross A285 road
Map 19	063	N50° 54.803'	W00° 38.488'	Track junction
Map 20	064	N50° 54.441'	W00° 37.926'	Track junction
Map 20	065	N50° 54.402'	W00° 37.319'	Track junction
Map 20	066	N50° 54.464'	W00° 36.968'	Bignor Hill car park
Map 20	067	N50° 54.587'	W00° 36.157'	Grave
Map 21	068	N50° 54.470'	W00° 35.814'	Track junction
Map 21	069	N50° 53.884'	W00° 34.403'	Cross A29 road
Map 21	070	N50° 53.837'	W00° 33.310'	Cross country lane
Map 22	071	N50° 53.952'	W00° 32.927'	Bridge over River Arun
Map 22	072	N50° 54.025'	W00° 32.358'	Leave B2139 road
Map 22	073	N50° 54.195'	W00° 31.927'	Road junction
Map 22	074	N50° 54.188'	W00° 31.839'	Leave road
Map 22	075	N50° 54.158'	W00° 31.215'	Gate & stile
Map 23	076	N50° 54.190'	W00° 30.413'	Join track
Map 23	077	N50° 54.145'	W00° 29.540'	Track junction
Map 23	078	N50° 54.111'	W00° 28.747'	Track junction
Map 23	079	N50° 54.051'	W00° 28.347'	Turn-off to Storrington
Map 25	080	N50° 53.656'	W00° 26.641'	New barn
Map 25	081	N50° 53.755'	W00° 26.032'	Gate on track
Map 25	082	N50° 53.791'	W00° 25.812'	Turn-off to Washington
Map 25	083	N50° 54.279'	W00° 25.030'	Join track
Map 25	084	N50° 54.251'	W00° 24.885'	Join road into Washington
Map 25	085	N50° 54.304'	W00° 24.306'	Frankland Arms, Washington
Map 25	086	N50° 54.189'	W00° 24.382'	Road junction, Washington
Map 25	087	N50° 53.807'	W00° 24.344'	Steep section of track
Map 26	088	N50° 53.617'	W00° 23.643'	Track junction
Map 26	089	N50° 53.757'	W00° 23.351'	Gate on track
Map 26	090	N50° 53.779'	W00° 22.928'	Chanctonbury Ring
Map 26	091	N50° 53.637'	W00° 22.612'	Gate on track
Map 26	092	N50° 53.409'	W00° 22.421'	Track junction
Map 26	093	N50° 53.269'	W00° 22.001'	Track junction
Map 27	094	N50° 53.219'	W00° 21.675'	Turn-off to Steyning
Map 27	095	N50° 52.669'	W00° 20.972'	Track junction
Map 29	096	N50° 52.403'	W00° 17.958'	Turn-off A283 road

MAP	REF	GPS WAYPOINT		DESCRIPTION
Map 29	097	N50° 52.430'	W00° 17.094'	Car park
Map 29	098	N50° 52.881'	W00° 15.991'	Join road to Truleigh Hill YH
Map 30	099	N50° 52.919'	W00° 15.461'	Truleigh Hill
Map 30	100	N50° 53.063'	W00° 13.763'	Turn-off to Fulking
Map 30	101	N50° 52.937'	W00° 13.213'	Gate
Map 31	102	N50° 53.092'	W00° 12.744'	Devil's Dyke Pub
Map 31	103	N50° 52.978'	W00° 12.254'	Gate on path
Map 31	104	N50° 53.309'	W00° 11.663'	Road crossing
Map 31	105	N50° 53.349'	W00° 11.466'	Gate into woodland
Map 31	106	N50° 53.410'	W00° 10.968'	Gate on path
Map 32	107	N50° 53.743'	W00° 10.001'	Join road
Map 32	108	N50° 53.923'	W00° 09.837'	Crossroads, Pyecombe
Map 32	109	N50° 54.056'	W00° 09.593'	Car park at golf club
Map 32	110	N50° 54.026'	W00° 08.687'	Track crossroads
Map 32	111	N50° 54.227'	W00° 08.718'	Track junction
Map 33	112	N50° 54.027'	W00° 07.845'	Turn-off to Dower Cottage
Map 33	113	N50° 54.146'	W00° 07.327'	Dew pond
Map 33	114	N50° 54.046'	W00° 06.278'	Car park, Ditchling Beacon
Map 33	115	N50° 53.940'	W00° 05.814'	Turn-off to Ditchling
Map 34	116	N50° 53.910'	W00° 04.709'	Road crossing
Map 34	117	N50° 53.876'	W00° 04.387'	Turn-off to Plumpton
Map 34	118	N50° 53.759'	W00° 03.198'	Turn-off to Lewes
Map 35	119	N50° 53.259'	W00° 03.666'	Gate at track junction
Map 35	120	N50° 53.000'	W00° 03.295'	Leave track through gate
Map 35	121	N50° 52.505'	W00° 02.808'	Through gate & stile
Map 35	122	N50° 52.426'	W00° 03.190'	Small hut and pylon
Map 35	123	N50° 51.977'	W00° 03.268'	Steps
Map 35	124	N50° 51.977'	W00° 03.487'	Bridge over A27 road
Map 35	125	N50° 51.872'	W00° 02.952'	Pass under railway
Map 36	126	N50° 51.548'	W00° 03.227'	Through gate
Map 36	127	N50° 51.224'	W00° 03.463'	Through gate
Map 36	128	N50° 51.025'	W00° 03.266'	Through gate, follow fence
Map 36	129	N50° 51.278'	W00° 02.526'	Through gate by dew pond
Map 36	130	N50° 51.032'	W00° 01.876'	Join track
Map 37	131	N50° 50.673'	W00° 01.557'	Track, Swanborough Hill
Map 37	132	N50° 50.086'	E00° 00.479'	Leave track through gate
Map 38	133	N50° 50.009'	E00° 00.149'	Through gate, cross track
Map 38	134	N50° 49.566'	E00° 00.315'	Through gate onto track
Map 38	135	N50° 49.795'	E00° 01.061'	Road junction, Southease
Map 38	136	N50° 49.805'	E00° 01.562'	Bridge over River Ouse
Map 38	137	N50° 49.888'	E00° 01.849'	Level crossing
Map 38	138	N50° 49.804'	E00° 02.228'	Gate after bridge over A26
Map 39	139	N50° 49.875'	E00° 03.090'	Trig point & dew pond
Map 39	140	N50° 50.092'	E00° 03.667'	Gate onto track
Map 39	141	N50° 50.063'	E00° 04.114'	Masts, Beddingham Hill
Map 39	142	N50° 50.069'	E00° 04.468'	Gate on path
Map 40	143	N50° 50.018'	E00° 04.987'	Car park, Firle Beacon
Map 40	144	N50° 50.029'	E00° 06.497'	Trig point, Firle Beacon
Map 40	145	N50° 49.527'	E00° 07.208'	Gate, Bo Peep
Map 41	146	N50° 49.108'	E00° 07.823'	Gate on path

MAP	REF	GPS WAYPOINT		DESCRIPTION
Map 41	147	N50° 48.659'	E00° 08.550'	Track junction
Map 42	148	N50° 48.405'	E00° 09.581'	Church, Alfriston
Map 42	149	N50° 48.689'	E00° 09.581'	Plough & Harrow, Litlington
Map 43	150	N50° 47.440'	E00° 09.628'	Through stile on path
Map 43	151	N50° 47.098'	E00° 09.471'	Steps up through forest
Map 43	152	N50° 46.707'	E00° 09.699'	Track junction
Map 43	153	N50° 46.398'	E00° 09.559'	Crossroads, Westdean
Map 43	154	N50° 46.499'	E00° 09.244'	Road crossing, Exceat
Map 44	155	N50° 45.905'	E00° 09.085'	Turn off track
Map 44	156	N50° 45.909'	E00° 09.508'	Stile on path
Map 44	157	N50° 45.376'	E00° 09.578'	Haven Brow
Map 44	158	N50° 45.310'	E00° 09.793'	Short Brow
Map 44	159	N50° 45.198'	E00° 10.139'	Rough Brow
Map 44	160	N50° 45.143'	E00° 10.376'	Brass Point
Map 45	161	N50° 44.995'	E00° 10.792'	Sarsen stone
Map 45	162	N50° 44.957'	E00° 11.020'	The 'Eighth' Sister
Map 45	163	N50° 44.910'	E00° 11.284'	Baily's Hill
Map 45	164	N50° 44.570'	E00° 11.462'	Memorial pillar
Map 45	165	N50° 44.766'	E00° 11.667'	Went Hill
Map 45	166	N50° 44.585'	E00° 12.075'	Car park, Birling Gap
Map 46	167	N50° 44.302'	E00° 12.901'	Belle Tout Lighthouse
Map 46	168	N50° 44.112'	E00° 13.870'	Path near Shooters Bottom
Map 47	169	N50° 44.335'	E00° 15.220'	Lookout point
Map 47	170	N50° 44.634'	E00° 15.478'	Fork in path
Map 47	171	N50° 45.113'	E00° 16.027'	End of SDW coastal route
Map 49	172	N50° 47.518'	E00° 12.825'	Jevington Tea Gardens
Map 50	173	N50° 47.222'	E00° 14.083'	Turn-off to Willingdon
Map 50	174	N50° 47.196'	E00° 14.162'	Trig point
Map 50	175	N50° 46.658'	E00° 14.575'	Concrete dew pond
Map 51	176	N50° 45.901'	E00° 14.776'	Road crossing
Map 51	177	N50° 45.729'	E00° 15.000'	Finger post
Map 47	171	N50° 45.113'	E00° 16.027'	End of SDW inland route

APPENDIX B – TAKING A DOG

TAKING DOGS ALONG THE WAY

Many are the rewards that await those prepared to make the extra effort required to bring their best friend along the trail. However, because the South Downs is a prime sheep-farming area your dog may have to be on a lead for much of the walk.

You shouldn't underestimate the amount of work involved, though. Indeed, just about every decision you make will be influenced by the fact that you've got a dog: how you plan to travel to the start of the trail, where you're going to stay, how far you're going to walk each day, where you're going to rest and where you're going to eat in the evening etc.

If you're also sure your dog can cope with (and will enjoy) walking 10 miles or more a day for several days in a row, you need to start preparing accordingly. Extra thought also needs to go into your itinerary. The best starting point is to study the town & village facilities table on pp30-1 (and the advice below), and plan where to stop and where to buy food.

Looking after your dog

To begin with, you need to make sure that your own dog is fully **inoculated** against the usual doggy illnesses, and also up to date with regard to **worm pills** (eg Drontal) and **flea preventatives** such as Frontline – they are, after all, following in the pawprints of many a dog before them, some of whom may well have left fleas or other parasites on the trail that now lie in wait for their next meal to arrive. **Pet insurance** is also a very good idea; if you've already got insurance, do check that it will cover a trip such as this.

On the subject of looking after your dog's health, perhaps the most important implement you can take with you is the **plastic tick remover**, available from vets for a couple of quid. These removers, while fiddly, help you to remove the tick safely (ie without leaving its head behind buried under the dog's skin).

Being in unfamiliar territory also makes it more likely that you and your dog could become separated. For this reason, make sure your dog has a **tag with your contact details on it** (a mobile phone number would be best if you are carrying one with you); you could also consider having it **microchipped** for further security.

When to keep your dog on a lead

● **On cliff tops** It's a sad fact that, every year, a few dogs lose their lives falling over the edge of the cliffs. It usually occurs when they are chasing rabbits (which know where the cliff-edge is and are able, unlike your poor pooch, to stop in time).

● **When crossing farmland**, particularly in the lambing season (around May) when your dog can scare the start of the trail, causing them to lose their young. Farmers are allowed by law to shoot at and kill any dogs that they consider are worrying their sheep. During lambing, most farmers would prefer it if you didn't bring your dog at all. The exception is if your dog is being attacked by cows. A couple of years ago there were three deaths in the UK caused by walkers being trampled as they tried to rescue their dogs from the attentions of cattle. The advice in this instance is to let go of the lead, head speedily to a position of safety (usually the other side of the field gate or stile) and call your dog to you.

● **On National Trust land**, where it is compulsory to keep your dog on a lead.

● **Around ground-nesting birds** It's important to keep your dog under control when crossing an area where certain species of birds nest on the ground. Most dogs love foraging around in the woods but make sure you have permission to do so; some woods are used as 'nurseries' for game birds and dogs are only allowed through them if they are on a lead.

What to pack
You've probably already got a good idea of what to bring to keep your dog alive and happy, but the following is a checklist:

● **Food/water bowl** Foldable cloth bowls are popular with walkers, being light and take up little room in the rucksack. You can get also get a water-bottle-and-bowl combination, where the bottle folds into a 'trough' from which the dog can drink.
● **Lead and collar** An extendable one is probably preferable for this sort of trip. Make sure both lead and collar are in good condition – you don't want either to snap on the trail, or you may end up carrying your dog through sheep fields until a replacement can be found.
● **Medication** You'll know if you need to bring any lotions or potions.
● **Tick remover** See above
● **Bedding** A simple blanket may suffice, or you can opt for something more elaborate if you aren't carrying your own luggage.
● **Poo bags** Essential.
● **Hygiene wipes** For cleaning your dog after it's rolled in stuff.
● **A favourite toy** Helps prevent your dog from pining for the entire walk.
● **Food/water** Remember to bring treats as well as regular food to keep up the mutt's morale. That said, if your dog is anything like mine the chances are they'll spend most of the walk dining on rabbit droppings and sheep poo anyway.
● **Corkscrew stake** Available from camping or pet shops, this will help you to keep your dog secure in one place while you set up camp/doze.
● **Raingear** It can rain!
● **Old towels** For drying your dog.

What to pack
When it comes to packing, I always leave an exterior pocket of my rucksack empty so I can put used poo bags in there (for deposit at the first bin we come to). I always like to keep all the dog's kit together and separate from the other luggage (usually inside a plastic bag inside my rucksack). I have also seen several dogs sporting their own 'doggy rucksack', so they can carry their own food, water, poo etc – which certainly reduces the burden on their owner!

Cleaning up after your dog
It is extremely important that dog owners behave in a responsible way when walking the path. Dog excrement should be cleaned up. In towns, villages and fields where animals graze or which will be cut for silage, hay etc, you need to pick up and bag the excrement.

Staying with your dog
In this guide we have used the symbol 🐕 to denote where a hotel, pub or B&B welcomes dogs. However, this always needs to be arranged in advance and some places may charge extra. Hostels (both YHA and independent) do not permit them unless they are an assistance (guide) dog; smaller campsites tend to accept them, but some of the larger holiday parks do not. Before you turn up always double check whether the place you would like to stay accepts dogs and whether there is space for them; many places have only one or two rooms suitable for people with dogs.

When it comes to eating, most landlords allow dogs in at least a section of their pubs, though few restaurants do. Make sure you always ask first and ensure your dog doesn't run around the pub but is secured to your table or a radiator.

Henry Stedman

INDEX

Page references in bold type refer to maps

Map key

🏠 Where to stay	📖	Library/bookstore	●	Other
○ Where to eat and drink	🕲	Internet	CP	Car park
Λ Campsite	🏛	Museum/gallery	⊗	Bus station
⊠ Post Office	✚	Church/cathedral	⊙	Bus stop
ⓔ Bank/ATM	☏	Telephone	Rail line & station
ⓘ Tourist Information	☑	Public toilet	Park
	□	Building	082 GPS waypoint

South Downs Way	Stile	Water
Other path	Gate	Stream/river
4 x 4 track	Cliffs	Trees/woodland
Tarmac road	Bridge	Beach
Steps	Fence	Lighthouse
Slope	Wall	Golf course
Steep slope	Hedge	32 Map continuation

TRAILBLAZER'S LONG-DISTANCE PATH (LDP) WALKING GUIDES

We've applied to destinations which are closer to home Trailblazer's proven formula for publishing definitive practical route guides for adventurous travellers. Britain's network of long-distance trails enables the walker to explore some of the finest landscapes in the country's best walking areas. These are guides that are user-friendly, practical, informative and environmentally sensitive.

● **Unique mapping features** In many walking guidebooks the reader has to read a route description then try to relate it to the map. Our guides are much easier to use because walking directions, tricky junctions, places to stay and eat, points of interest and walking times are all written onto the maps themselves in the places to which they apply. With their uncluttered clarity these are not general-purpose maps but fully edited maps drawn by walkers for walkers.

● **Largest-scale walking maps** At a scale of just under 1:20,000 (8cm or 3^1/$_8$ inches to one mile) the maps in these guides are bigger than even the most detailed British walking maps currently available in the shops.

● **Not just a trail guide – includes where to stay, where to eat and public transport** Our guidebooks cover the complete walking experience, not just the route. Accommodation options for all budgets are provided (pubs, hotels, B&Bs, campsites, bunkhouses, hostels) as well as places to eat. Detailed public transport information for all access points to each trail means that there are itineraries for all walkers, for hiking the entire route as well as for day or weekend walks.

Coast to Coast *Henry Stedman*, 6th edition, £11.99
ISBN 978-1-905864-57-7, 268pp, 110 maps, 40 colour photos

Cornwall Coast Path (SW Coast Path Pt 2) 4th edition, £11.99
ISBN 978-1-905864-44-7, 3526pp, 142 maps, 40 colour photos

Cotswold Way *Tricia & Bob Hayne* 2nd edition, £11.99
ISBN 978-1-905864-48-5, 204pp, 53 maps, 40 colour photos

Dorset & South Devon (SW Coast Path Pt 3) *Stedman & Newton*, £11.99
ISBN 978-1-905864-45-4, 336pp, 88 maps, 40 colour photos

Exmoor & North Devon (SW Coast Path Pt I) *Stedman & Newton*, £11.99
ISBN 978-1-905864-43-0, 192pp, 68 maps, 40 colour photos

Hadrian's Wall Path *Henry Stedman*, 4th edition, £11.99
ISBN 978-1-905864-58-4, 224pp, 60 maps, 40 colour photos

Offa's Dyke Path *Keith Carter*, 4th edition, £11.99
ISBN 978-1-905864-65-2, 240pp, 98 maps, 40 colour photos

Peddars Way & Norfolk Coast Path *Alexander Stewart*, £11.99
ISBN 978-1-905864-28-7, 192pp, 54 maps, 40 colour photos

Pembrokeshire Coast Path *Jim Manthorpe*, 4th edition, £11.99
ISBN 978-1-905864-51-5, 224pp, 96 maps, 40 colour photos

Pennine Way *Stuart Greig*, 4th edition, £11.99
ISBN 978-1-905864-61-4, 272pp, 138 maps, 40 colour photos

The Ridgeway *Nick Hill*, 3rd edition, £11.99
ISBN 978-1-905864-40-9, 192pp, 53 maps, 40 colour photos

South Downs Way *Jim Manthorpe*, 5th edition, £11.99
ISBN 978-1-905864-66-9, 192pp, 60 maps, 40 colour photos

Thames Path *Joel Newton*, 1st edition, £11.99
ISBN 978-1-905864-64-5, 256pp, 99 maps, 40 colour photos

West Highland Way *Charlie Loram*, 5th edition, £11.99
ISBN 978-1-905864-50-8, 208pp, 60 maps, 40 colour photos

'The same attention to detail that distinguishes its other guides has been brought to bear here'.
THE SUNDAY TIMES

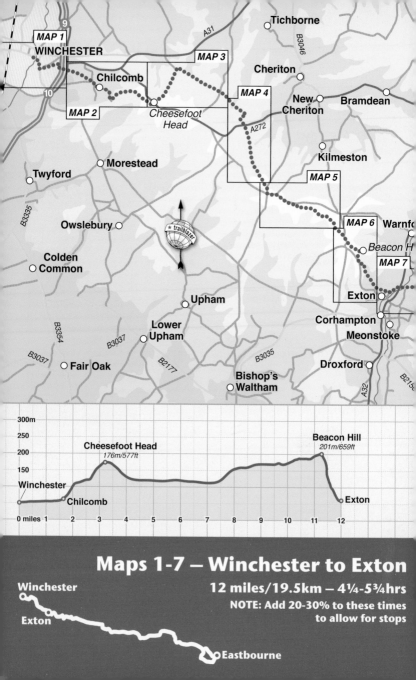

MAP 1

9

WINCHESTER

10

MAP 2

Chilcomb

A31

MAP 3

Cheesefoot
Head

MAP 4

A272

Tichborne

B3046

Cheriton

New
Cheriton

Bramdean

Kilmeston

MAP 5

MAP 6

Warnfo

Beacon H

MAP 7

Exton

Twyford

B3335

Morestead

Owslebury

Colden
Common

★ trailblazer

Upham

Lower
Upham

B3354

B3037

B3037

Fair Oak

B2177

Corhampton

Meonstoke

Droxford

A32

B215

Bishop's
Waltham

B3035

300m
250
200
150
100

Cheesefoot Head
176m/577ft

Beacon Hill
201m/659ft

Winchester

Chilcomb

Exton

0 miles 1   2   3   4   5   6   7   8   9   10   11   12

Maps 1–7 – Winchester to Exton

12 miles/19.5km – 4¼-5¾hrs

**NOTE: Add 20-30% to these times
to allow for stops**

Winchester

Exton

Eastbourne

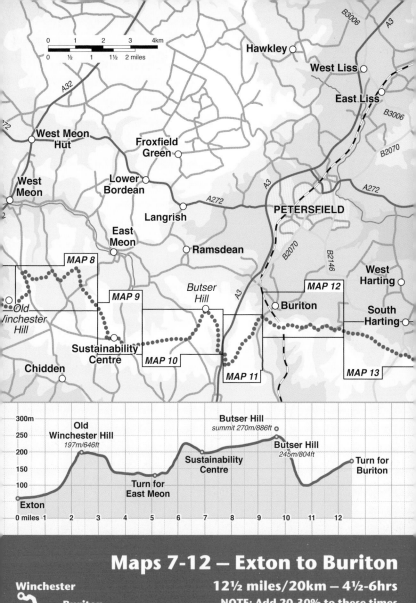

0   1   2   3   4km
0   ½   1   1½   2 miles

A32

Hawkley

West Liss

East Liss

B3006

A3

B2070

A272

West Meon
Hut

Froxfield
Green

West
Meon

Lower
Bordean

Langrish

A272

PETERSFIELD

A3

B2070

B2146

East
Meon

Ramsdean

West
Harting

MAP 8

MAP 9

Butser
Hill

MAP 12

Buriton

South
Harting

Old
Winchester
Hill

Sustainability
Centre

MAP 10

MAP 11

MAP 13

Chidden

300m

250

200

150

100

Old
Winchester Hill
197m/646ft

Butser Hill
summit 270m/886ft

Butser Hill
245m/804ft

Sustainability
Centre

Turn for
Buriton

Exton

Turn for
East Meon

0 miles 1   2   3   4   5   6   7   8   9   10   11   12

Maps 7-12 – Exton to Buriton

12½ miles/20km – 4½-6hrs

**NOTE: Add 20-30% to these times
to allow for stops**

Winchester

Buriton

Exton

Eastbourne

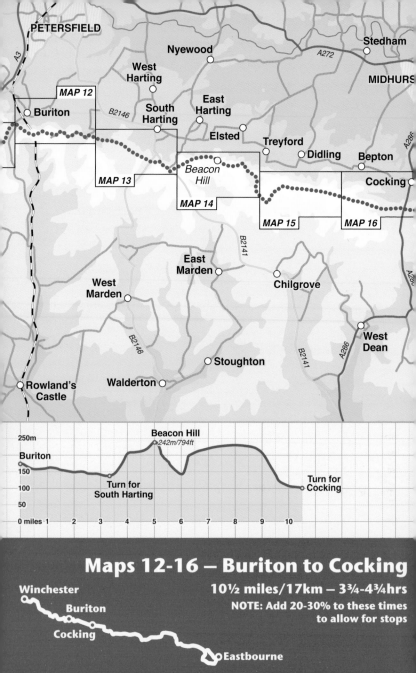

PETERSFIELD

Stedham

Nyewood

A272

West Harting

MIDHURS

MAP 12

East Harting

Buriton

B2146

South Harting

Elsted

Treyford   Didling

A286

Bepton

MAP 13

Beacon Hill

Cocking

MAP 14

MAP 15

MAP 16

B2141

East Marden

Chilgrove

A26

West Marden

A286

West Dean

B2146

B2141

Stoughton

Walderton

Rowland's Castle

250m

Beacon Hill
242m/794ft

Buriton

Turn for Cocking

150

Turn for South Harting

100

50

0 miles 1   2   3   4   5   6   7   8   9   10

Maps 12-16 – Buriton to Cocking

10½ miles/17km – 3¾-4¾hrs

NOTE: Add 20-30% to these times to allow for stops

Winchester

Buriton

Cocking

Eastbourne

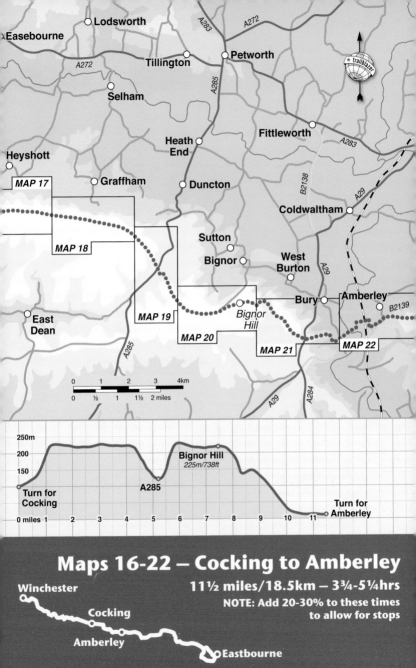

MAP 17

MAP 18

MAP 19

MAP 20

MAP 21

MAP 22

Lodsworth

Easebourne

A272

A283

A272

Petworth

Tillington

A285

Selham

Fittleworth

A283

Heath
End

B2138

Heyshott

Graffham

Duncton

A29

Coldwaltham

Sutton

A285

Bignor

West
Burton

A29

Amberley

East
Dean

Bignor
Hill

Bury

B2139

A285

A29

A284

| 0 | 1 | 2 | 3 | 4km |
| 0 | ½ | 1 | 1½ | 2 miles |

250m

200

150

Bignor Hill
225m/738ft

A285

Turn for
Cocking

Turn for
Amberley

0 miles 1   2   3   4   5   6   7   8   9   10   11

Maps 16-22 – Cocking to Amberley

11½ miles/18.5km – 3¾-5¼hrs

NOTE: Add 20-30% to these times
to allow for stops

Winchester

Cocking

Amberley

Eastbourne

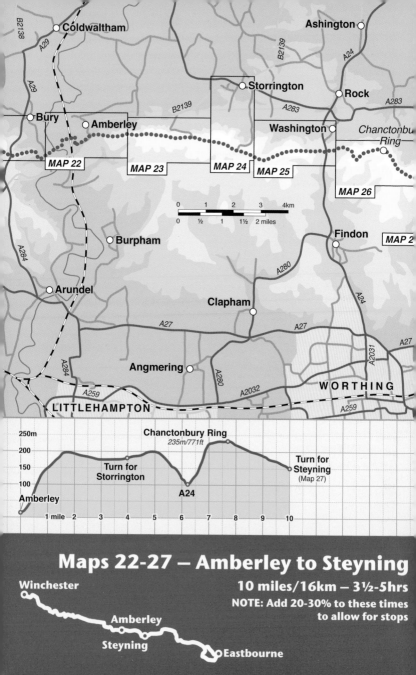

MAP 22

MAP 23

MAP 24

MAP 25

MAP 26

MAP 2

Coldwaltham

Ashington

Storrington

Rock

Bury

Amberley

Washington

Chanctonbury Ring

Burpham

Findon

Arundel

Clapham

Angmering

WORTHING

LITTLEHAMPTON

250m

200

150

100

Chanctonbury Ring
235m/771ft

Turn for
Storrington

Turn for
Steyning
(Map 27)

A24

Amberley

1 mile 2 3 4 5 6 7 8 9 10

Maps 22-27 – Amberley to Steyning

10 miles/16km – 3½-5hrs
NOTE: Add 20-30% to these times
to allow for stops

Winchester

Amberley

Steyning

Eastbourne

B2138

A29

A29

A24

B2139

A283

A283

B2139

A284

A280

A24

A280

A2031

A27

A27

A27

A284

A259

A280

A2032

A259

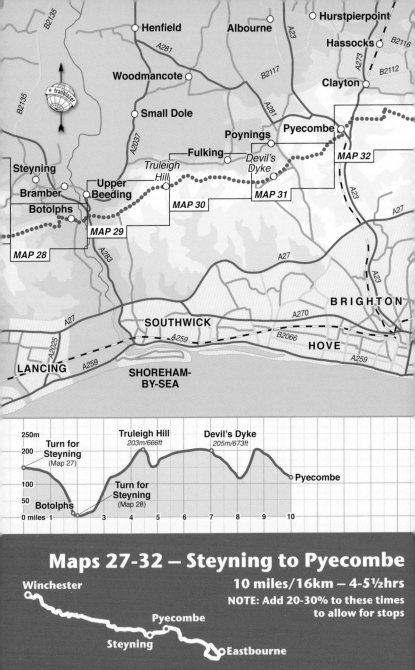

Maps 27-32 – Steyning to Pyecombe

10 miles/16km – 4-5½hrs

NOTE: Add 20-30% to these times to allow for stops

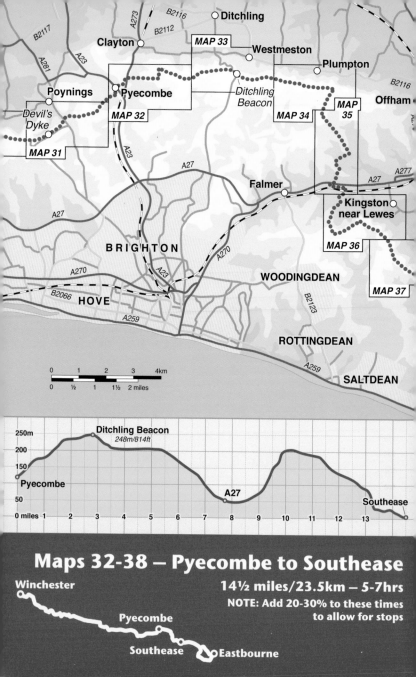

Maps 32-38 – Pyecombe to Southease

14½ miles/23.5km – 5-7hrs

NOTE: Add 20-30% to these times to allow for stops

Winchester

Pyecombe

Southease Eastbourne

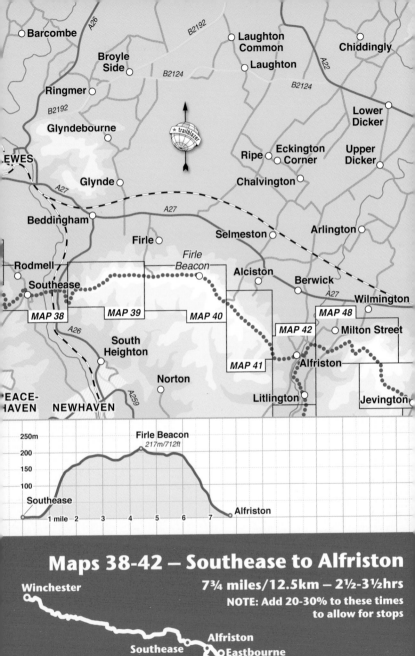

Maps 38-42 — Southease to Alfriston

7¾ miles/12.5km — 2½-3½hrs

**NOTE: Add 20-30% to these times
to allow for stops**

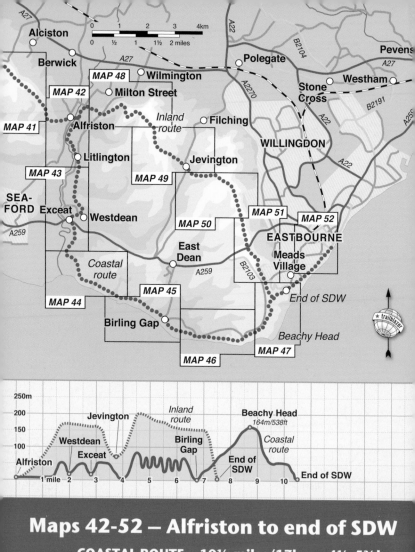

Maps 42-52 – Alfriston to end of SDW

COASTAL ROUTE – 10½ miles/17km – 4¼-5¾hrs
INLAND ROUTE – 7½ miles/12km – 2¾-3½hrs
NOTE: Add 20-30% to these times to allow for stops
Add 1½ miles for end of SDW to Eastbourne centre

TRAILBLAZER TITLE LIST

Adventure Cycle-Touring Handbook
Adventure Motorcycling Handbook
Australia by Rail
Australia's Great Ocean Road
Azerbaijan
Coast to Coast (British Walking Guide)
Cornwall Coast Path (British Walking Guide)
Corsica Trekking – GR20
Cotswold Way (British Walking Guide)
The Cyclist's Anthology
Dolomites Trekking – AV1 & AV2
Dorset & Sth Devon Coast Path (British Walking Gde)
Exmoor & Nth Devon Coast Path (British Walking Gde)
Hadrian's Wall Path (British Walking Guide)
Himalaya by Bike – a route and planning guide
Inca Trail, Cusco & Machu Picchu
Japan by Rail
Kilimanjaro – the trekking guide (includes Mt Meru)
Morocco Overland (4WD/motorcycle/mountainbike)
Moroccan Atlas – The Trekking Guide
Nepal Trekking & The Great Himalaya Trail
New Zealand – The Great Walks
North Downs Way (British Walking Guide)
Offa's Dyke Path (British Walking Guide)
Overlanders' Handbook – worldwide driving guide
Peddars Way & Norfolk Coast Path (British Walking Gde)
Pembrokeshire Coast Path (British Walking Guide)
Pennine Way (British Walking Guide)
Peru's Cordilleras Blanca & Huayhuash – Hiking/Biking
The Railway Anthology
The Ridgeway (British Walking Guide)
Siberian BAM Guide – rail, rivers & road
The Silk Roads – a route and planning guide
Sahara Overland – a route and planning guide
Scottish Highlands – The Hillwalking Guide
Sinai – the trekking guide
South Downs Way (British Walking Guide)
Thames Path (British Walking Guide)
Tour du Mont Blanc
Trans-Canada Rail Guide
Trans-Siberian Handbook
Trekking in the Everest Region
The Walker's Anthology
The Walker's Haute Route – Mont Blanc to Matterhorn
West Highland Way (British Walking Guide)

For more information about Trailblazer and our
expanding range of guides, for guidebook updates or
for credit card mail order sales visit our website:

www.trailblazer-guides.com

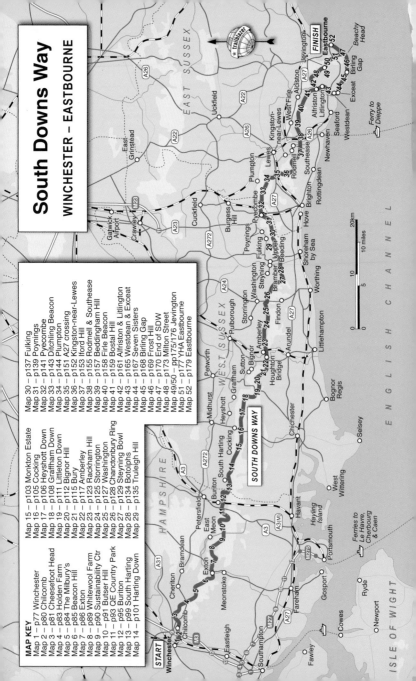

South Downs Way

WINCHESTER – EASTBOURNE

SOUTH DOWNS WAY